BODY
BY design

The Anatomy and Physiology of the Human Body

For thou hast possessed my reins: thou hast covered me in my mother's womb. I will praise thee; for I am fearfully and wonderfully made: marvellous are thy works; and that my soul knoweth right well. My substance was not hid from thee, when I was made in secret, and curiously wrought in the lowest parts of the earth. Thine eyes did see my substance, yet being unperfect; and in thy book all my members were written, which in continuance were fashioned, when as yet there was none of them.

Psalm 139:13-16

By
Dr. Alan L. Gillen

Master
Books
A Division of New Leaf Publishing Group

BODY
BY design

First Printing: May 2001
Sixth Printing: March 2009

Graphic Artist: Mike Daily

For information write:

Master Books®
P.O. Box 726
Green Forest, AR 72638

ISBN-13: 978-0-89051-296-8
ISBN-10: 0-89051-296-5
Library of Congress Catalog Number: 00-102650

Printed in the United States of America

Please visit our website for other great titles:
Download FREE study guides
www.masterbooks.net

For information regarding publicity for author interviews, contact the publicity department at (870) 438-5288.

Dedicated to Jayne, Earl, and Barbara Gillen

All scripture quotations taken from the
King James (Authorized) Version of the Bible.

BODY BY design

CONTENTS

Preface

Body by Design describes the wonder, beauty, and creation of the human body. While writing this book on the human body I had the sense of working on several books at once. I wanted to capture the essence of its anatomy and physiology, the interwoven components in each body system as creation evidence, and to provide special explorations in each body system. These explorations include disease aspects of body systems, current events, and classic (historic) and contemporary explorers. Although an evolutionary origin of humans is now assumed among most professional biologists, this has not always been the case. Most of the foundation laid in human anatomy, microbiology, and pathology was by done by scientists who believed in creation. Therefore, I have made it a goal to tell biographically about some of the famous explorers of the human body. In addition, I also hoped to convey an appreciation for the vast evidence that supports a creation or design view of the human body by rendering medical facts in an appealing style.

This book, *Body by Design*, continues the approach I began in *The Human Body: An Intelligent Design*. It is not a sequel in the strictest sense because each volume stands alone and is written at different reading levels. Also, *The Human Body: An Intelligent Design* emphasizes physiological evidences for creation and *Body by Design* emphasizes anatomical evidences for creation in the human body. It also follows a pattern begun with *Fearfully and Wonderfully Made* and *In His Image* in that it gives credit to the Creator for forming and fashioning the human body and denies it is a product of evolution. The two books by Dr. Paul Brand and Phillip Yancey emphasize spiritual analogies of human body with the church, medical missions, and the varying roles within the body, whereas my books focus on more in-depth human biology and apologetics of the Christian faith.

I begin each major section with a survey of the basic anatomical parts of each system in the human body and how they function. Since Vesalius first declared the human body the most wondrous of the world's wonders, several hundred years of scientific discovery have only served to underscore his words. The body is far more wondrous than Vesalius could have imagined. Up until the late 18th century, science was seen as a direct search for God. When Vesalius, Harvey, Leonardo da Vinci, and Newton made their discoveries, they believed their results taught humanity about God as well. The created world, they felt, revealed His nature. Not many people approach science that way any more.

The organization of the book is built around a universal organization of human anatomy, the systems approach. It is like most texts, where most chapters are devoted to one of 11 body systems. Some medical texts use a regional approach to anatomy, where one body region, such as the thoracic region, is treated at a time. Most popular books on the human body, as well as most anatomy and physiology texts, assume an evolutionary origin of man. This book is somewhat unique in that it is built around the widely accepted physiological themes but provides a distinct, creationist approach to the human body. I wrote *Body by Design* to help readers understand the human body from a biblical perspective. The objectives for this book include 1) to describe the designed structures and purposeful functions for each of the 11 systems in the human body; 2) to explain selective in-depth explorations in each body system; 3) to compare and contrast the interwoven pattern observed in cloth/fabric with the design seen in each human body system; 4) to provide examples of disease in each of the body systems from a clinical and/or creation perspective; and 5) to explain the historical, classical, and contemporary explorations in anatomy and physiology (beginning with Vesalius, Father of Modern Anatomy) and trace the design model of the human body through the year 2000 (technology-based research projects of today). The book should serve as a reference for biology students because it provides questions to study and definitions of basic biology terms. Many of these new terms can be found in a glossary. Finally, after reading this book, the student should better understand that we have been made fearfully and wonderfully and that we serve an awesome God.

Foreword
Marvelous Interweaving

Could we — *Homo sapiens* — have just come into existence through a series of evolutionary changes over thousands of years? Careful examination of the human body reveals that macroevolution of *Homo sapiens* is not possible. The more intricately one explores human anatomy and physiology, the more obvious creation by a Master Creator becomes. The more scientific research discovers about the functioning of the human body, the more obvious a planned, "intelligent design" by God becomes.

High school and college anatomy and physiology textbooks usually present an evolutionist view without presenting accurate, truthful explanations of what is known and what is theory. Even in clinically oriented texts that used to be "neutral," such as human anatomy, physiology, and microbiology, we now see Darwinian philosophy and medicine interwoven throughout. Logical reasoning and statistical explanations for these "new" developments of human structure, function, and disease are not discussed. References from other scientists that mention God are not accurately quoted, or worse, not acknowledged at all.

Body by Design presents human anatomy and physiology clearly, accurately, and truthfully. Purposeful, intricate design of structure and function are discussed. The evidence for logical, deliberate design by God is interwoven into a detailed explanation of the human body systems. Body system relationships to one another are explored. Students are challenged to think through the evidence — the facts as we know them today — and to consider the statistical likelihood of macroevolution. The end result is an effective, interwoven presentation of anatomy, physiology, and creation.

Body by Design defines the basic anatomy and physiology in each of the 11 body systems, as do many texts. However, the unique contribution of this book is the evidence it provides for design in each of these systems through description of their basic biology. *Body by Design* also contains biographical information about famous biologists like Vesalius, Harvey, Starling, Pasteur, Lister, and Cuvier, revealing that a design view of the body is not new. Instead, this is a common view held through the ages. Only in recent times have biologists been so antagonistic toward the idea of a Creator being responsible for the origin of mankind. Additionally, the book compares and contrasts the viewpoints of creation/design with macroevolution on specific human traits.

Tables assist the reader with understanding relationships between design and purpose. Figures provide details of key anatomical structures and physiologic principles. Clear examples are used to explain relationships between structure, function, and intelligent design. **Focus** boxes stimulate thinking and provide practical application of the information presented. **"Check Your Understanding"** questions, at the conclusion of each chapter, go beyond rote memory to stimulate process thinking and reasoning.

Body by Design achieves a marvelous interweaving of anatomy, physiology, and creation. Only high school and college students who are willing to explore the intricacies of human anatomy and physiology in a logical, thought-provoking manner should venture into this textbook.

Inis Jane Bardella, M.D., FAAFP
Assistant Professor
Department of Family Medicine and Clinical Epidemiology
University of Pittsburgh School of Medicine

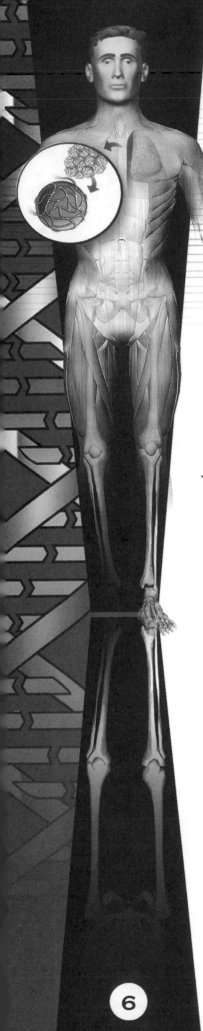

RECOGNIZING DESIGN IN THE HUMAN BODY

CHAPTER 1

"For thou hast possessed my reins: thou hast covered me in my mother's womb. I will praise thee; for I am fearfully and wonderfully made: marvelous are thy works; and that my soul knoweth right well. My substance was not hid from thee, when I was made in secret, and curiously wrought in the lowest parts of the earth. Thine eyes did see my substance, yet being unperfect; and in thy book, all my members were written, which in continuance were fashioned, when as yet there was none of them"

(David, Ps. 139:13–16).

The powerful, unceasing beating of the heart, the intricacy of blood clotting, the complex, camera-like eye, the double helix pattern in DNA, and the skillful hand of a surgeon are all examples of intricate designs found in the human body. The origin of these patterns is a topic that has fascinated biologists since the time of the ancient Greeks. It was not until the time of Vesalius (1514–64), however, that the dissection of cadavers was allowed in the study of human anatomy. It was also during this era that the scientific method was first used by William Harvey (1578–1657) in human physiology, and that good biology began to demand proof from experiments, not just "logical" and speculative thinking. Beginning with the **Reformation** time period (and later during the **Renaissance**) man began to really understand "wisdom of the inward parts" and to seek to understand products of the Creator's design and plan for the human body. In those days, many explorers of the human body began "*thinking God's thoughts after Him.*"

The Webster's dictionary defines **design** as a plan, a scheme, a project, or a purpose with intention or aim. Today, many are asking whether these observed designs are the product of evolution or if they are the "fingerprints" of a master creator. Many biologists view man as the product of cosmic evolution from some hominid ancestor. Still other biologists question this naturalistic model of human descent because there is a unique plan and pattern to the human body. Today, many biologists are reconsidering design and are seeing *Homo sapiens* (literally, man who is wise) as the pinnacle of design because of his spectacular cell biology, anatomy, and physiology.

The Fabrica View of the Human Body

Thou didst form me from my mother's womb.

The Psalmist, in his song of praise to God, is beautifully picturing the weaving together of a human being within the womb. However, the Psalmist had no idea of how scientifically true his picture was. In the Old Testament era, man had never heard of DNA or RNA, the helical and symmetrical molecules that are woven together to produce the blueprint of life. Yet with great accuracy, the Psalmist depicts the skillful fabric of the human body.

During the Great Reformation, a Belgian anatomist and physician began to unlock the mysteries of the human body. Andreas Vesalius (figure 1.1), born in Brussels in 1514, changed anatomy forever. Vesalius, a devout Roman Catholic, understood there to be a Master Craftsman behind the fabric design in the human body. During the 1530s, Vesalius developed a great interest in anatomy by studying the body parts of human cadavers. After completing a medical degree, he taught young medical students by performing dissections as he lectured. Vesalius did not follow the traditional approach of merely reading from books as he taught anatomy. Ancient Roman physicians such as Galen had studied the body parts by dissecting animals. Vesalius, however, turned to human corpses for his dissections. His radical methods enabled him to write the text *De Humani Corporis Fabrica* (The Fabric of the Human Body), the most accurate and comprehensive book on human anatomy ever written in his time. The seven-volume work was completely illustrated with handmade engravings by Vesalius himself. These diagrams vividly proved the theme of a divine designer in the interwoven human body.

Because of his great work, Vesalius was appointed as royal physician to Phillip II in Madrid. In 1564, Vesalius died in a shipwreck after a trip to the Holy Land, but he lived on in his masterpiece, *Fabrica*. This book boldly challenged hundreds of Galen's teachings on how the body operates. Many traditional anatomists attacked Vesalius' book, but failed in every attempt. No matter where the opponents looked, they were rebuffed with the accuracy of details he used in describing the human body and the vivid drawings depicting the interwoven designs. Both text and drawing could be verified by dissection of human cadavers.

Everywhere a scientist studies in the human body, he is confronted with a designer behind the seamlessly interwoven design of the lymphatic, immune, circulatory, respiratory, and digestive systems. Like the idea in Vesalius' *Fabrica*, many body systems illustrate the blueprint of a divine weaver, craftsman, or artificer. The interwoven complexity, along with the organs' intricacies, defies chance. The infinitely low probability of macroevolution occurring by mutations and selection points to an intelligent designer. There must have been a Creator to make such a beautiful fabric of the body systems, all originating from a microscopic blueprint called DNA.

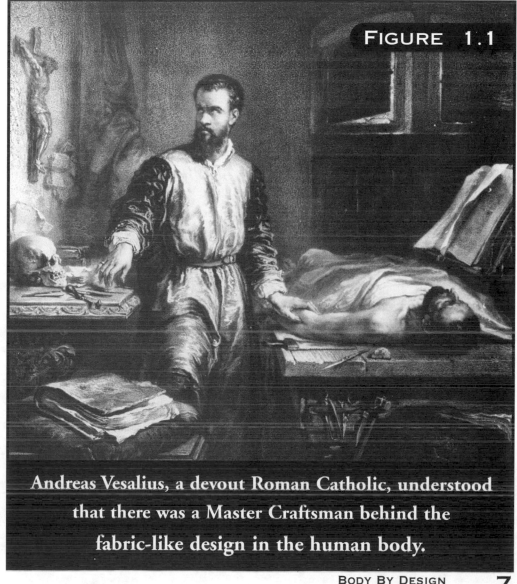

FIGURE 1.1

Andreas Vesalius, a devout Roman Catholic, understood that there was a Master Craftsman behind the fabric-like design in the human body.

The intertwining design of the human body will be shown in the manual by the fabric of DNA, embryonic development, muscle construction, alveoli of lungs, convoluted tubules of kidneys, capillaries of lymphatic and circulatory systems, intertwining nature of heart chambers, and many other body systems.

BOOK OBJECTIVES

The purpose of this book is to:

- Describe the designed structures and purposeful functions for each of the 11 systems in the human body;
- Explain selective in-depth explorations for interwoven components and body parts for each system;
- Compare and contrast the interwoven design observed in cloth/fabric with the patterns seen in each system of the human body;
- Provide examples of disease in each of the body systems from a clinical and/or creation perspective; and
- Explain the historical Reformation viewpoint of anatomy and physiology.

We begin with Vesalius, Father of Modern Anatomy, and trace the creation model of the human body through the year 2000, including the technology-based research projects of today.

Many of the terms that are useful in discussing such a plan can be found in the glossary.

The complexity of the human body is direct evidence against macroevolution. All the interwoven parts of the body point to an intelligent Creator. In the early 1990s, Dr. Charles Thaxton argued for the intelligent design of the human body. His argument is called the principle of uniform experience. To illustrate the complex nature of this principle, one needs to look at the formation of a beautiful tapestry in a weaver's loom. First, a fabric designer needs to sit down and design the blueprint for the tapestry. She needs to decide which colors to use and what type of pattern she will use the colors in. The seamstress must also decide what type of fabric she will use for the tapestry. She cannot randomly pick colors and fabrics, for they must coordinate and complement each other. Next, the weaver must decide how to mix and intertwine the strands of thread. On a simple loom, she will weave the secondary threads under and over the primary threads. Each individual thread meshes tightly against the next thread. Slowly, carefully, the designer weaves together her beautiful

picture, one thread at a time. When the seamstress has finished her picture, she releases it from the loom.

All customers who look at the tapestry see only the one complete fabric. However, if one would look close enough, he could see all the individual threads seamlessly woven together. Anyone looking at the rich tapestry and the vibrant colors would immediately praise the designer, because they realize that only a Master Designer could produce such a magnificent work of art. Yet, the very same people will turn around and claim that the complex human body happened by chance. The body, however, is woven together just like a tapestry. For example, look at the interwoven complexity of a single skeletal muscle. When one initially glances at a muscle, he sees a tough, translucent mass of tissue. Under the microscope, however, the amazing interwoven design manifests itself. Each muscle is composed of muscle fiber bundles (figure 1.5). In each fiber, many myofibrils and nuclei are enclosed within a common sarcolemma. Each myofibril contains numerous sarcomeres, arranged end to end in a single file. There are millions of sarcomeres in a single muscle with each overlapping the next one in a long string. These sarcomeres have two parts to them. Thin actin filaments surround a thick myosin filament. When the actin filaments contract across the myosin filament, the muscle contracts. The muscle will not move until every sarcomere is contracting the same way. Therefore, nerves repeat the message to other neighboring muscle fibers.

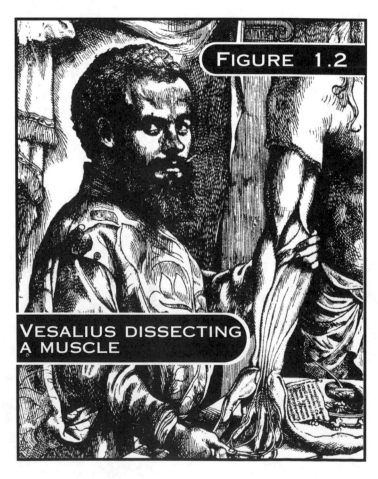

FIGURE 1.2

VESALIUS DISSECTING A MUSCLE

All of these individual parts are needed just to make one single muscle contract. Yet, there are nearly 700 muscles in the human body. Indeed, the complexity of the human muscle must have come from the blueprint of a master weaver. Just as one would acknowledge the intelligent causation of a tapestry, so also must one acknowledge the intelligent designer of the human body. This chain of logic, which compares the making of a tapestry to the formation of a human muscle, illustrates the principle of uniform experience (figure 1.3).

The Human Body and Its Design

What a piece of work is a man! How noble in reason,
how infinite in faculty, in form and moving how express
and admirable, in action like an angel,
in apprehension how like a god!
Shakespeare

Awesome, incredible, or ingenious are some of the adjectives that men through the ages have used to describe the order found in the human body. The splendor of the human body can only be described in superlative terms! When one considers the movement in the hand of a concert pianist, the thought processes in the brain of a heart surgeon, the eye focus required of a seamstress, and the muscle coordination that propels a world-class gymnast, it is difficult to imagine this body plan has happened by chance. A naturalistic explanation alone cannot account for the incredible complexity and optimal integration in human anatomy and physiology. All these life processes require precise movement, coordination, and communication among the body's cells.

The human body consists of 11 organ systems, four basic body tissues, and dozens of different specialized cells. The human body is mostly made up of an estimated 30 to 100 trillion cells, with most estimates counting over 75 trillion cells. This is quite a range. Perhaps this range is so vast because of the diversity of human sizes from Billy Barney, a famous circus midget, to Hakeem Olajuwon and Shaquille O'Neil (NBA stars). Most of these cells can be seen with a light microscope. Some 100 million are red blood cells (RBC) and several hundred million are nerve cells. The human body is truly a highly organized and coordinated system!

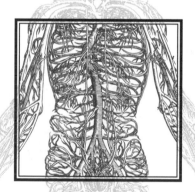

Human Body Systems

The Bible calls the human body a "temple" (1 Cor. 3:16). If the body is a temple, it is surely the most elaborate one ever wrought. It is a marvel of architecture, complete with domes, windows, arches, and thousands of miles of intricate passageways. But this is no placid, subdued temple. It is far from it. Every cell of the body, every fiber of its being blazes with activity. The human body is a bustling place, even when asleep. It is always building, renovating, reproducing, and growing. It converts one energy form into another. It sends and receives messages, it fends off intruders, and it performs the most amazing balancing acts.

This human temple is constructed according to levels of organization that increase in size and complexity. Cells form the basic structural and functional units of life; they are the smallest living parts of our bodies. The most complex level is the systems level. Anatomical evidence of design can be seen in every level from the simplest to the most complex levels of organization.

Humans are complex creatures; they require many levels of organization to keep things running properly. Groups of similar **cells** come together to form **tissues**; tissues unite to form **organs**. Two or more organs, along with their associated structures, join forces to perform certain vital functions, such as digestion or reproduction. This group of organs working together is called a **system**. The complete creature comprises various systems. God's pride (declaring it very good), the human body, is composed of 11 distinct but interrelated systems. They all seem to possess an interwoven fabric design, bearing the signature of a master craftsman (Eph. 2:10).

From a biological standpoint, the ultimate goals underlying all the body's internal activities are survival and reproduction. The Bible tells us that we are to be good stewards of the temple God has given us and that man is to be fruitful (for survival) and multiply (for reproduction). With our large, sophisticated brains, we humans can set many goals for ourselves, but our bodies are run largely by systems designed to ensure that we survive and reproduce.

The human body may be considered to have 11 systems (table 1.1), each with its own job but all highly interdependent. The main job of the skeletal system is to protect our inward parts and to support us. Muscles help us move and respond to external stimuli. The task of the nervous and endocrine systems are to maintain order among the body's trillions of cells. Both the digestive and the respiratory systems provide raw materials for our daily lives and for growth and both carry off wastes. The circulatory system transports nutrient- and oxygen-rich blood throughout the body. The excretory system rids us of liquid waste, while the nervous system interprets and responds to stimuli from outside our bodies as well as from those inside. The job of the reproductive system is to ensure the survival of mankind. The integumentary system holds the whole package together and helps protect us from invading microbes. It works with the major systems that marshal protection against germs

TABLE 1.1 Organ Systems with their Main Components and Main Functions

ORGAN SYSTEM	DESIGNED STRUCTURE	PURPOSEFUL FUNCTION	INTERWOVEN COMPONENTS
1. DIGESTIVE	Mouth, pharynx, esophagus, stomach, intestines, rectum, anus, liver, pancreas, and gall bladder	Food processing (ingestion, digestion, absorption, elimination)	villi: capillaries & lacteal
2. CIRCULATORY	Heart, blood vessels, blood	Internal distribution of materials	twisting (helical) inside arteries & veins; capillary junctions with each body system
3. RESPIRATORY	Lungs, trachea, other breathing tubes	Gas exchange (uptake of oxygen)	alveolus, capillaries
4. IMMUNE AND LYMPHATIC *	Bone marrow, lymph nodes, thymus, spleen, lymph vessels, white blood cells	Body defense (fighting infections and cancer)	lymphatic capillaries, spleen, thymus reticular fibers in spleen, lymph nodes
5. EXCRETORY	Kidneys, ureters, urinary bladder, and urethra	Disposal of metabolic wastes; regulation of osmotic balance of blood	juxtamedullary nephron with peritubular capillaries
6. ENDOCRINE	Pituitary, thyroid, pancreas	Coordination of body activities between hormone-secreting glands (e.g. digestion, metabolism)	nerve/endocrine junction in pituitary stalk
7. REPRODUCTIVE	Ovaries, testes, and associated organs (egg and sperm)	Procreation, physical intimacy	umbilical cord, uterine blood supply, double helix in germ cells Seminiferous tubules, epididymis
8. NERVOUS	Brain, spinal cord, nerves	Coordination of body activities; sensory organs detection of stimuli	astrocytes and various neuroglial cells cauda equina, plexuses, pain network
9. INTEGUMENTARY	Skin and its derivatives (e.g. hair, claws, skin glands)	Protection against mechanical injury, infection, drying out	dermis glands, hair, and nerve network
10. SKELETAL	Skeleton (bones, ligaments, cartilage)	Body support, protection of internal organs	osteon (haversian system in compact bone)
11. MUSCULAR	Skeletal muscles	Movement, locomotion	sarcoplasmic reticulum, with T-tubules

* Anatomical structures in our body's defense system are collectively known as the *lymphatic system* and the functional body defenses system are known as the *immune system.*

and toxins. These body defenses include the immune system and the lymphatic system.

If one system fails, the others are affected, either directly or indirectly. Let us explore how these 11 systems do their jobs in the chapters ahead, for herein lies the wonder that differentiates our living bodies from even the most exquisite temple.

Human Body as a Machine

Another classic word picture used to describe the human body is one that envisions it as a complex machine. The body and a machine both perform work. This analogy is not new. Renaissance scholars, including the famous artist and scientist Leonardo da Vinci, used it. At the close of the 15th century, Leonardo da Vinci made the most comprehensive study of the human body, yet he saw neither superfluous nor defective structure in man. In fact, he described human anatomy as one of beauty and complexity. In addition, he made sketches of the body in a study of proportions, and compared them with the most sophisticated machines of his time. Because the body was so masterfully engineered like a "machine," it has been the subject of many artists' works through the centuries.

This machine analogy is still applicable today. Each part of the body has its own job. The parts work together to keep the body alive, much as the parts of an automobile work together to make it run. The skin, for example, protects the body as paint protects the metal on a car. Food serves as fuel for the body as gasoline powers a car engine. The human body wears out and breaks down if not properly maintained. If a machine requires a blueprint and an architect, how much more does the plan of the human body logically demand that it have a Maker?

Remember, however, that the human body is not as simple as a machine made by people. If a car breaks down, its broken parts can be replaced. If some parts of the body wear out and break down completely, they cannot so easily be replaced to make the body as good as new. Many parts, such as the hair and outer layers of skin, however, are continually being replaced as older portions die and fall off. Unlike a machine, the body can heal itself, within limits, as illustrated in the case of a broken bone that forms a collar and a wound that disappears as the tissue is restored.

Basic Themes of Human Physiology

There are basic principles, or themes, that can be observed in all 11 of the human body systems. These themes include 1) relationship of structure to function; 2) steady state of metabolism, or homeostasis; 3) interdependence among body parts; 4) short-term physiological adaptation; 5) maintenance of boundaries; and 6) the triple scheme of order, organization, and integration. These themes are widely acknowledged by physiologists and are consistent with a creation perspective of the human body. In fact, I believe each of these themes are physiological evidences for a creation model of the human body.

The **correlation of structure and function** can be explained by stating that, in general, the physical form of human tissue, organ, or system is related to its function. Two examples of this are 1) the composition of bone that makes it both strong and relatively light to handle the body's weight, and 2) the longitudinal separation in the heart that keeps unoxygenated from oxygenated blood. Both are exquisite demonstrations of form being related to function.

The human body maintains itself in equilibrium, a steady state known as **homeostasis**. This concept is based upon feedback that prevents small changes from becoming too large and harmful. Changes occur between internal and external environments, and between interstitial fluid (the fluid between our cells) and intracellular fluid. In this way the body stays in balance, but not everyone's balance is exactly the same. "Thermostat wars" inside the house frequently happen when family members are at home — one member is hot and the other is cold. Clearly, the body's hypothalamus or body "thermostat" has a unique best setting. The body will regulate its temperature by a negative feedback mechanism by either shivering to warm the body when it is cold or sweating to cool the body when it is hot.

Another example of homeostasis and negative feedback is glucose regulation by insulin and glucagon. The pancreas is considered both an exocrine and endocrine gland. The endocrine function of the pancreas secreting insulin in the blood is controlled by the amount of glucose in the blood. The pancreatic cells that control blood glucose levels are called Islets of Langerhans. Insulin and glucagon work as a check and balance system regulating the body's blood glucose level. Insulin is antagonistic to glucose. It decreases the blood glucose concentration by accelerating its movement out of the blood and through the cell membranes of the working cells. This topic will be explored in chapter 13.

As glucose enters the cells at a faster rate, the cells increase their metabolism of glucose. All sugary and starchy foods, such as bread, potatoes, and cakes, are broken down into glucose. In this form they can be absorbed by every cell in the body, including the cells in the liver, which store glucose in the form of glycogen. Cells absorb glucose and generate ATP, using the energy released from the sugar.

ATP is generated in the cell's mitochondria, resulting in energy storage and the production of carbon dioxide and water as byproducts. This aerobic process is the body's principle source of energy and it cannot take place without insulin. One type of diabetes occurs when the pancreas fails to secrete enough insulin and so fails to regulate the glucose concentration in the blood. The normal glucose level for an average person is about 80 to 120 milligrams of glucose in every 100 milliliters of blood. If the beta cells of the pancreas secrete too little insulin, an excess of glucose collects in the bloodstream causing diabetes mellitus, the most common disorder of the endocrine system.

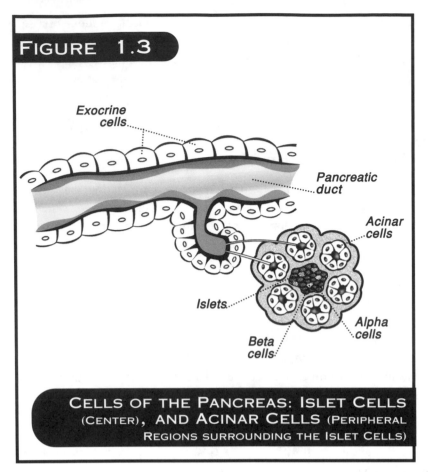

FIGURE 1.3

Exocrine cells

Pancreatic duct

Acinar cells

Islets

Beta cells

Alpha cells

CELLS OF THE PANCREAS: ISLET CELLS (CENTER), AND ACINAR CELLS (PERIPHERAL REGIONS SURROUNDING THE ISLET CELLS)

Many early anatomists believed that body parts share a common thread uniting them; they are **interdependent with each other.** These early workers noted that the body is one unit, though it is made up of many different types of cells and tissues. They all form one body. Related terms that other scientists have used to describe this phenomenon of interdependence include an **adaptation package, cell team, compound traits, emergent properties, interwoven components, irreducible complexity, molecular team,** and **synergism.** This resulting condition of interdependent body parts working together is synergistic such that the sum of their action is greater than the addition of separate, individual actions.

Two examples of the marvelous advantage resulting from this cooperation at all levels from the molecular to the systematic are 1) the amazing interdependence of many parts for focusing the lens in the human eye, and 2) the irreducible complexity involved in the cascade (meaning one effect must occur in order for the next level of effect to happen) of biochemical reactions required for blood clotting.

Adaptation allows living cells to adjust to change in the external environment. Short-term change is facilitated by

physiological adaptation. An example of this would be an adjustment of oxygen level in our bloodstream as we change altitude. Oxygen pressure in the atmosphere decreases at higher altitudes. The athlete who is conditioned at sea level won't breathe as efficiently at high altitude stadiums compared with those who train at higher altitudes. If the body remains living and training at higher altitudes over a period of months, however, then it will physiologically adapt to this altitude by increasing the level of a hormone called **erythropoietin.** This hormone increases the number of red blood cells and, in turn, the oxygen available to body tissues also increases. This adaptation gives greater "wind" to the athlete competing in "mountain" arenas.

Every living organism must be able to **maintain its boundaries** so that its inside structures remain distinct from its outside chemical environments. Every human body cell is surrounded by a cell membrane that encases its contents and allows needed substances to enter while restricting the entry of potentially damaging or unnecessary substances. Additionally, the integumentary system, or skin, encloses the whole body. The integumentary system protects internal organs from drying out, from bacterial invasion, and from the damaging effects of an unbelievable number of chemical substances and physical factors in the external environment.

Finally, the triple theme of **order, organization, and integration** can be clearly seen in many of the human body systems. These themes will be discussed most in chapter 11 on the nervous system. The levels of organization from least complex to most complex are molecules, cells, tissues, organs, organ systems, and organisms. A plan and purpose can be seen through the structure and function of an information system, leading us to believe the parts of animal and human bodies are the work of an intelligent designer. This argument may apply from the molecular level to the gross anatomical level.

AGING THEORY: WHY DOES THE BODY WEAR OUT?

One of the topics of great interest to cell biologists and physicians is **aging**. Why do we age and are there limits to how long we live? These are just two of the questions that scientists and theologians alike are asking. Evolutionists believe we can extend human life longer and longer if only we have the technology. Yet, the Bible does seem to indicate that we will all die and that there are upper limits to how long we may live. On the other hand, creation scientists believe there was a time in human history that man could live to great ages, even into the 900-year life span. (Most evolutionists scoff at such an idea.) This was prior to the great flood of Noah's day. In this age, however, a median age between 70 and 80 is most common, with an upper limit of about 130 years.

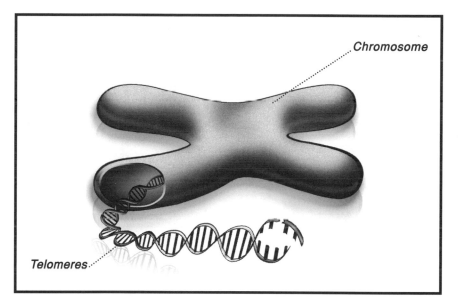

Chromosome

Telomeres

Why do we age?

Cells in the human body will eventually wear out and die. It is enough to simply say that there are biological laws that dictate that all fixed structures will eventually wear out. This is true, but biological machinery has a built-in program that has the ability to repair itself. Human and animal cells don't keep dividing, repairing, and renewing our body parts forever. If worn-out cells could be replaced by newly manufactured ones, then none of your parts would wear out and you could live forever. You might die of an automobile accident or microbial infection, but you would not die of "old age." Our organs, however, do wear out. The cells within can multiply for a while, but not forever. After a finite number of times, they simply stop dividing and eventually die.

Cell biologists have found that ordinary cells will divide between 80 and 90 times. It appears that telomeres, on the tips of each chromosome, control the number of times a cell can reproduce. Every time the cell divides, it is as if a bead is snipped off, shortening the **telomere**. Once all the beads are gone, cell division can no longer take place. From then on, each cell runs down and new ones do not replace it. Scientists discovered that DNA polmerase copies only part of the DNA sequence at the telomere. Each time a chromosome replicates it loses 50–100 DNA base pairs. Cell division ultimately stops when there is too much loss of DNA, and the cell dies because of damage it sustains in the course of aging. So even if you avoid any sort of fatal accident or disease, you will virtually succumb to organ failure and eventually death.

Events like infectious disease, accidents, mutations, and environmental toxins may speed the process of decay. A basic physical law, **entropy**, only accelerates disorder, and thus, aging. Unfortunately, the bad news is that we are all going to die. The good news is that those who trust in Jesus Christ, the Creator, for their lives, will someday get to "trade in" this old body for a new one. This new body will never grow old and die. And that is something to celebrate!

BASIC TERMINOLOGY FOR BODY BY DESIGN

Figure 1.4
Planes and Sections of the Human Body

The human body may also be described in terms of the planes, or imaginary flat surfaces, that pass through it. A sagittal plane is a plane that divides the body into right and left sides. A midsagittal (or medial) (2) passes through the midline of the body and divides the body into equal right and left sides. A frontal, or coronal plane (1), is a plane that divides the body into anterior (front) and posterior (back) portions. A transverse, or cross section (horizontal) (3) plane divides the body into superior (upper) and inferior (lower) planes. When you study body structure, you will often view it in a section, meaning that you look at only one surface of the three-dimensional structure. Figure 1.4 illustrates how three different sections were prepared from the three planes of reference. Each section can provide a different view of the thorax and its contents, the vital organs. The intelligent designer made our bodies in 3-D! A good anatomy student can learn to visualize a body part from any angle in his/her mind. This is a good skill to have when entering the health professions or biology. Practice of this skill will make you a better creation biologist.

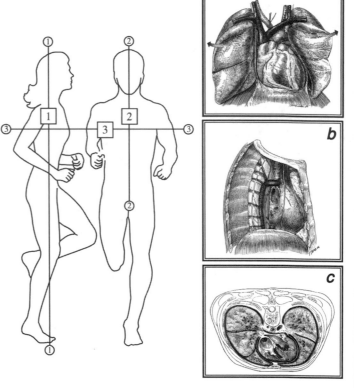

Planes • 1. Coronal 2. Midsagittal 3. Transverse
Sections • a. Coronal section b. Sagittal section c. Transverse section

Figure 1.5
A Living Design: The Creation of a Human Muscle

This chain of logic that compares the making of a tapestry to the formation of a human muscle illustrates Dr. Thaxton's principle of uniform experience. The hands of God and Adam, DNA, myofibrils from a muscle fiber, a motor nerve unit, and muscles of the arm are pictured. All of these individual parts are needed just to make one single muscle contract. Yet, there are nearly 700 muscles in the human body. Indeed, the complexity of the human muscle must have come from the genetic blueprint of a Master Weaver. In everyday experience, one would never conclude that random chance events could produce a beautiful interwoven tapestry but that it is the end product of a weaver (intelligent designer). Logic demands that highly interwoven, intricate designs must also have an intelligent cause.

The Principle of Uniform Experience

Creation of man

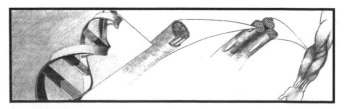

Genetic Blueprint for muscles • A myofibril • Bundle of muscle fibers • Muscles and tendons making up the arm

CHECK YOUR UNDERSTANDING

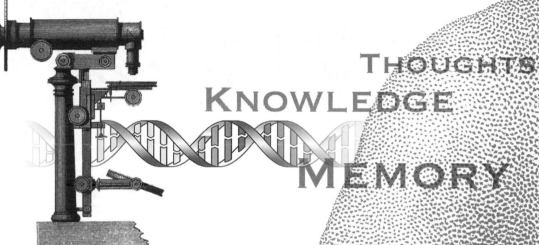

THOUGHTS

KNOWLEDGE

MEMORY

Two Views of Origins

1. How can you recognize design in the human body?

2. List the 11 systems in the human body. Which of these systems is easiest to recognize? Hardest to recognize?

3. Name six physiological themes that are consistent with the concept of intelligent design. Which of these themes could be applied to all body systems?

4. How does the body reveal wisdom in the inward parts (Job 38:36)?

5. The anatomical masterpiece *De Humani Corporis Fabrica* was the work of Vesalius. Explain why he may have been a creationist in thinking. Also, discuss the impact of Vesalius on the advancement of anatomy and medicine when he based his human anatomy upon cadaver dissection rather than animal dissection.

6. Why must scientists be critical thinkers and sometimes oppose the popular thinking of the day? How does this apply to evolutionary dogma of this day?

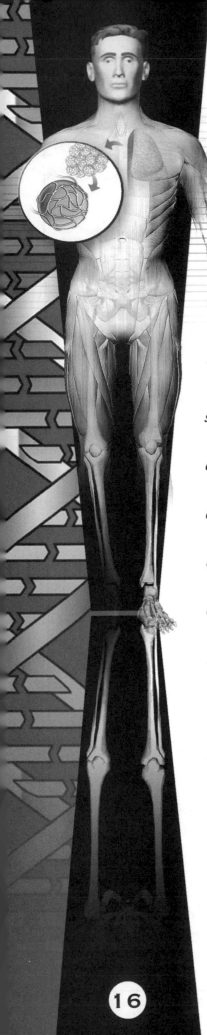

ORIGINS
OF THE
HUMAN BODY

CHAPTER 2

"If it could be demonstrated that any complex organ existed, which could not possibly have been formed by numerous, successive slight modifications, my theory would absolutely break down."

(Charles Darwin, The Origin of Species)

There are two basic views regarding the origin of the universe, the earth, life, and man — the naturalistic view and the **creation** (or **design**) view. The naturalistic view incorporates the belief in macroevolution (molecule to man), which has never been observed. It assumes that all life on earth is somehow related and that the origin and descent of all living things can be explained through a natural, mechanistic, random process. This concept, in the extreme, does not allow for the possibility of supernatural activity. **Macroevolution** has a long history that dates back to the ancient Greeks, but it became more popular in the 19th century as it found new support in speculations popularized by Charles Darwin in his book *The Origin of Species*, published in 1859.

Darwin's Theory of Macroevolution

The essence of the Neo-Darwian theory is that all life can be traced to a single ancestor through purely natural means. The plants, animals, and other organisms that surround us are products of random **mutation,** acted upon by **natural selection**. This is commonly referred to as **descent with modification.** According to Darwin, nature acts like a breeder, scrutinizing every organism. When useful new traits appear, nature preserves them and passes them on to succeeding generations, while harmful traits are eliminated. Over time, these small changes accumulate until organisms develop new limbs, organs, or other parts. Eventually, organisms change so drastically that they bear no resemblance to their original ancestor.

Many evolutionists believe that all this happens with no purposeful input. In their view, chance, physiochemical laws, and nature run the whole show. In *The Origin of Species*, for example, Darwin wrote,

"If it could be demonstrated that any complex organ existed, which could not possibly have been formed by numerous, successive, slight modifications, my theory would absolutely break down. But I can find no such case."

In Darwin's time, however, no one appreciated the amazing complexity of living things. Back then, cells were thought to be little more than tiny blobs of gel. In recent years, Richard Dawkins, a biologist at Oxford University, in his book, *The Blind Watchmaker*, has popularized the neo-Darwinian theory. The essence of Richard Dawkins' argument is that given enough time (millions of years) and materials (billions of individuals), many genetic changes will occur so that, as a result, slight improvements occur in structures such as the eye. Natural selection will favor these small improvements and they will spread through a population over many generations.

Little by little, one improvement at a time, the system becomes more and more complex, eventually resulting in a fully functioning, well-adapted organ. This does not mean that evolution can produce any conceivable structural change. For example, life forms do not have and probably will never have electronic gadgets. But evolution may be used as an explanation for complex structures, if we can imagine a series of small intermediate steps leading from the simple to the complex.

Because natural selection will act on every one of those intermediate steps, no single one can be justified on the basis of the final structure toward which it may be leading. Each step must stand on its own as an improvement that confers in itself an advantage on the organisms that possess it. Some changes will lead "upward" in overall evolutionary progress; still other changes, usually temporary ones, will go "downward." It is like a parking garage with ramps leading to different levels. You must travel the ramp to ascend or descend. Sometimes evolution goes three steps forward and two steps backward (like the so-called imperfections in life forms), but the overall progress is still forward.

TABLE 2.1 — Predictions of the Human Body

CATEGORY	MACROEVOLUTION	CREATION SCIENCE
Body parts	Low level of order Numerous vestigial organs (useless organs that are "leftovers")	Highly ordered No "useless organs" All have some function from the creation
Development	Several vestigial organs Development repeats evolution	Organs fully functional Purposeful development Versatile use of embryological structures
Inheritance	Blending/gradual transitions between offspring	Mosaic design Distinct traits, kinds separate
Mutations	Occasionally beneficial	Basically harmful or lethal with only a few which are beneficial in certain environments
Natural selection	Creative process	Conservation process Weed-out device for harmful mutations
Nature of man	Slightly different from other primates "Misfits are disposable"	Distinctive and superior from all primates No "misfits" All have value
Organization	Chaotic at times A product of tinkering by nature	Ordered most of the time Divine craftsman
Race*	Various races represent different levels of evolution Came from multiple stocks Some races viewed as inferior with less "fit" traits.	All races are equal, descended from one family; "nations" of the earth have varying skin color, but all are people in the human race. Variation adds richness to culture and human experience.
Relationship among body	Independent parts Mechanistic properties	Interdependent parts Coordinated properties

*Race is frequently defined as a population within a species that is genetically distinct in some way. In humans, skin color and other physical features usually determine the definition for various races. Traditionally, *Homo sapiens* have been divided into three to six races based upon skin color (amount of melanin), cultural patterns, and prominent nose features. The classical evolutionary depiction of race frequently led to prejudice. In contrast, creationists view all people groups as equal. From a biblical viewpoint, terms like "nations," "people groups," or "tribes" better describe diversity seen in man.

CHANGES IN THE COMMON COLD

What does microevolution, or variation, look like up close? Biologists have found that there are more than 100 serotypes of rhinoviruses that are responsible for most of our common colds. The diversity of colds can be attributed, in part, to various rhinoviruses that have been modified over time. **Rhinoviruses** have an RNA **genome**, whereas living organisms usually store their genetic information as DNA. Most importantly, replicating RNA, unlike DNA, lacks proofreading enzymes to check that the correct bases have been added to the growing chain. Since RNA lacks the ability to proofread its genetic message, RNA viruses change more rapidly than do DNA viruses. As the RNA replicates, it averages about one mistake per 10,000 nucleotides copied. As DNA replicates its complementary strand, it makes one mistake in every million to ten million nucleotides. It is estimated that up to 2 percent of the nucleotides in the RNA genome in a virus are altered every year. Consequently, antigenic drift of rhinoviruses can be attributed, in part, to point mutations.

When a mutation in RNA occurs within a virus, a change may also occur on the viral protein coat. This viral protein coat contains antigens that elicit varying antibody responses in the human body. The **immunoglobulin** A (IgA) antibodies are produced by plasma cells in the mucous membrane of the nose. IgA binds antigens on the capsid of the virus particle preventing the virus from attaching and penetrating the cell. This interaction leads to recovery. The protein coat in a cold virus changes over time. This gradual change is sometimes referred to as **antigenic variation**. This factor may help account for the diversity of rhinoviruses, the variety of cold symptoms, and cold severity.

Each rhinovirus has 20 outer "protein" coats that can vary in composition. When common cold viruses change over time, it is the rearrange-ment in their antigen or protein coat. There are four **viral protein antigens** on the outer capsid (VP1, VP2, VP3, and VP4). The reason that we keep catching the common cold is because there are so many different rhinoviruses — each classified by their particular antigen combination. Even when our body can build immunity against one virus, there may be another hundred that it has to defend against. It takes a lifetime to build immunity to the majority of cold viruses in one's environment.

Boundaries to Common Cold Changes

The story of common cold viruses is like that of dog breeds. Although there are many different breeds descending from a common ancestor in the distant past, dogs are still dogs. We see this in rhinoviruses, as well as in plants and animals. DNA and RNA allow for many variations on a common theme. Although there may be great diversity to rhinoviruses, there are boundaries to their change. The genetic "blueprint" in all living things has its limits set by the disastrous consequences that inevitably happen when too many mutations add up. There are boundaries to a given gene pool. This fits with the concept of **stasis,** or limited change seen in nature. The principle that "**like begets like**" seems to be corroborated. Variation has it limits. There are boundaries to how far the changes can occur. This microevolution of rhinoviruses is an example of **recombination** and stasis, not a model of naturalistic descent with modification. Despite these many minor changes, those pesky viruses that cause the common cold will not mutate into an HIV (the AIDS virus), nor Ebola, nor even the "related" influenza virus. Finally, although we may keep catching the common cold, there is no need to worry that someday your disease will turn into AIDS, hemorrhagic fever, or even the flu. Relax — it is just a cold and gone in two weeks!

Electron Micrograph of Rhinoviruses

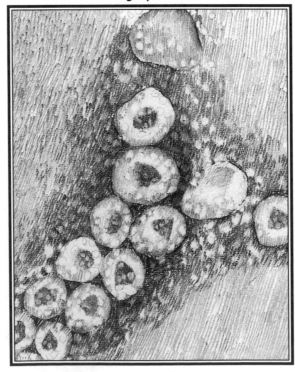

TABLE 2.2	"Macro" vs. "Micro" Evolution*	
TYPES	**MACRO**	**MICRO**
Gene Pool	Expansion There are no "misfits"	Same, conserving, oscillating genes
Direction	Upward, vertical	Sideways, horizontal
Selection	Creation of new, "good" phenotypes	Conservation of "good" phenotypes
New Forms	Expansion of "kinds" All life from one (or more) common life forms.	Expansion of subspecies Possible expansion of species No new "kinds" Variation

* Evolution = change, change in gene frequency, change in morphology

Predictions About the Nature of the Human Body

Two views of origins are summarized in table 2.1. Although neither the naturalistic view nor the intelligent design view can be proven scientifically in the ultimate sense, each theory has predictions that may be tested. This table compares each view's predictions about the human body's origins, genetics, development, organs, and systems, as well as form and function.

The term **evolution** here is used with caution, because it has a variety of meanings. It means different things to different people. Evolution can mean 1) change within a kind over time; 2) change from one kind to another kind due to the Darwinian mechanism of random variation and natural selection; and 3) descent with modification (all life forms being related).

Proponents of both **naturalistic descent** and creation models believe in the first definition of evolution, which is biological change within a kind (microevolution). Views two and three above involve macroevolution, a process that has never been observed in nature. These views differ in the amount of evolution, or biological change, that has taken place in microorganisms, plants, animals, and people over time. Table 2.2 summarizes the difference between micro- and macroevolution. Creationists can agree with most interpretations of microevolution, or variation within kinds (see Disease Focus 2.1).

Proponents of naturalistic descent see man as related not only to other primates but also to bacteria, protozoans, fungi, plants, and invertebrates. In the naturalistic view, the mechanisms of natural selection, mutations, immense periods of time, and chance physiochemical laws are assumed to be sufficient to explain the vertical, developmental macro-evolution of all life forms.

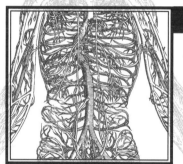

In contrast, proponents of intelligent design, while agreeing that current life forms may differ somewhat from their ancestors eons ago, believe the evidence from the fossil record and anatomy favor a model of **variation** (one with limited change or stasis) rather than macroevolution. Yes, some species may have undergone speciation (within their kind), such as in bacteria, *Drosophila* (fruit flies) or Galapagos finches. The evidence for variation or **microevolution** (limited change within a kind) is compatible with the creation view.

Intelligent Design

In 1802, William Paley, in his book *Natural Theology*, made the observation that if you were walking through the woods and you were to see two objects, a stone and a pocket watch, lying on the ground and asked yourself about the origin of these objects, you would not hesitate to say that the watch was a product of a watchmaker and the stone was likely a product of weathering, erosion, and fragmentation of a larger rock. As you studied and looked at the watch gears, springs, and screws, you most likely would deduce the watch was produced by conscious design and was the handiwork of a watchmaker. You would not deduce this about the stone, because its surface and features are much more random. The inference is inevitable that the watch must have had a maker. Paley argued that like the watch's arrangement, the anatomy of the human eye or the hand with its opposable thumb logically demand a divine **artificer** (craftsman) because of their complexity. The mechanisms proposed in macroevolution are insufficient to explain the seemingly perfect design in the human body.

Paley provided the first substantial, logical argument for creation or design theory. This is the concept that sees living organisms as the product of careful and conscious design and creative acts. A close examination of life forms

FIGURE 2.1

MT. RUSHMORE

reveals the details of structure and function so perfectly formed that they cannot be explained by chance physiochemical laws alone. The watch shows clear evidence of organization because of the way the components are put together to achieve a purpose.

How High Can You Jump?

Suppose your neighbor came to you saying that he had been exercising and wanted to impress you with his athletic ability. "Today, I cleared four feet in the high jump." You would have no reason to doubt him. If on successive days, he came to you bragging of his new athletic prowess being a foot higher each time, then you would probably start wondering about the truth after he claimed he cleared more than six feet. If he were one of the best athletes in the world (like Olympian Carl Lewis), then a seven-foot leap would be as far as you could possibly trust him. If he qualified himself and said he used a pole vault to complete the jump then you might believe him up to a point, perhaps as high as 20 feet.

If your neighbor kept coming to you to brag about his jumping to a mountaintop, such as jumping to the top of Mount Rushmore (figure 2.1) and standing on top of the carved president heads, you would not just harbor doubt but figure him to be a liar or lunatic. If he wanted to convince you that he was not telling a fairy tale, he might then qualify himself and tell you that he used scaffolding in several leaps. Then you would want to know where his scaffolding had gone after the jumps. Perhaps he would say, "*Oh it disappeared!*" If you pressed him further to provide evidence of this scaffolding, he tells you that he took it apart and used it to make his son's treehouse. His story is very convenient. Because it is difficult to prove him a liar, you change the topic of conversation to an NBA game or some other topic.

This allegory of high jumping can be applied to evolution. Microevolution refers to changes that can be made in one or a few simple jumps, whereas macroevolution refers to changes that appear to require large jumps. Darwin's proposal that relatively tiny changes can occur in nature was an important conceptual advance.

There seems to be strong evidence that one or two species of Galapagos finches change into clusters of species. We observe bacteria evolving from the antibiotic-sensitive condition into new strains that are resistant to antibiotics. Rhinoviruses, those that cause the common cold, may owe their diversity to mutation, selection, and diverse immune systems of the human body. Bacteria and viruses do change over time within their kind, but never become new types of microbes causing new diseases.

Dawkins' proposal, however, in *The Blind Watchmaker* and *Climbing Mount Improbable*, insists that entire new organs, organ systems, and species have come about by means of numerous mutations acted upon by natural selection over long periods of time. This is like an argument that someone jumped to the top of Mount Rushmore. Dawkins' argument for evolving major human body organs and complex systems is like your neighbor who claimed to have climbed Mount Rushmore with scaffolding that no longer exists.

SUMMARY

In summary, the Darwinian macroevolution view and Paley's intelligent design theory provide two very different perspectives on the development of the human body. Table 2.1 summarizes these two views of origins. You will want to compare the predictions of these two views and evaluate the data that support each one. According to Darwin, nature tinkered for a long time and human body parts were the result. For Paley, a divine artificer (craftsman) was responsible for the design seen in human anatomy. Which one is true? You are challenged to make a choice:

> *Choose you this day whom ye will serve; whether the gods which your fathers served that were on the other side of the flood, or the gods of the Amorites ... but as for me and my house, we will serve the Lord (Josh. 24: 15).*

Today's choice can be compared to a decision the ancient Israelites had to make between Jehovah and the Amorite gods. Today a worker in science must choose between the Creator and the blind forces of macroevolution. I believe that after all the evidence is examined, you will find new confidence in the biblical summary of creation:

> *For by him were all things created, that are in heaven, and that are in earth, visible and invisible, whether they be thrones, or dominions, or principalities, or powers: all things were created by him, and for him: And he is before all things, and by him all things consist (Col. 1:16–17).*

Before one can have faith, one must understand Jesus as the master Craftsman. Creation came after God (Jesus) acted. This is the foundation.

CHECK YOUR UNDERSTANDING

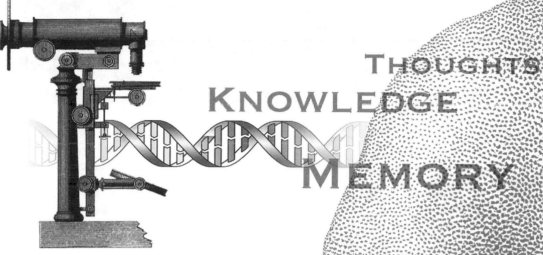

THOUGHTS
KNOWLEDGE
MEMORY

Two Views of Origins

1. How has evolution (molecules-to-man) affected thinking in the 20th century? How do you think it will affect people in the new millennium?

2. Compare and contrast the definition of evolution by creationists and evolution.

3. Explain the difference between micro- and macroevolution.

4. How is variation in humans (and other creatures) a lot like the concept of microevolution?

5. Explain two views on the presence of tonsils and wisdom teeth in your body.

6. Why do you suppose Charles Darwin rejected the earlier view of intelligent design proposed by William Paley?

7. How does one's world view of man's origin affect his/her living?

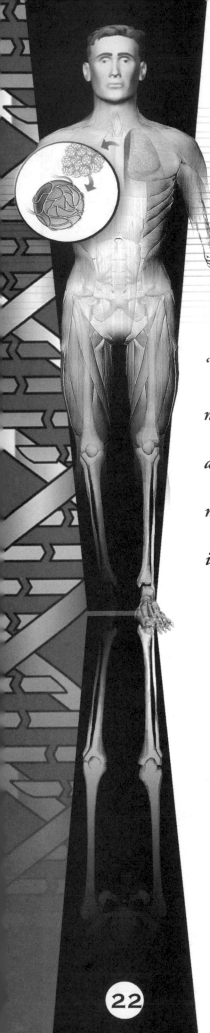

"The secret of (human)

membership lies locked

away inside each cell

nucleus, chemically coiled

in a strand of DNA."

(Paul Brand, M.D. [1980, 45])

The most basic unit of the body is the cell. In the cell we find various parts, like the cytoplasm, ribosomes, endoplasmic reticulum, and the nucleus. It is in the nucleus that we find one of the most fundamental molecules of life, **deoxyribonucleic acid (DNA)**. DNA serves as a "blueprint for life." Observations of living cells confirm that most of the development in the human body is both coded for and controlled by DNA.

The nucleus releases another molecule, **ribonucleic acid (RNA),** into the cytoplasm and eventually to the ribosome to direct protein synthesis. DNA, along with RNA, eventually directs the stages of development in the embryo. DNA consists of a simple but elegant pattern. The DNA bases are the language of biology. Like a blueprint for a building, these bases determine the details of the body form and function.

Three themes that can be seen in development in human cells, organs, and organ systems include 1) many living organisms and their parts can best be described as mosaics, thus, comparable to artwork; 2) each body cell clearly illustrates a coordinated complexity; and 3) each body part is fully functional.

DNA and Design Theory

Deoxyribonucleic acid, otherwise known as DNA (figure 3.1), is the blueprint of every human body and controls all the heredity of it. In 1953, the American biochemist James Watson and the British biochemist Frances Crick discovered that DNA was made of bases linked together in a double helix, looking like a long, twisted ladder. Each side of the "ladder" has alternating molecules made of deoxyribose sugar with an attached nitrogen base and phosphate. The four possible nitrogen bases are called **adenine (A), cytosine (C), guanine (G),** and **thymine (T)** (exclusive to DNA), or **uracil (U)** (exclusive to RNA). These bases are connected to each other by weak hydrogen bonds. Adenine (A) always pairs up with thymine (T), and cytosine (C) always pairs up with guanine (G). The joined base pairs form the "rungs" of the ladder. Each unit of DNA contains a sugar molecule, a phosphate molecule, and a nitrogenous base. This unit is called a nucleotide, and looks like the "rung" and the short section of ladder attached to it.

Each DNA strand has millions of atoms all fibrously connected into this long, twisted "ladder" in an extremely orderly fashion, giving the exact blueprint for the entire body. The "ladder" of DNA is so long that every human cell has about three feet of DNA in it, all coiled up into a tremendously compact coil. More amazing, however, than this interwoven system is the Creator who made it all. Nothing can compare to Him who not only made the huge stars in heaven, but also made the most compact coded information known to man, called DNA. It is worth noting that we are now finally able to map out the coded DNA on many large computers in the **Human Genome Project**; yet the architect made the intertwined, coded, string of life inside the tiny cell long before computers were invented.

Deoxyribonucleic acid (DNA) is the most perceptible example of interwoven design in the human body. Its abstruse structure and irreducible complexity are also evidence of a supernatural contrivance. Everything from phenotypic qualities of a human to the helicases and topoisomerases that comprise the DNA replication apparatus are so complex, characteristically delineated, and interwoven, that special creation is evident and evolutionary theories are nothing short of speculation.

In humans, the synthesis of a new strand of DNA occurs at the rate of about 3,000 nucleotides per minute, which in itself is evidence enough to disprove chance occurrence. Clearly, the cellular machinery involved in DNA replication must work with great precision and fidelity. Simple flaws in replication can lead to severe phenotypical disorders such as **sickle cell anemia**. DNA replication involves an intricate system of checks and balances. The main "proofreading" unit of this system is the **DNA polymerase**. This polymerase is so accurate that it averages a mere one error per billion base-pair duplications. This keeps the mutation load to a tolerable level in large genomes such as those in humans that contain 3 billion nucleotide pairs. The whole mechanism of DNA replication would fail if every integral part were not present; so, the idea of descent with modification is invalid in that all parts had to be present or no function would exist.

There are many solid evidences that descent with modification is not likely to happen. For instance, by studying **cytochrome C** gene comparisons, every plant and animal is approximately the same molecular distance from any bacterial species. No molecular evidence exists that points to any intermediates that might fill or have filled the space between bacteria and higher organisms. The sequence divergence of cytochrome C from bacteria to humans is 64–66%. This evidence is very important because natural selection is supposed to be a selective force that preserves any slight positive variation. Due to the fact that no intermediates (or evidence of past intermediates) exist, the whole idea of macroevolution and descent with modification is logically impossible. There are many other mechanisms involved in DNA

FIGURE 3.1

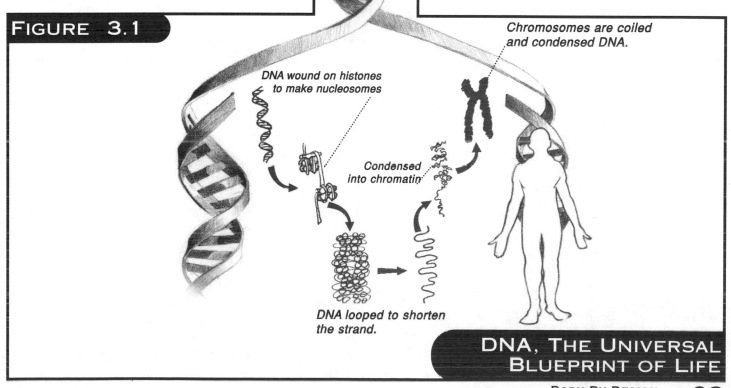

DNA wound on histones to make nucleosomes

Chromosomes are coiled and condensed DNA.

Condensed into chromatin

DNA looped to shorten the strand.

DNA, THE UNIVERSAL BLUEPRINT OF LIFE

IDENTICAL TWINS ARE UNIQUE

People often explain the nearly identical phenotypes of **monozygotic** (identical) twins by saying they contain the same genes. This is not precise. A gene can only exist in one place at any given time. The statement should be that identical twins contain progeny replicas of the same parental genes. This simple idiomatic expression suggests that most people do believe that the progeny replicas of a gene actually are identical. If the human genome contains 50,000 to 100,000 genes, could one deduce that all of these genes are exactly alike in identical twins?

A human life emerges from a single fertilized egg cell, which is a tiny sphere about 0.1 mm in diameter. That cell gives rise to literally hundreds of billions of cells during fetal development alone. The average adult human body contains around 65 trillion (6.5×10^{13}) cells. With little exception, each of these cells contains a progeny replica of each of the 50,000 to 100,000 genes. Do identical twins have identical replicas of these genes in all 65 trillion cells? If this is so, the process by which the genes are duplicated must be extremely accurate. Moreover, the cells of the body are not static. In some tissues, new cells are continuously replacing old or dead cells. A good example of this would be in bone marrow of a healthy person. The bone marrow cells produce approximately 2 million red blood cells per minute. The process by which these are duplicated is very accurate, but not all of the progeny replicas of genes in the body are identical. The human haploid genome contains some 3×10^9 nucleotide pairs of DNA that must all be duplicated with every cell division. Therefore, the idea that identical twins are in fact identical is limited to their genotype at conception. Over time, identical twins look and behave differently. Identical twins often have different destinies as adults. God designed every human specifically and individually with its own identity and purpose in life.

---

replication that point to special creation and show an interwoven, complex design as Dr. Michael Behe points out in the book *Mere Creation*.

DNA primarily determines the phenotype (outward appearance) of a human. DNA is supercoiled and forms chromatin. DNA is woven together with protein in a unit called a **histone** (figure 3.1). **Chromatin** is further coiled to form a **chromatid**. Two chromatids combine to form a **chromosome**. Chromosomes group together in the nucleolus of the cell. The cells group together to form tissues. Tissues group together to make organs. Organs group together to make organ systems, and organ systems group together to form an organism. Figure 3.1 illustrates the supercoiled design from the molecular to the organism level. Throughout the whole scheme, DNA determines and directs cellular processes that control everything from the blood type to facial features and hair color in humans. DNA, in a word, is the blueprint of life patterned and carefully assembled by the Creator.

DNA is such an efficacious proof of intelligent design and example of interwoven complexity that words fall short of adequate expression. It is interesting to note that by Charles Darwin's own test, evolution fails. He said in his book *The Origin of Species*: "If it could be demonstrated that any complex organ existed which could not possibly have been formed by numerous, successive, slight modifications, my theory would absolutely break down." If DNA does not demonstrate this, nothing else does. It is amazing that the more man learns about himself, the more he sees the Creator's interwoven craftsmanship in the human body.

DNA: Key to Understanding Design

The word, *fabrica* (or *fabricae*) is Latin for craft, trade, industry, workmanship, and process of building, construction, and production. A related word, *fabre*, is an adverb that means skillfully. Fabric is frequently used as an adjective to describe a tapestry, interwoven quilts, mosaics, and cross-stitching.

We see parallels in Scripture and body design. Henry Morris says in the annotations of *The Defender's Study Bible* reading for Psalm 139:15: "'curiously wrought' means 'embroidered,' a striking description of the double-helical DNA molecule program which organizes part by part the beautiful structure of the whole infant." In Psalm 139:16, his annotation on **fashioned**, reads: "The embryo is being fashioned in a way analogous to the way in which God 'formed' (same word) the body of Adam from the dust of the earth (Gen. 2:7)." In another highly respected study Bible, Charles Ryrie states that in Psalm 139:13, "'Didst form' means to acquire by creation, implying weave me in my mother's womb." Ryrie also concurs with Morris that "weave" is a good paraphrase of this passage. Like the helical symmetry of DNA woven in the DNA blueprint of life; God's will for our life is a woven tapestry.

Fluid Mosaic Model of the Cell

Many living organisms and their parts can best be visualized as **mosaic patterns**. Mosaics in nature mirror artwork. The tapestry of an Amish quilt represents a mosaic, blending home economics principles with an artistic vision. Both have patterns and designs in which contrasts exist between colors, pigments, and structures.

Biological mosaic patterns are most readily seen in cell structure. The cell membrane is a collage of many different proteins

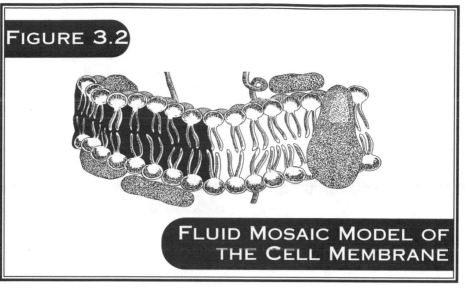

FIGURE 3.2

FLUID MOSAIC MODEL OF THE CELL MEMBRANE

embedded in the fluid matrix of the **lipid bilayer**. The lipid bilayer is the main fabric of the cell membrane, but the protein composition (within the bilayer) determines the specific functions of most cell membranes. Proteins in and on this bilayer have been described by some as "sailboats on a lake." The cell membrane and other intracellular membranes have their unique sets of proteins.

For example, more than 50 protein kinds have been found in the plasma membrane of red blood cells. In fact, biologists refer to the best model of the cell membrane as a **fluid mosaic model.** This model (figure 3.2) describes the cellular

---

DISEASE FOCUS 3.1

DISCOVERY OF SICKLE CELL ANEMIA

James Herrick, a Chicago physician, and Ernest Irons, a medical intern, examined the blood cells in one of their patients in 1904. They noticed that the red blood cells of the young man were thin and elongated. Their shape was remarkably different from the donut-shaped red blood cells of other patients. Herrick and Irons had examined numerous blood samples but had never come across this. They repeated sampling blood from the man with the same result. The red blood cells of the patient were shaped like the sickle that farmers used to harvest grain at that time.

The patient was a young college student and had been experiencing periods of weakness and dizziness. On the outside, the patient seemed like a normal, healthy 20-year-old. He complained that his major problem was fatigue. An extensive physical exam found curious enlargements of the heart and lymph nodes. The patient had mentioned that his heart always seemed to be pounding fast even while he was resting. Further blood

tests showed that he was anemic. His hemoglobin level was half as much as it should have been. **Hemoglobin** is a complex protein found in red blood cells that carries oxygen from the lungs to the tissues. Herrick and Irons were puzzled by their observations. Herrick kept an in-depth account of the patient's symptoms for six years before publishing his finding in a paper. The patient died in 1916 at age 32, from severe damage to the kidney caused by the anemia.

James Herrick was the first to publish a study on sickle cell anemia — the first inherited disease to be fully understood at the molecular level. It was not until 1949 that Linus Pauling documented the difference between the hemoglobin of a normal red blood cell and those with **sickle cell anemia**. Later, in 1957, Vernon Ingram found that the sixth amino acid of the b-chain of sickle cell hemoglobin was glutamic acid. In normal healthy hemoglobin, the amino acid is valine. Other than this single DNA mutation with an amino acid change, sickle cell and normal hemoglobin are identical.

proteins embedded in mosaic patterns within a lipid bilayer. This newer model reflects a change when proteins are embedded into the original lipid layer. All this intricacy fits with the creation concept that the cell is the result of a divine craftsman who has skillfully planned this beautiful cell membrane. These mosaic patterns in membranes facilitate transport between cells and screen toxins, as well as pathogens, across this important boundary.

Irreducible Complexity of the Cell

Each human body cell clearly illustrates a coordinated complexity. Prominent scientist Dr. Michael Behe has compiled this evidence. Biochemist Behe, author of *Darwin's Black Box*, points out that the simplest self-replicating cell has the capacity to produce thousands of different proteins and other molecules, at different times and under variable conditions. Synthesis, repair, and communication are functions that take place in virtually every cell. According to Behe, many processes in the cell exhibit irreducible complexity.

An **irreducibly complex system** is one that requires several interacting parts to be present and functioning at the same time. The removal of one (or more) of the parts causes the whole system to malfunction. Destroy one part and the whole falls apart — losing any beneficial adaptation or selective advantage. The purported mechanism of evolution, on the other hand, is that a new trait will confer a **survival advantage**, and thus enable its possessors to compete better than organisms without the trait. In macroevolution, any new trait would have to be completely developed; no halfway measures would do. Given this requirement, new features are so complex that neo-Darwinian gradualism is very improbable because an incompletely developed trait would confer no selective advantage.

Many cellular processes will not work unless every part is present and functioning. One such process is the transport of proteins across the cell membrane. Proteins do not just float around freely inside of cells. To paraphrase Michael Behe, **eukaryotic cells** have a number of different compartments, like rooms in a house. When a protein is made it has to get from the compartment where it's made to the compartment where it's supposed to be.

Consider what is involved in simply moving a protein through a compartment wall. Cells have two fundamentally different ways of doing this – **gated transport** and **vesicular transport**. In gated transport, the compartment wall is equipped with a "gate" and a chemical "sensor." If a protein bearing the right "identification tag" approaches, the sensor opens the gate and allows the protein to pass through. If one with the wrong tag comes near, the gate stays shut.

Note that all three components — the gate, the sensor, and the tag — must be in place for transport to occur. Most biochemical systems in the cell are much more complex than this. The total cooperation of many organelles produces an effect greater than the sum of the individual organelles. Biologists refer to this cooperative effect as an **emergent property** of the cell. Do you think this cooperation happened by chance?

Marks of Design

Michael Denton, a molecular biologist, wrote a controversial book in the 1980s called *Evolution: A Theory in Crisis*. He says that the "puzzle of perfection" in living things critically challenges any theory of evolution that is based on chance mutations. New discoveries in biology are opening up new levels of detail in the workings of the human body and are revealing ever more precise functioning.

Every cell type and organ in the body is necessary and useful, and within each organ there is an incredible inner precision. The liver, the body's largest internal organ, is a multifaceted, vital organ — one without which people cannot live long. Indeed it is only one of many organs which, when working properly, illustrate great efficiency and order in complexity.

Cells in the immune system illustrate the emergent property concept. This cell-team action produces a result that is greater than the individual parts. This is one of the "puzzles of perfection" that Dr. Denton describes in his book. The effective body defense of the immune system comes from the cooperation of many cells including monocytes, lymphocytes, and **macrophages** ("big eaters" of harmful chemicals and pathogens). The ability of macrophages to recognize, apprehend, and destroy bacteria depends on the coordinated activity of many cells. The cytoskeleton, lysozyme, and the plasma membranes function in phagocytosis. Like many other bodily functions, the immune system depends on the contribution of each and every cell type.

Every organ in the body is fully functional and useful, and within each organ there is an incredible inner order that provides precise, coordinated functioning. Today's scientific tools of investigation are much more powerful than any during Darwin's day. Scientists can now explore most of the complex, interlocking biochemical systems.

As cell biologists discover numerous biochemical cascades, they have learned that these reactions act in perfect harmony. The human body is able to facilitate these activities when they are needed and it can inhibit them when they are not needed.

The sequence of commands is programmed in the DNA code that directs almost all cellular processes. Such microscopic precision is dazzling!

It is a mathematical absurdity to suggest that billions of complex cells could all coordinate their precise molecular activities by blind chance and natural selection. The inadequacy of the theory on body organs arising by chance is well illustrated in the human kidney. There is an elegance of design manifest in the kidney. It combines many wondrous and clever adaptations to control water and electrolyte homeostasis, as well as blood pressure. At this same time, the kidney concentrates and eliminates wastes from the body in urine.

In chapters 4 to 16 there are dozens of examples of intricate design, including the structure of the hand, the extraordinary excretory system, the dynamic digestive system, the blood-clotting mechanism, the impressive immune system, and the biology of vision. Neo-Darwinism falls short, lacking a scheme of explanation for these intricate systems. Because there is no simpler level to which they can appeal, macroevolutionists can't explain how these systems arose. There are no detailed mechanisms for the origin of living cells.

Some professional creationists carry this criticism of macroevolutionism over to the study of biological code chemicals. Unlike the complexity of a snowflake that derives its structure from the nature of the materials it is made from, the complexity of genetic information is independent of the nature of nucleic acids that record it. The nucleic acids are merely the vehicle by which this marvelous biological information is carried. Intelligent causation once again is strongly suggested.

The Remarkable Fit of Body Tissues

The principle that structure is the basis of function applies to the cells and tissues as well. **Histology** is the study of tissues that are defined as a group of similar cells forming a definite and continuous fabric, usually having a comparable function. The function of tissues is limited by its structure, as illustrated by epithelium. It can do only as much as its structure will "allow." The structure of each type of epithelium fits its function. Some of the major tissue types from four regions of the body are depicted in figure 3.3.

Can you identify the major types?

Pseudostratified columnar epithelium (I) has cells (like bricks on end) with relatively large cytoplasmic volumes. It is often located where secretion or active absorption of substances are important functions, like those found in the trachea. Dust or foreign particles are escalated out of the body by means of cilia and mucous.

Simple cuboidal epithelium (II) is specialized for secretion and makes up the epithelia of the thyroid gland shown. These cells (like sugar cubes) secrete hormones into the bloodstream. In contrast, **simple squamous epithelium (III)** is relatively leaky tissue. These cells (like floor tiles) are specialized for exchange of materials by diffusion. These epithelia are found in such places as the linings of blood vessels and air sacs (alveoli) of the lungs.

A **simple columnar epithelium (IV)** has cells with relatively large cytoplasmic volumes, and is often located where secretion or active absorption of substances are important functions. The stomach and intestines are lined by a columnar epithelium that secretes digestive juices and absorbs nutrients.

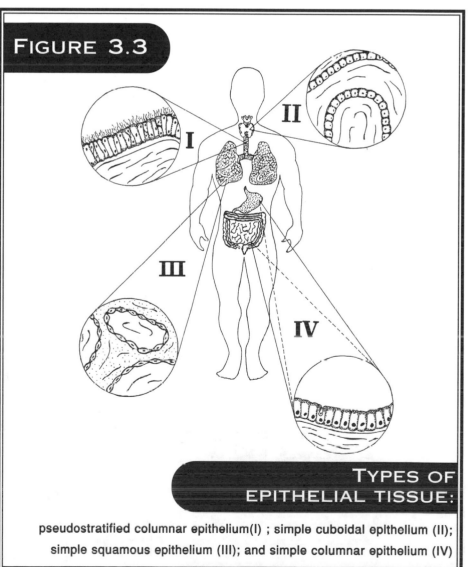

FIGURE 3.3

TYPES OF EPITHELIAL TISSUE:

pseudostratified columnar epithelium(I) ; simple cuboidal epithelium (II); simple squamous epithelium (III); and simple columnar epithelium (IV)

Structure and Function: A Planned Relationship

Given a choice of dissection tools, you would not make an incision in a preserved specimen with a blunt probe, nor would you use scissors to separate delicate blood vessels that are attached. Ideally, you would use a sharp scalpel to make an incision and a blunt probe to separate the blood vessels in your dissection. The structure of an instrument determines its function. In other words, a device fits its structure and form fits function.

In like manner, structure and function are correlated at all levels of biological organization. This theme is a guide to anatomy at its many structural levels, from molecules to organisms (figure 3.4). Analyzing a biological structure gives us clues about

what it does and how it works. Conversely, knowing the function of a structure provides insight about its construction.

Structure/function relationships may be seen at every level of the body, as well as the interwoven design pattern. Figure 3.4 illustrates this. Interacting atoms form interwoven molecules, such as DNA. Biologically important molecular units (like **histones**) form organelles that combine to form cells, such as heart muscle cells. Groups of cells combine to form tissues with specific function, such as cardiac muscle. Two or more tissues combine to form an organ, such as the heart. The heart is one component of the circulatory system that includes blood and blood vessels. All the organ systems combine to create a complete human being, *Homo sapiens*.

The Creator, in His wisdom, makes use of a well-organized and orderly plan to make a whole person. No detail is forgotten and no provision is lacking for a purposeful life. How amazing!

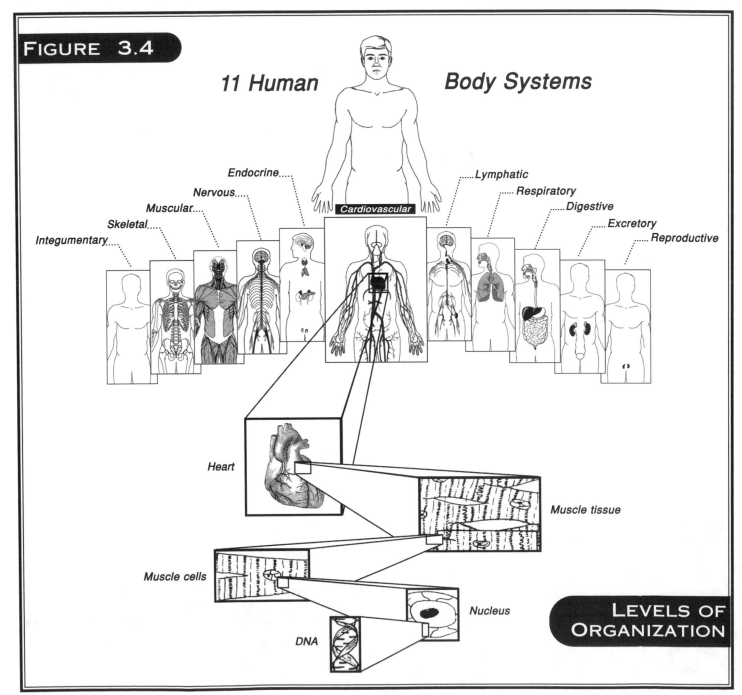

FIGURE 3.4

11 Human Body Systems

Integumentary
Skeletal
Muscular
Nervous
Endocrine
Cardiovascular
Lymphatic
Respiratory
Digestive
Excretory
Reproductive

Heart
Muscle tissue
Muscle cells
Nucleus
DNA

LEVELS OF ORGANIZATION

CHECK YOUR UNDERSTANDING

THOUGHTS
KNOWLEDGE
MEMORY

DNA and Development

1. How is the concept of a mosaic an evidence for intelligent design?

2. Describe the fluid mosaic membrane of the cell.

3. Explain the principle of uniform experience and how it relates to the intelligent design inference.

4. Illustrate how you might recognize design in DNA in living systems.

5. What are the four types of tissues found in the body? Describe how structure is related to the function for each tissue type.

6. Define the different levels of complexity in the human body, starting with DNA and ending with one of the systems in the body.

Thine hands have made me and fashioned me together round about; yet thou dost destroy me. Remember, I beseech thee, that thou hast made me as the clay; and wilt thou bring me into dust again? Hast thou not poured me out as milk, and curdled me like cheese? Thou hast clothed me with skin and flesh, and hast fenced me with bones and sinews. Thou hast granted me life and favour, and thy visitation hath preserved my spirit

(Job 10:8–12).

In the last chapter we explored the biblical and the biological basis for the helical, interwoven design. David recognized that he was fearfully and wonderfully made. Then, 3,000 years later, the spiral blueprint for all life, DNA, was elucidated. In this chapter we explore human body development and see further the wisdom behind the Scriptures implying a curiously wrought pattern. Like David, Job not only recognized his Creator but also realized that God had fashioned him with skill and purpose. The intelligent Designer had made Job as a delicate, intricate vessel for His use. In the midst of suffering, Job wondered why God would create something expensive, beautiful, and finely stitched (like designer clothing) and then, for no reason, discard what He had taken so much time to make. After all, God made his skin, digestive tract, and blood vessels with many layers (**tunics**) and fashioned his body framework with the strength of bones, tendons, and muscles. All these body parts were sewn, stitched, and woven together with such wondrous care. God had granted him life and favor for so long, yet in this moment of anguish God seemed to be disposing of this fine craft!

Eventually, we see that all that happened to Job was no accident. In fact, his life pattern and body structures were not random. Perhaps Job could only see the black and gray threads strung below the tapestry, but God was cross-knitting a tapestry above that the angels could see. The angels saw the beautiful picture interlaced with gold and silver, along with the black threads — a masterpiece for all eternity to see. Not only was Job's body intertwined with color, but so was his life testimony.

Reproductive System

The reproductive system is the only body system that is not necessary for the survival of an individual, but is necessary for the survival of mankind. In man, the "act of marriage"

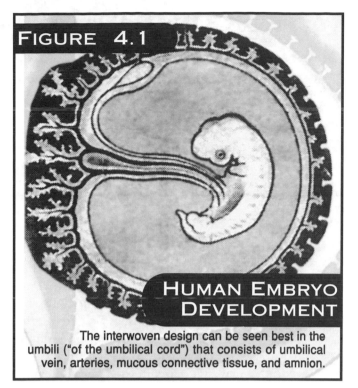

FIGURE 4.1

HUMAN EMBRYO DEVELOPMENT

The interwoven design can be seen best in the umbili ("of the umbilical cord") that consists of umbilical vein, arteries, mucous connective tissue, and amnion.

functions in physical intimacy, as well as in reproduction. This is the system that serves mankind to fulfill the biblical mandate to "be fruitful and multiply."

Because the reproductive organs are located in the same area of the body, and share some functions, they often are treated together with the excretory system. You might say that men and women have different types of "plumbing," and consequently are treated by physicians differently by design. The systems of the male and female are each geared toward fulfilling specific roles. The male's reproductive system is designed to generate sperm cells containing half of the genetic material necessary for the development of a baby and deliver that material to the female's reproductive system. The female's reproductive system is designed to generate an **ovum**, or egg, that carries the other half of the genetic material, to be fertilized by the **sperm** cells from the male. The female's reproductive tract is also made to support the gestating **embryo** and later the **fetus** (figure 4.1), until the baby is born, about nine months after fertilization.

Pregnancy occurs as a result of the fertilization of an ovum by sperm. With fertilization, cell division (mitosis) begins, and the fertilized egg develops into a mass of cells called the **morula** that move through the uterine tube (also fallopian tube or oviduct) into the uterus. The morula continues to divide until it becomes a hollow clump of about a hundred cells called the **blastocyst**. About seven or eight days after fertilization, the blastocyst settles on the wall of the uterus. Some of the cells covering the blastocyst, known as the **trophoblast**, begin to invade the endometrium and grow into cords that anchor the blastocyst to the wall of the uterus. The trophoblast eventually develops into the **placenta**.

The **blastocyst** is composed of two layers — the upper ecto-

derm layer, and the lower endoderm layer. An amniotic cavity and "yolk sac" soon appear in the blastocyst. The amnion lines the chorion, the outermost envelope that furnishes a protective and nutritive covering for the zygote, as the fertilized egg is now called. The embryonic disk, a flat area in the ovum in which the first traces of the embryo are seen, is suspended from the chorion and is composed of three germ layers, the **ectoderm**, **mesoderm**, and **endoderm**. All organs of the embryo are developed from these three germ layers.

From the ectoderm, the nervous system, sense organs, the epidermis, and others are developed. The circulatory, excretory, skeletal, muscular, and reproductive systems are developed from the mesoderm. The endoderm produces the respiratory and digestive systems, along with their linings.

Pregnancy lasts for about nine months and can be divided into approximately three equal parts called trimesters. The first trimester is the period in which all the various different parts of the baby are formed. During the second and third trimesters the organs needed for the baby to survive in the outside world develop and mature, and the fetus continues to grow in size and weight.

The first sign of pregnancy is usually when the menstrual cycle is interrupted by the fertilization and implantation of the embryo cell in the uterus. Other signs of early pregnancy are nausea, more frequent urination, and a sense of fullness or tenderness in the breasts. Nausea usually occurs early in the day and then subsides, hence the phrase "**morning sickness**," but some women can suffer from actual vomiting. Nausea and vomiting normally cease after the first three months of pregnancy.

A doctor will probably want to give women a physical examination, in addition to performing lab tests, to confirm pregnancy. There are various signs a doctor looks for in the examination: changes in a woman's breasts and changes in the shape and size of the uterus, vaginal lining, and cervix. In a pregnant woman the lining of the birth canal becomes blue as a result of the increase in blood flowing to it. The cervix softens so that it is possible to feel the rest of the uterus clearly through it. The uterus softens as well and becomes larger and rounder than usual. From the doctor's internal examination it is possible to estimate how many weeks pregnant a woman is. During the first trimester the growth of the uterus is rapid, and feeling the uterus at this stage is done more accurately than later in pregnancy.

Embryo at Six Weeks

From a single cell, the embryo (which is one of the largest cells in the human body but still far too small to be seen with the naked eye), grows in length during the first six weeks of intrauterine life to about 5 mm (0.2 inch). During the embryonic period the main parts of the neck and face develop, as do the bones, nerves, muscles, genitals, and some sense organs. The spinal cord, brain, ears, and eyes have started their development. The tissue from which the lungs form appears as well as the earliest parts of the stomach, liver, pancreas, intestines, and kidneys. There are two pairs of limb buds, from which the arms and legs will take shape. The simple heart has started to beat.

By the time a child has been developing for only nine weeks in the mother's womb, all the organs are formed and the external features are established. At this point in time, the child is classified as a fetus. By the end of 12 weeks, when the child is three inches long, every detail of basic structure is developed. The fetal period, which begins at week 9 and culminates at birth, is characterized by tremendous growth and the specialization of body structures.

By 16 weeks of intrauterine life, the fetus is about six inches long and weighs about six ounces. The blood vessels show through the delicate, semi-transparent skin, and the body is bright pink. Downy, fine hair is starting to grow over the whole surface of the skin, and the eyebrows and eyelashes are beginning to emerge. The joints of all the limbs are moving, the fingers and toes have separated and are fully formed, and the toenails and fingernails are grown in. The sex of the fetus can clearly be determined as the external genital organs are developed. Although the lungs are very poorly developed, the chest of the fetus moves from time to time as if it were breathing. The fetus is now moving a lot but it is still too early for the mother to feel.

A pregnancy lasts for approximately 267 days (nine months). As the date of conception is not always known, it is usual to calculate the date of delivery from the start of the last menstrual period. When a mother fails to note the date of her last period or had previously been on contraceptives, a doctor may want an ultrasound examination which gives remarkably accurate information on the age of the fetus. Even if the exact date of conception is known, a doctor will frequently give a range of dates covering a 2–3 week period for the estimated date of birth.

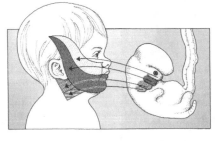

The structures in an embryo that evolutionists call gill slits actually have an important developmental function.

Fabrica Design: The Umbilical Cord

The **umbilical cord** is the communicating channel between the placenta and the fetus. It sends waste products from the fetus to the placenta and returns the blood from the placenta to the fetus. At birth the arteries in the umbilical cord constrict and close, stopping the blood flow to the placenta. Soon after the birth the umbilical cord is cut short and securely clamped. The fabrica or interwoven design may be seen in the umbilical cord and its associated connecting parts between mother and child. The associated parts include the embryo's chorion and the mother's endometrium (figure 4.1).

Every Part Essential

There are certain areas of human genetics and embryology in which researchers expect to expand their current knowledge. Two of these are the regulation of gene expression and the mapping of the entire human genome. The role of the vast majority of DNA that has not yet been assigned a function has been inappropriately named "junk" DNA. Research published in early 1992 demonstrated that an intron, which is thought to be a non-coding region of DNA, plays a role in the function of transfer RNA, which is critical to protein synthesis. Additional research has revealed other functions of this so-called "junk" DNA. Indeed, each genetic component seems to be essential for body function. Even the so-called "vestiges" are fully functional organs. In human development, there are few (if any) wasted parts in the fetus and embryo. The concept of there being useless or vestigial body parts is an outdated idea that has largely been disproved.

Recapitulation Revisited

Ernst Haeckel, a German anatomist, first proposed the recapitulation idea that **ontogeny recapitulates phylogeny** (development replays macroevolution) over 100 years ago. Better known as the biogenetic "law," it claims that in its development each embryo passes through abbreviated evolutionary phases that resemble the developmental stages of its ancestors. Evolutionary theory states that man evolved from fish and amphibians, which have gills, and then point to the "gill slits" which human embryos are said to have in one stage of their development. Evolutionists base the recapitulation idea on the faulty assumption that any body part superficially resembling another in animals must have a common origin.

This idea was dismissed for a number of years by professional biologists but it keeps cropping up. Anti-creationist Dr. Ken Miller, for example, has recently tried to give credibility to this 19th century thinking in a recent *Life* magazine article. This article, in a speculative essay format, contains beautiful photographs of vertebrate embryos, intended to convince readers of its scientific merit.

Does ontogeny repeat phylogeny? No, not at all, says Dr. Jonathan Wells, a noted Ph.D. embryologist. Wells says Miller's evidence for the recapitulation idea is the "Piltdown hoax" of 1990s embryology. The following evidence stands against **Haeckel's discredited biogenetic law**:

1. The so-called "yolk sac" is really a blood sac. Blood cells originate from blood islands in the structure. Later, bone

Sexually Transmitted Diseases and the Fear Factor

*"Be not wise in thine own eyes: fear the Lord, and depart from evil. It
shall be health to thy navel, and marrow to thy bones" (Prov. 3: 7–8).*

Sexually **transmitted diseases** (STDs) is a general term that refers to as many as 20 different illnesses. These are transmitted by sex, usually through the exchange of body fluids such as semen, vaginal fluid, and blood. STDs such as herpes can be acquired by kissing or close contact with infected areas — not just intercourse. If left untreated, STDs can cause permanent damage that may leave you blind, brain-damaged, or sterile. **HIV (human immunodeficiency virus)** disease often leads to AIDS (acquired immune deficiency syndrome), which can cause death. The most common STDs are chlamydia, herpes, gonorrhea, genital warts, syphilis, hepatitis B, crabs, and trichomoniasis.

Who gets STDs? They infect men, women, and children. Mothers can also give STDs to their babies. Anyone at any age can be a victim. It is not true that having had a STD once and having been cured prevents one from getting it again. Anyone who has sex can get a sexually transmitted disease, and millions do. More than 4 million people get chlamydia each year. Genital herpes affects an estimated 30 million Americans, with as many as 500,000 new cases reported each year. There are over 1 million cases of gonorrhea each year. And syphilis, once thought to be on the decline, has made a comeback in the last few years.

Sexually transmitted diseases merit special attention in a biology course because of the enormous number of infected individuals in our society. Some estimates suggest that an astronomical 25 million people may have some form of sexually transmitted disease. Syphilis, the ancient scourge, continues to be a significant problem in modern society; gonorrhea accounts for a million recorded cases annually; and several "new" STDs are among the most common of all diseases in Americans, including chlamydia and ureaplasmal urethritis.

STDs can be prevented and most can be cured. Yet, there are two reasons for alarm. STDs are increasing among young people ages 14–21, and medical doctors are seeing more patients that have resistant bacteria to antibiotic treatment. Many feel invincible, yet few realize the long-term consequences of illegitimate sex. Unless people begin to obey God's laws and obey God's commandments (the fear factor), STDs will likely follow the trend of increasing worldwide. We reap the consequences of what we sow.

---

marrow develops from this tissue in the human fetus.

2. The so-called "gill slits" are really wrinkles in the throat region. This body tissue becomes the palatine tonsils, middle ear canal, parathyroid gland, and thymus.

3. The so-called "tail" is in reality four fused bones called the coccyx that serves as attachment for vitally important muscles (used in defecation, for example). The coccyx is also necessary for good posture and support.

In fact, neither gills nor their slits are found at any stage in the embryological development of any mammal, including man. These folds in the neck region of the mammalian embryo are not gills in any sense of the word and never have anything to do with breathing. They are merely inward folds, or wrinkles, in the neck region resulting from the sharply down-turned head and protruding heart of the developing embryo. None of the reputable medical embryology texts that we checked claimed that there are "gill slits" in mammal development.

To say that people have a "tail bone" is to assume "human evolution" from a tailed, vertebrate ancestor. Anatomically speaking, this bone is the **coccyx**. It has nothing to do with the tail that we usually associate with monkeys or dogs. In the developing human embryo, before it is covered with important muscles of the lower intestine, the coccyx only looks like a tail. There are a number of embryonic structures that superficially look like something else. Evolutionists use these developing structures to make their case for macroevolution. However, science has shown each structure is fully functional for development, such as what we have seen with the coccyx. Still, the "gill slit" myth is perpetuated in many college biology textbooks as evidence for macroevolution. The fictitious "gill slits" of human embryos discussed by Haeckel, for example, are supposed to represent the "fish" or "amphibian" stage of man's "evolutionary ancestors." Most professional embryologists no longer believe this "gill slits" myth of the biogenetic "law." Even evolutionist Dr. P. Ehrlich said:

> *This interpretation of embryological sequences will not stand under close examination. Its shortcomings have been almost universally pointed out by modern authors, but the idea still has a prominent place in biological mythology.*

Embryologist Dr. E. Blechschmidt reveals some of his frustration with the persistence of this myth: "The so called basic law of biogenetics is wrong. No buts or ifs can mitigate this fact. It is not even slightly correct or correct in a different form. It is totally wrong." Yet, in many introductory biology textbooks, embryological recapitulation is offered as evidence for evolution. Ever since Darwin, the argument from similarity comprises much of the case for the general theory of evolution. It is assumed that similarity provides evidence for an evolutionary relationship and the degree of similarity predicts its proximity in time. Neither of these propositions is supported by scientific data.

"Vestigial" Organs Are Fully Functional

One topic of interest to anatomists over the years has been rudimentary or **vestigial** organs. A vestigial structure is a body part that apparently has no function, and is presumed to have been useful in ancestral species. Like the anatomical anomaly story discussed in the previous section, alternative research techniques and new ways of studying old topics have shed fresh insight on the study of vestigial organs.

Medical research now confirms that over one hundred body parts once considered "vestigial" do have functions. Some examples of previously imagined "vestigial" organs include the adenoids, appendix, thymus, tonsils, and lymph nodes. Extensive research studies have now shown that each of the above organs and tissue is a part of our impressive immune system.

Tonsils Are Needed in Fighting Respiratory Infections

Many of the organs once classified as vestigial were found to be composed of lymphatic tissue, and hence, have an immune function. Two medically important organs routinely removed in former days were the tonsils (palatine tonsils) and the adenoids. The long-held assumption was that tonsils were useless or vestigial, and hence tonsillectomies were frequent. **Tonsillitis** was over-diagnosed (swollen tonsils during a cold), and the routine removal of tonsils by surgery was all too common. Most physicians thought it best to remove these useless (vestigial) organs when the tonsils were irritated for more than a few days.

Tonsils were first suspected as a cause of health problems because of a connection between tonsil size and severity of respiratory infection. When children have the greatest severity of colds, tonsils swell. In the 1930s, over half of the children had their tonsils and adenoids removed. Then medical scientists learned that tonsils are important to young people in helping to establish the body's defense capabilities by producing antibodies. Once these defense mechanisms develop, the tonsils shrink to a smaller size in adults. Tonsils are important in the growth of the immunological system.

Tonsils are the first line of defense against respiratory viruses and bacteria. After learning these facts in 1971, a medical doctor is reported as saying that "If there are one million tonsillectomies done in the United States, there are 999,000 that don't need doing." For decades, millions of children were victims of evolutionary medical malpractice.

Drawing Conclusions

Notice how flawed thinking yields false conclusions. We wonder how many malpractice suits might have been filed because of the error of removing fully functional organs. There is danger when scientists make errors in their conclusions. Many lives could have been spared. The number of severe colds and prolonged throat infections could have been reduced if physicians had not removed so many tonsils. In most cases, children would not have been exposed to the danger of this needless surgery. In addition, they would have had the benefit of a fully developed immune system to help fight respiratory diseases. In conclusion, the health of many individuals could have been improved if physicians had realized that tonsils and **adenoids** are fully functional.

Until very recently, vestigial organs were interpreted as strong evidence favoring macroevolution. For well over a century, the vestigial organ argument was considered one of the strongest supporting data of evolution and some writers still consider it to be a strong support for evolution. But of the approximately 180 vestigial organs compiled by researchers around the year 1900, it is now agreed that most of these have at least one function in the body. After examining the few organs that are still generally believed to be vestigial by evolutionists, it is now thought that each of these has at least one function.

In addition to the previously named organs of the immune system, the coccyx, **plica semilunaris**, and **pineal gland** were once considered examples of useless vestigial organs. Researchers have found that most of these so-called vestigial organs also play several roles. Some are back-up organs, operative in unusual situations or during only certain stages of the organism's life. Such information has been very slow to find its way into the textbooks of biology and origins. For example, several major functions of the so-called nictitating membrane in the human eye were delineated in the 1920s, yet some science text writers still label them "vestigial." Finally, I echo the conclusions of Bergman and Howe:

> *Since virtually all of the so-called vestigial organs are shown to have functions, macroevolutionists can no longer credibly claim that evolution is the only origins model that will accommodate these scientific data. Individuals who are not fully indoctrinated with evolutionary philosophy will be able to see that all body organs function harmoniously. Dispelling the concept of vestigial organs allows the Creator's work in biology to be viewed scientifically as neither evolutionary, defective, nor capricious, but as evidence for His handiwork and design.*

CHECK YOUR UNDERSTANDING

THOUGHTS

KNOWLEDGE

MEMORY

Reproductive System and Development

1. List at least three organs of the reproductive system.

2. What is the overall function of the reproductive system?

3. Describe an interwoven part of the reproductive system.

4. Describe how the layers around the growing fetus develop and function to protect the growing embryo. How is this evidence for an intelligent designer?

5. What is the term for infectious diseases that are transmitted through intimate contact of the reproductive organs?

6. Explain recapitulation theory. Name the person who conceived this idea and name its modern-day proponent.

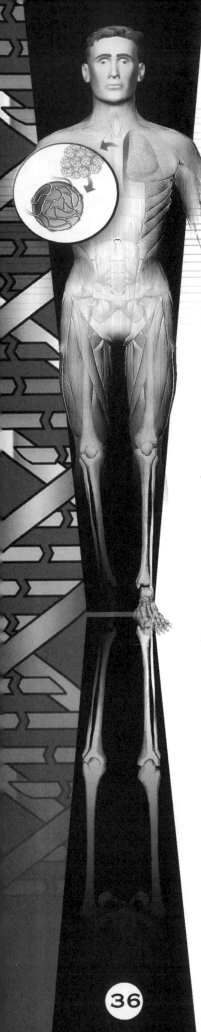

"Bone is power. It is the bone to which the soft parts cling, from which they are, helpless, strung and held aloft to the sun, lest man be but another slithering earthnoser."

Richard Selzer (Brand and Yancey)

Bones: A Study in Design Engineering

One of the more familiar types of connective tissue to the anatomist and layperson alike is bone tissue. Perhaps the simplest anatomy to understand is the skeleton, and the easiest place to observe the relationship of form to function are its individual bones. Anatomy and physiology students are impressed with the robust, intricate, sculpted design of bone. Why is this? Perhaps it is due to the function and structure of bone, and the interaction and fit of various bones, much like mechanical objects. Fossilized bones, too, have an ancient mystery surrounding them; their very existence is explained by one's world view. Convinced that "form follows function," we will first consider the functional importance of bones with regards to our physical make-up and survival.

Bones will be examined not only for their mechanical function but also for the role that the largest and smallest bones have in our anatomy and physiology. Since human skulls (mostly shattered and incomplete) and teeth are some of the most important fossil specimens used to speculate about the strange fiction of "human evolution," we will look at these, too. Special attention will be given to the dynamic nature of bone as a living, growing tissue. We will see how our **endoskeleton** grows in response to the physical demands an individual places upon it.

An ultrastructural study of bone will show special cells that break down, maintain, or add bone deposits in a very detailed and orchestrated fashion according to daily physical demands. These cells must work together in a precisely coordinated fashion. An imbalance of the activity of these cell types will result in serious conditions like **osteoporosis**.

Skeletal System

The skeleton is the framework of the human anatomy, supporting the body and protecting its internal organs (figure 5.1a).

How Do You Identify a Real Skeleton From a Plastic One?

Authentic skeletons usually have an off-white appearance, fake ones have a bright white appearance. Real skeletons are quite porous and have ridges where healing took place on breaks and bone fractures. Artificial ones have smooth surfaces; everything is symmetrical and perfect. Authentic skeletons have imperfections. In fact, when I studied anatomy at Baylor College of Medicine, I never saw a "perfect" skeleton. Every authentic skeleton in the **cadaver** room has either nicks, extra bumps, or fractures on bone surfaces. In general, every skeleton has minor deformities at birth and sustains evidence of trauma through adulthood. Life is traumatic and brings various bumps and bruises. The skeleton records life's knocks, breaks, cuts, and even marks of healing. This is why ancient bones, skulls, and skeletons tell us much about our historic past. You can tell an authentic skeleton from a replica, cast, or fake skeleton by its composition and "marks." You will be less likely to be fooled by a forgery if you are aware of these identifying features. They are also valuable for revealing to medical doctors and dentists a person's medical history for planning diagnosis and treatment in the present. Physicians and dentists learn a lot from authentic skeletons, skulls, bones, and teeth so they can help you understand your body and its health.

FIGURE 5.1

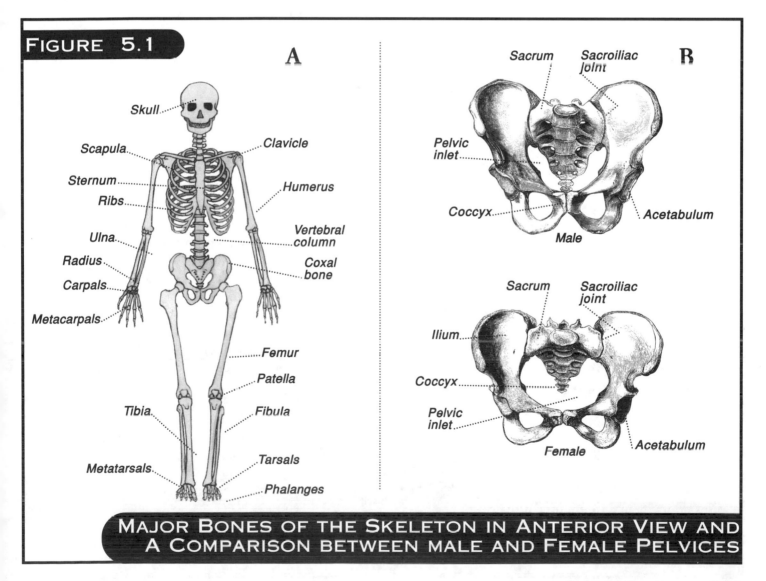

A

- Skull
- Scapula
- Sternum
- Ribs
- Ulna
- Radius
- Carpals
- Metacarpals
- Clavicle
- Humerus
- Vertebral column
- Coxal bone
- Femur
- Patella
- Tibia
- Fibula
- Metatarsals
- Tarsals
- Phalanges

B

- Sacrum
- Sacroiliac joint
- Pelvic inlet
- Coccyx
- Acetabulum

Male

- Sacrum
- Sacroiliac joint
- Ilium
- Coccyx
- Pelvic inlet
- Acetabulum

Female

MAJOR BONES OF THE SKELETON IN ANTERIOR VIEW AND A COMPARISON BETWEEN MALE AND FEMALE PELVICES

Two hundred and six bones compose the adult skeleton, over half of which are in the hands and feet. Most of the bones are connected to other bones at flexible joints, which lend the framework a high degree of flexibility. An old spiritual sings that the footbone is connected to the legbone and the legbone is connected to the thighbone. In truth, every bone is connected to another, with one exception. Only the **hyoid bone** is not directly connected to another bone in this **articulation**. It anchors the tongue and is attached to the styloid processes of the skull by ligament. The skeletons of male and female bodies are essentially the same, with the noteworthy exceptions being that female bones are usually lighter and thinner than male bones, and the female pelvis is shallower and wider than the male's (figure 5.1b). This latter difference makes childbirth easier.

Bones (or **osseous material**) serve a number of diverse purposes in the human anatomy. In addition to providing structure, protection, and support for the organs of the body, bones also house marrow, which produces blood cells. The bones also store the calcium deposits which the body may access, via resorption, when needed. Additionally, bones detoxify the system by removing heavy metals, such as lead and arsenic, as well as other toxins, from the bloodstream. Osseous tissue itself is made of water (about 1/4 of the bone weight), organic material (about 1/3 of the bone weight, most of which is the protein, collagen) and inorganic minerals (calcium, phosphorus, and magnesium predominate, though iron, sodium, potassium, chlorine, and fluorine are also present in small amounts). Most bones (except the cranium) are initially pre-formed in cartilage and are then ossified as the newborn develops (figure 5.2).

Bones and the Skeleton

Two basic classification methods exist to categorize the bones of the body. These two classification systems are based upon anatomical location (axial or appendicular), and shape (long, short, flat, and irregular). **Axial bones** are the 80 bones which lie along the central, vertical axis of the body and support and protect the head and torso. They include the skull and the spinal (vertebral) column. **Appendicular bones** include the 126 bones that comprise the appendages, including the shoulders and hips, arms and legs, hands and feet, and fingers and toes. The shape classifications include **long bones** (such as the radius, humerus, and femur), the **short bones** (such as the carpals, tarsals, and manual and pedal phalanges), **flat bones** (such as the sternum, skull bones, and scapulae), and **irregular bones** (such as the vertebrae).

DISEASE FOCUS 5.1

Arthritis, the Greatest Crippler

Arthritis, afflicting an estimated more-than-50-million Americans, is the country's chief cause of physical disability and is a combination of Greek words meaning "joint" and "bone." Arthritis causes the joint to swell painfully, and eventually the joint becomes inflamed. This group of diseases appears in many forms. One is old-fashioned **gout**; more prevalent is **osteoarthritis**, which produces the aches and hobbled joints of old age; and the form most feared is **rheumatoid arthritis**, which often attacks young adults and persists into advanced age.

Arthritis strikes body joints or connective tissues with painful and disabling effect. But why it attacks and how it can be prevented is unanswered. One theory surmises that the body literally turns on itself, an **autoimmune disease**.

Doctors are still a long way from controlling this great crippler. Typical results of rheumatoid arthritis appear in two finger joints; the disease-damaged tissue deteriorates so much that it is immobilized in the knobby, misshapen deformity that is characteristic of advanced cases of rheumatoid arthritis.

Sometimes, a normal finger joint induces certain cells to multiply unnaturally at the synovial membrane (it normally secretes fluid to lubricate the joint). When the synovial membrane swells, it will cause discomfort in the joints. The second joints are a favorite target of the disease, but other finger joints and the wrist, too, may be affected. As the synovial tissue grows and unhealthy body defenses eat cartilage-covering tissues away, the arthritis grows. Rheumatoid arthritis creeps into the joint itself, centering on the ends of the bones and even erodes the bone. Eventually, in late stages of the disease, the bone is destroyed, rendering the joint useless.

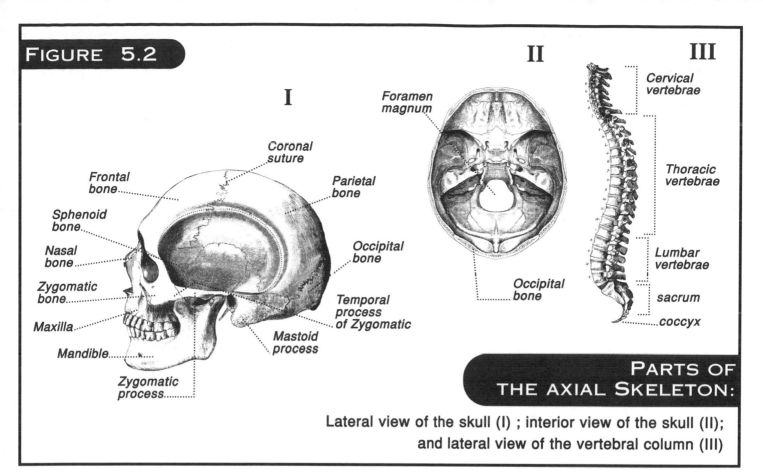

FIGURE 5.2

I

Coronal suture
Frontal bone
Parietal bone
Sphenoid bone
Nasal bone
Occipital bone
Zygomatic bone
Temporal process of Zygomatic
Maxilla
Mandible
Mastoid process
Zygomatic process

II

Foramen magnum
Occipital bone

III

Cervical vertebrae
Thoracic vertebrae
Lumbar vertebrae
sacrum
coccyx

PARTS OF THE AXIAL SKELETON:

Lateral view of the skull (I) ; interior view of the skull (II); and lateral view of the vertebral column (III)

The skull is one of the principal groups of bones in the human anatomy. The skull consists of 26 bones: 8 bones form the **cranium**, which houses the brain and ear ossicles, plus 14 facial bones, which form the front of the face, jaw, nose, orbits, and the roof of the mouth. Three more bones make up the inner ear **ossicles**, and 1 more, the **hyoid** bone, is in the neck and is attached to the **temporal** bone by ligaments. The bones of the skull include the **frontal** bone (which makes up the forehead and roof of the orbits), the **occipital** bone (which forms the back and base of the skull), two **parietal** bones (which form the roof and upper sides of the skull), and two temporal bones (which form the lower sides of the skull and house the inner ear ossicles). The lower rearmost part of each temporal bone is called the **mastoid process,** but because it is separated from the temporal bone proper by a suture, it is often considered a separate bone. The **sphenoid** bone forms the central base of the skull and spans the skull from side to side, the greater wings forming side plates of the skull.

The sections of the **ethmoid** bone are positioned between the orbits, forming the walls and roof of the nasal cavity, while the three middle ear ossicles (stapes, malleus, and incus) are located within the temporal bones on each side of the skull. The U-shaped hyoid bone is found in the neck, and is attached by ligaments to the temporal bones. In the face, the two **maxillary** bones form much of the orbits, nose, upper jaw, and roof of the mouth, while the **zygomatic** (malar) bones form the cheeks. The lachrymal bones are located on the inner sides of the orbits and are attached to the ethmoid

and maxillary bones. Within the nasal cavity, the vomer is located in the low center and forms the thin flat bone of the nasal septum, while two inferior urbinates form the lower sides of the cavity and two palate bones form the floor of the nasal cavity as well as the roof of the mouth. The mandible is the only movable part of the skull, forming the lower jaw and mounting the teeth.

The bones of the skull, with the exception of the mandible, are held together by very thin sutures, or seams, in which the periosteum of the individual bones interweave with each other, and are cemented by a fibrous, connective tissue. In the newborn, these sutures are not yet developed, with the bones being attached by cartilage that ossifies over time as the bones of the skull fuse together. The most evident external sutures of the cranium include the **coronal suture**, joining the frontal and parietal bones; the **sagittal suture**, joining the parietal bones to each other; the **lambdoid suture**, joining the occipital and parietal bones; and the **squamous suture**, joining the temporal and sphenoid bones to the parietal bone on each side of the skull. The **pterion** is the short segment of the suture joining the squamous and parietal bones.

The bones of the skull also feature a number of **sinuses** (cavities) and **foramina** (the plural of **foramen**, meaning hole or opening). Four pairs of sinuses flank the nasal cavity (and are therefore called paranasal sinuses). Two are found in the maxillary bone, and are called maxillary sinuses. The sphenoid bone forms two paranasal sinuses called the sphenoids and the ethmoid bone forms the two paranasal sinuses called ethmoids.

FIGURE 5.3

Baby (primary) teeth
Incisor (8 total)
Canine (4 total)
Molar (8 total)
Total = 20 deciduous teeth

Molars..........
Canines..........
Incisors..........

Lateral View of
Baby Skull (left side)

The teeth are the perfect example of God's marvelous works because they are fashioned in particular shapes to accomplish specific purposes of chewing food. These include incisors for cutting, cuspids for grasping, bicuspids for tearing, and molars for grinding. The Creator provides two sets of teeth in a person's lifetime. Early in life, 20 primary (or deciduous) teeth erupt from the bony dental alveolus and are with us until about fourteen years of age. Permanent teeth start to absorb the roots of primary teeth and will replace them from around the age of six and until the age of fourteen.

An adult has approximately 32 permanent teeth. Adults have more molars than children do. The last set of molars is called the wisdom teeth. These erupt between the ages of 17 and 25 years. In some cases, people do not have wisdom teeth at all and for others they have to be removed. These teeth are not vestigial organs, but are fully functional "grinders."

Adult (secondary) teeth
Incisor (8 total)
Canine (4 total)
Bicuspid (8 total)
Molar (12 total)
Total = 32 permanent teeth

Incisors   Canines Bicuspids   Molars

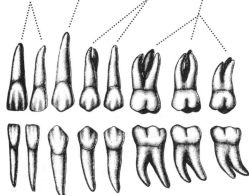

Lateral View of
Adult Skull (left side)

COMPARISON OF DECIDUOUS (PRIMARY) TEETH IN NEWBORN BABY WITH PERMANENT TEETH (SECONDARY) IN AN ADULT

Additionally, the frontal sinuses are located in the frontal bone just behind the roof of each orbit. The foramen magnum is a large, round opening in the base of the skull that admits the spinal cord, while at the base of each temporal bone is the external auditory meatus, which serves as the auditory canal. Two more openings, one on each side of the skull, can be found in the frontal processes of zygomatic bones, and are called, therefore, zygomatofacial foramina. On each side of the mandible, just below the lower canines, are the mental foramina. These **facial foramina** serve to admit blood vessels and nerves through and into the bones.

The teeth are mounted in the maxillary bone and the mandible and are brought together for chewing by the hinge-like motion of the mandible (the lower jawbone). An adult will usually grow 32 teeth, but will most commonly only retain 28 teeth due to the extraction of four wisdom teeth. The teeth are evenly arrayed on the **maxilla** and mandible. The details of skull anatomy may seem trivial, but are quite important to your dentist. Actually, if your dentist neglects these details during your next office visit, you may walk away in great pain and will grow in appreciation for this anatomical trivia.

The Teeth

The teeth are formally considered to be accessory digestive organs, but as they are osseous tissue as well as integral to the structure of the skull, they deserve to be treated with the skeletal system. The average adult human has 16 teeth, anchored in the maxilla and 16 in the mandible. Chewing is accomplished by moving the mandible in proximity to the maxilla so that the teeth of the two bones are brought together, cutting, grinding, and tearing food. The teeth are paired, with two of each variety in the top row and two of each in the bottom, with every tooth in the top row matching one in the bottom as well. In the adult, the 16 teeth in a row consist of 4 **incisors** (2 central, 2 lateral), 2 **canines**, 4 **premolars** (also called bicuspids), and 6 **molars** (also called tricuspids). In the child, however, the 4 premolars and the back 2 molars are missing in the deciduous (non-permanent) teeth. Because it is usually between the age of 18 and 21 that the last 2 molars grow in, these teeth are often called "**wisdom teeth.**"

Bone as Tissue

Our skeletal frames are more than just scaffolding that holds us erect; they serve as the structures upon which we hang all that we are. Our bones are the anchors to which muscles attach, and they act as the levers and fulcrums for our daily activities. They are strong, sturdy, and cradle and protect our vital organs, yet they are light in weight. They house the marrow that produces our blood and act as storehouses for phosphorous and calcium.

Bones are far from rigid, lifeless structures. Nerves etch their surfaces; blood vessels interweave them. Bones bustle with metabolic activity. Break one and you will immediately understand how sensitive they can be. By studying a bone from someone who died centuries ago, a physical anthropologist can tell the sex, size, general health, diet, and age of the bearer.

The body of an adult contains about 206 bones (figure 5.1a). The reason for the "about" is that bones fuse and/or separate over our lifetime. In a few rare instances, some people have an extra vertebrate or rib, most likely due to genetic reasons. The reason for more bones in babies (higher than an adult) is that some bones, particularly those of the pelvis and skull, converge and grow together as the child grows.

Bones start forming in the first two months of fetal life and continue to grow long after birth. Long bones, such as the leg and arm bones, grow mostly where plates of cartilage separate the bone shafts from their ends. These cartilage cells grow, then die, leaving spaces for blood vessels and bone-forming cells called **osteoblasts**. As the osteoblasts multiply, they move outward, invading the cartilage and pushing the knobby ends of the bone farther away from each other. Cells left behind begin forming new bone.

The process continues into young adulthood, when the bones stop growing. You will see the significance of this continued process of development as evidence for creation when you read the boxed section called "**Creation Focus 5.2: Buried Alive.**" All else being equal, the genetic code determines our assigned height. The pituitary gland, working on instructions from our genes, "tells" the bones to stop growing. The ends of each bone solidify, and bone growth ceases. That's a clue in determining the age of skeletons, ancient or modern, and that's why anthropologists inspect the condition of the bone ends. The end of growth does not mean bones become inert. New bone is constantly forming, while other cartilage is being torn down and reabsorbed — a form of renovation.

Bone that receives sustained stress is replaced more quickly than bone that does not. Bones are far more complicated than they look from the outside. A cavity that runs along the center of bones holds yellow marrow, fat cells, and blood vessels. The ends of these bones enclose red bone marrow, which produces blood cells. The central cavity connects to the rest of the bone through an intricate labyrinth of small channels. These run through spongy material surrounding the cavity and out to a fibrous membrane that covers the bone, called the periosteum. The periosteum carries the blood supply and the nerves that make the bones sensitive to pain.

Bones come in various shapes and sizes, which reflect their varied functions. Long bones, such as the femur, act

DESIGN FOCUS 5.2

Buried Alive

Bones have generated an interest not just among health professionals, but archaeologists and anthropologists also. This interest in bones, particularly skulls, is because they give clues to mankind's past history and hints at our origins. Fossilized bones, too, have an ancient mystery surrounding them; their very existence is explained by one's world view. One of the promising lines of research on **Neanderthal** man is of cranium development. Think of a baby's soft head. It is fashioned with cartilage as well as bone. Our skull gradually changes over time from fetus to infant to adolescent to adult. This has been known for some time. But more recently Dr. Jack Cuozzo has found that our skull continues to change in our old age, and assuming man could live to 150, 200, 300, or even 500 years of age, this pattern of change would produce an individual that looked remarkably like Neanderthal man.

Dr. Jack Cuozzo, a research orthodontist for over 30 years, in his book *Buried Alive*, explains Neanderthal man skeletons. His studies show that the human head does not stop growing as we age. Contrasting the measurements of people's heads when they were 19, in their late forties, and some at age 80, he discovered that the head changed in the following manner: 1) the brow ridge came forward; 2) the jaw came forward; 3) the nose got bigger; 4)

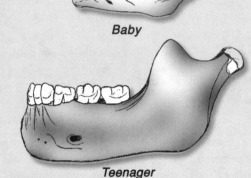

Baby

Teenager

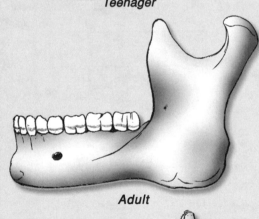

Adult

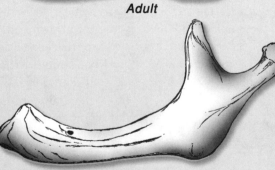

Old Person

the chin came forward; 5) the cheeks came forward and flattened out; 6) the teeth came forward; 7) the back of the head started to point out.

Some of the measurements show that the nose moved 1.3 mm in 30 years while the brow ridge moved forward and upward by 1.5 mm, while the cheek bone moved 1.1 mm in the same 30-year period. Dr. Cuozzo's associate (a Ph.D. biologist) then took the same data, plotted it, and extrapolated the growth out from 300 to 500 years. The 500-year age would be about the age of Noah and some of the other early people who lived for a long time. At 300 years, he illustrates pictures that showed man's jaw was square at the **gonial angle**, and the face was moving forward and downward. At 500 years, there was no chin point, a very long face, and a huge brow. His conclusion is that the large-browed Neanderthal man was just an old human and the features are a natural manifestation of aging. Neanderthal man represents one of the people groups that lived after the flood of Noah and dispersed into Europe during the Ice Ages. These conclusions are supported by over 30 years of fossil study. The idea that Neanderthals are an intermediate between an ape-like ancestor in man (because of heavy brows, sloping foreheads, and a slouched-over, gorilla-like posture) is false. The truth is that man has always been man (*Homo sapiens*) and he will always be the only creature made in the image of God.

as levers; short bones, such as those of the wrists, are rather cube-shaped and provide support and flexibility; flat bones are protective shields. The femur is the body's longest bone; the ossicles of the middle ear that vibrate to sounds, are among the smallest.

The skull, whose crucial function is to support and protect the brain, consists of no less than 26 bones, 8 of which constitute the **cranial vault**, or cranium. The cranial bones are connected at irregular seams, called **sutures**.

The Human Foot: Marvel of Engineering

The human foot is a marvel of engineering. The foot is highlighted by its specially designed arches and series of bones that allows one to either pound the gridiron or balance tip-toed for hours during a *Swan Lake* performance. You will be amazed at the design features of this complex, highly integrated system of dynamic tissue called bone.

Each **pes** (foot) is composed of an ankle, instep, and five toes. The **tarsus** (ankle) consists of seven tarsal bones that form the heel and the posterior portion of the **instep**. The instep is composed of five elongated **metatarsals** that form the ball of the foot and articulate with the tarsus. Ligaments connect the tarsals and metatarsals to form the arches of the foot.

A longitudinal arch stretches from the toe to the heel. The transverse arch extends across the foot. The arches provide a stable, springy support for the body. Design is seen even in the small details. Each toe has three **phalanges**, corresponding to those phalanges of the fingers, except for the big toe, which has only two phalanges and provides precise movement and balance in the foot.

Arches of the Foot

The foot has two arches that support the weight of the body and provide leverage when walking. The structure and arrangement of the bones held in place by ligaments and tendons form these arches. The arches are not rigid; they yield when weight is placed on the foot and spring back as the weight is lifted. The longitudinal arch is divided into medial and lateral parts. It is supported by the **calcaneus** proximally and by the heads of the first three metatarsal bones distally. The wedge, or keystone, of this part of the longitudinal arch is the **talus**. The shallower lateral part consists of the calcaneus, cuboid, and the fourth and fifth metatarsal bones.

The **transverse arch** extends across the width of the foot and is formed by the distal part of the calcaneus, navicular, and cuboid bones, as well as the proximal portions of the five metatarsal bones. The weakening of the ligaments and tendons of the foot decreases the height of longitudinal arch in a condition called the flat foot.

The foot is the humblest member of man's anatomy. The human foot with its five toes is a miracle of construction. It consists of 26 separate bones of various sizes and shapes bound together by a system of ligaments. It is supported by a complex array of muscles and supplied with a network of fibers and blood vessels. The different bones articulate in gliding joints, giving the foot a degree of elasticity and a

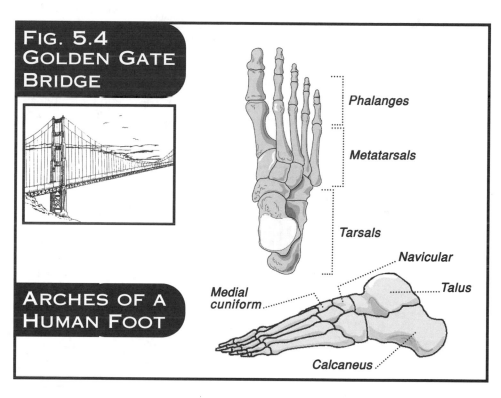

FIG. 5.4 GOLDEN GATE BRIDGE

ARCHES OF A HUMAN FOOT

Phalanges

Metatarsals

Tarsals

Navicular

Talus

Medial cuniform

Calcaneus

limited amount of motion. The arrangement of the bones is such that it forms several arches, the most important of these being the long arch from the heel to the ball of the foot.

These arches are held in place and supported by a complex network of strong muscles to carry the weight of the body, just as steel cables carry the load of a suspension bridge. The construction also gives elasticity to the foot, making walking, running, and other movements possible. The ability to walk and to move from place to place and to balance the tall upright body on a comparatively small pedestal is itself a most remarkable feature of the human body. If the foot were flat and rigid, fixed at right angles to the bone of the leg, walking would be difficult or impossible. The elastic arches also serve as shock absorbers to soften the jar resulting from walking on a hard surface.

The human foot is a miniature suspension bridge which is much more complicated than an ordinary bridge. Would anyone say that the Golden Gate suspension bridge just happened? Of course not, if he were truthful! But why do people assume that the even more intricate mechanism of the human foot could have just happened without intelligent cause or the workmanship of a master Engineer?

To add to the wonders of the human foot, we must also remember that it has been reproduced billions and billions of times in every human birth with exactly the same shape and form and with the same number of bones and tendons and nerves. It has both strength and agility, just like the famous Golden Gate Bridge, to handle varying weather conditions. And so we see that even the humble foot of man is one of the wonders of his body that glorifies the Creator's engineering genius.

Interwoven Parts

The compact bone layer features a number of foramina (openings) that allow the nutrient vessel(s) to tunnel through to reach the marrow cavity and spongy bone tissue within. Most bones have one main nutrient vessel that, by branching into a web of arterioles within the bone, feeds them, though the femur has two such nutrient blood vessels. The bone has one foramen for the entrance of each nutrient vessel and foramina at the extremities for the produced blood to exit the bone.

The **Perforating Canal** is located within the **Haversian canals** in the Haversian lamellae. These vessels carry the nutrients that nourish the bone tissue and carry newly generated blood cells and lymphocytes from the marrow to the bloodstream. The **marrow** (also called **medullary**) **cavity** is the region within the bone that houses the marrow, responsible for generation of blood cells. Yellow marrow is found in the upper ends of the humerus and femur and in many of the flat bones of the skull, vertebrae, ribs, sternum, and hip. The red marrow, also known as myeloid tissue, produces all types of blood cells except for lymphocytes and monocytes (that are formed primarily in the lymph nodes and the spleen). The osteocytes are bone cells responsible for producing and maintaining the dynamic nature of bone that has both a "soft," living inner component and a "hard" outer shell.

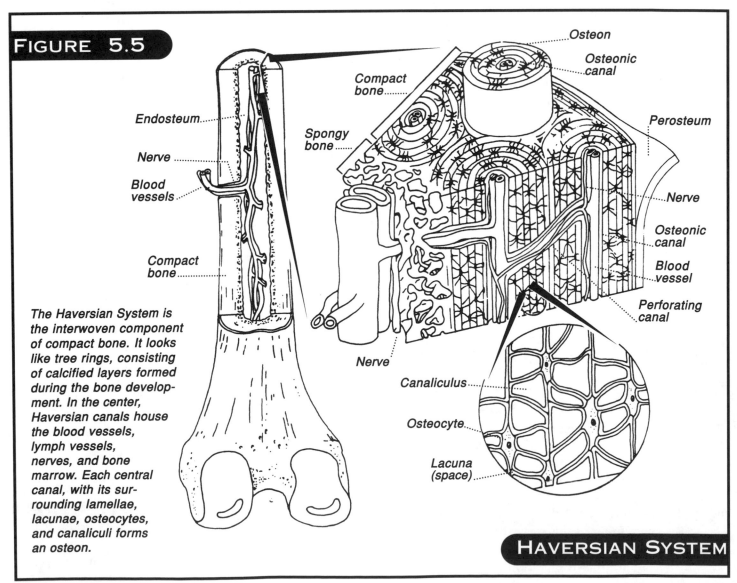

FIGURE 5.5

Osteon

Osteonic canal

Compact bone

Perosteum

Spongy bone

Endosteum

Nerve

Blood vessels

Compact bone

Nerve

Osteonic canal

Blood vessel

Perforating canal

Nerve

Canaliculus

Osteocyte

Lacuna (space)

The Haversian System is the interwoven component of compact bone. It looks like tree rings, consisting of calcified layers formed during the bone development. In the center, Haversian canals house the blood vessels, lymph vessels, nerves, and bone marrow. Each central canal, with its surrounding lamellae, lacunae, osteocytes, and canaliculi forms an osteon.

HAVERSIAN SYSTEM

CHECK YOUR UNDERSTANDING

THOUGHTS
KNOWLEDGE
MEMORY

Skeletal System

1. What are three of the main components or organs of the skeletal system?

2. What are the overall functions of the skeletal system?

3. Name and describe an interwoven part of the skeletal system applying the fabrica idea.

4. Discuss the differences between male and female pelvic girdles. How are these differences evidence for an intelligent designer?

5. What is a common degenerative condition of joints? Include symptoms.

6. Isaac Newton said, "In the absence of any other proof, the thumb alone would convince me of God's existence." Discuss the anatomical and physiological basis for such a confident assertion. (Include diagrams as needed.)

7. The foot has similar design features to a suspension bridge. Explain this analogy and include diagrams as needed.

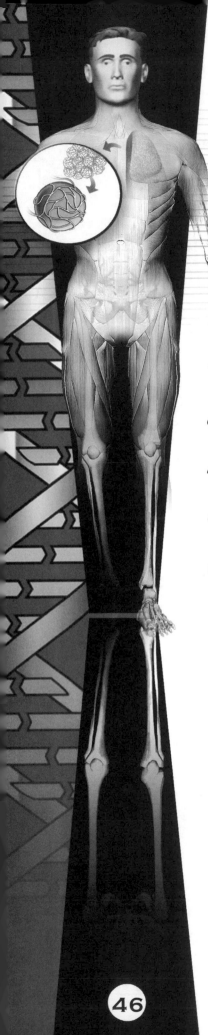

EXPLORING INTERWOVEN DESIGNS OF THE MUSCULAR SYSTEM

CHAPTER 6

"In the absence of any other proof, the thumb alone would convince me of God's existence."

(Isaac Newton)

Although bones and joints form the framework of the body, they cannot move the body by themselves. Motion results from the contraction and relaxation of muscles. Muscle tissue constitutes about 40 to 50 percent of the total body weight and is composed of highly specialized cells.

Design of Muscles

Design is inferred with the fabric of muscle construction. *Fabrica*, or *fabricae* in Latin, translates to craft, trade, industry, workmanship, or a process of building, construction, and production. *Fabre* (a related word) is an adverb that means "skillfully." A study of the art of Vesalius and da Vinci similar styles. Vesalius and da Vinci lived in the same time period, where their diagrams gave man a "heavenly" glory. Each sketch was a masterpiece. Many of their illustrations portrayed the interwoven fabric of the human body. Some of the patterns displayed contrasting threads, dark and light, as well as gold, silver, black, and white.

Muscular System Overview

The human body contains nearly 700 individual muscles anchored to the skeleton, which provide pulling power to allow mobility. These muscles constitute about 40 percent of your total body weight. The muscle's points of attachment to bones or other muscles are designated as origin or insertion. The point of **origin** is the point of attachment to the bone to which the muscle is anchored. The point of **insertion** is the point of attachment to the bone the muscle moves. Generally, the muscles are attached by tough fibrous structures called tendons. These attachments bridge one or more joints and the results of muscle contraction are movement of these joints. The body is moved primarily by muscle groups, not by individual muscles. These groups of muscles power all actions ranging from the threading of a needle to the lifting of heavy weights.

The overall function of muscle is motion. This includes movement such as walking and running, as well as movement of substances within the body. All three types of muscle tissue help move substances such as blood, food, sperm, and urine. Muscle helps to stabilize body positions and regulate organ volume. Skeletal muscle contractions maintain stable body positions and sustain posture. Contractions of smooth muscles block the exit of food from the stomach and urine from the urinary bladder for temporary storage. A byproduct of muscle contraction is the production of heat. Skeletal muscle contractions may generate 85 percent of all body heat to help maintain normal body temperature.

those nonsegmented around the appendicular skeleton (arms and legs), and those associated with the visceral skeleton (brachiometric muscles). All muscles have basically the same structure. Each muscle has an attachment at both ends, called the origin and insertion, and a fleshy contractile part, called the muscle **belly**. These muscles are attached either directly or indirectly (via tendons) to the bones, and work in opposing pairs (one muscle in the pair contracts, while the other relaxes) to produce body movements. The muscles work together to produce movement of a joint, to steady a joint, and to prevent movement in the direction opposite to those intended. As a rule, only the insertion bone moves. The shortening of the muscle as it contracts pulls the insertion bone toward the origin bone.

The origin bone stays put, holding firm while the insertion bone moves toward it. These muscles always tire with continued use and require rest.

Because of their cross-striped appearance under a microscope, these muscles are called **striated**. There are two types of striated muscle: dark fibers and light fibers. The dark fibers are a deep red color and predominantly produce slow, tonic movement. The light fibers are lighter in color and predominantly produce quick and contracted motions. Each muscle fiber is encased in a thin, transparent membrane called the **sarcolemma**. The fibers are subdivided longitudinally into minute **myofibrils** and **myofilament** encased in a fluid called **sarcoplasm**. The

Muscle Types

SKELETAL MUSCLE

The **skeletal muscle** cells that comprise about 40 percent of the body weight are voluntary. They are mostly attached to the bones to move the skeleton and are fast-acting and powerful. The voluntary muscles are of three series: those that are more or less arranged around the axial skeleton (head, neck, and trunk),

DESIGN FOCUS 6.1

An Anatomical Anomaly

Scientists must be cautious not to get too set in their ways. Good scientists are open to alternative explanations, as new data become available. This is true even in the old discipline of gross anatomy. *Gray's Anatomy* is the "bible" of human musculature, but even this "bible" may be incomplete. In 1996, Dr. Gary Hack, a research dentist, announced that he and his co-workers had found a new muscle in the face. Hack stumbled onto the structure while working on a cadaver so altered by previous dissections that he was forced to cut into the face from the front instead of the usual side approach. Hack found this new muscle, the **sphenomandibularis**, by cutting from an unconventional angle and exposing an unfamiliar muscle connecting the mandible (lower jawbone) to the sphenoid bone behind the base of the eye socket. He suspected that it stabilizes the jaw during chewing rather than actually moving the jaw. You might say that this finding has given researchers something to "chew on."

Hack still needs evidence to show that this new structure is indeed a separate muscle. In order for it to be considered a separate muscle, the sphenomandibularis must have its own nerve and blood supply, connect at both ends of the skeletal structure, and have a distinct function. But no matter what future findings may be, it is significant that no description of this structure is discussed in *Gray's Anatomy* or any other of the 15 "standard" anatomy textbooks.

Hack's research has now caused the classic reference, *Gray's Anatomy* to be revised. The moral of this story is that a study of an old subject with alternative methods and an open mind may reveal new information and insight into how the body works. His work illustrates not only the expanding knowledge of human anatomy, but also that scientists need to keep an open mind for new data that may contradict established preconceived ideas.

FIGURE 6.1

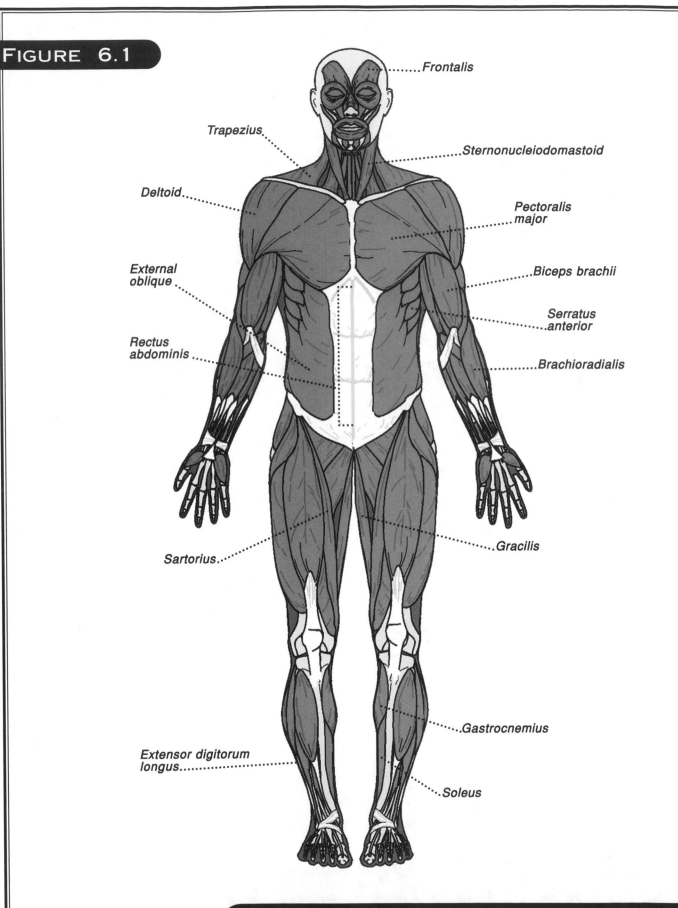

Frontalis

Trapezius

Sternonucleiodomastoid

Deltoid

Pectoralis major

External oblique

Biceps brachii

Serratus anterior

Rectus abdominis

Brachioradialis

Sartorius

Gracilis

Gastrocnemius

Extensor digitorum longus

Soleus

PRINCIPAL SUPERFICIAL SKELETAL MUSCLES IN ANTERIOR VIEW

FIGURE 6.2

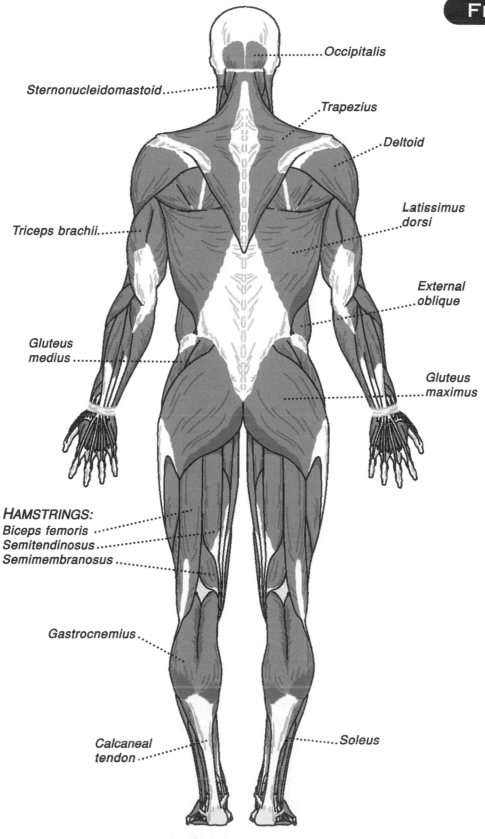

Occipitalis

Sternonucleidomastoid

Trapezius

Deltoid

Latissimus dorsi

Triceps brachii

External oblique

Gluteus medius

Gluteus maximus

HAMSTRINGS:
Biceps femoris
Semitendinosus
Semimembranosus

Gastrocnemius

Calcaneal tendon

Soleus

PRINCIPAL SUPERFICIAL SKELETAL MUSCLES IN POSTERIOR VIEW

muscle cells are elongated tubular structures with as many as several hundred nuclei and are actually a fusion of cells (**syncytia**). The muscle fibers are bound together in bundles of white fibrous connective tissue called **perimysia**. Striated muscles that are not directly under voluntary control include vocal cord muscles and the diaphragm.

CARDIAC MUSCLE

Cardiac muscle is red-colored involuntary muscle that contracts automatically and rhythmically, like a smooth muscle, but is striated, like skeletal muscle. The muscle is fast-acting and powerful. It is under the control of the autonomic nervous system and continuously contracts and relaxes throughout life.

SMOOTH MUSCLE

Smooth-muscle cells are not attached to the skeleton, but are found in the walls of the blood vessels, the digestive tract, and in the dermal layer of the skin. They react slowly to stimuli from the autonomic nervous system and perform actions such as forcing food through the intestines, transporting urine to the kidneys, and pumping blood through blood vessels. The muscle is nonstriated and consists of spindle-shaped, uninuclear cells that are not bound together, as in skeletal muscle. Like skeletal muscle, smooth muscle has fibrillae but without cross-striations. The muscles are involuntary, and are slow-acting, untiring, and weak in action.

Intertwining Neuromuscular Junctions

The nerve-muscle junction features a connection, or **synapse**, between an axon terminal and a group of muscle fibers. A space between the neural and muscular tissue is called the synaptic space. When a nerve impulse is transmitted to the axon terminal, it causes a **neurotransmitter** (chemical) to be released from small sacs, called **synaptic vesicles**, within the terminal, or knob. The neurotransmitter causes sodium ions to be transferred to the muscle fibers which, in turn, contract. The neurons are covered by an insulating, lipid-based coating, called the **myelin** sheath, which prevents stray neural signals from passing to other neurons or to other tissues.

Muscles work by contracting and relaxing. During contraction they shorten their length to bring the bone closer to their points of attachment on two different bones. Every muscle movement, therefore, is a pull. The fibers and fibrils of the muscle accomplish this pulling action. All skeletal muscles are made up of small fibers. The **fibers** are cylindrical in shape and are several centimeters long, with regular bands (striations) dividing them into sections. The fibers are made up of many cylindrical subunits called **fibrils**. These are the structures that actually contract. Muscular fibers are able to shorten 30 to 40

DISEASE FOCUS 6.1

Fibromyalgia

Fibromyalgia is a disorder characterized by muscle pain, stiffness, and easy fatigability. The cause is unknown and an estimated 3 million are affected in the USA. Fibromyalgia is a complex problem. It is a not only a multiple sclerosis-type problem but a problem of "central activation," too. The symptoms of muscle pain, depression, impairment and interruption of daily activities, and sleep pattern malfunction characterize fibromyalgia and its sister myofascial pain syndrome, multiple sclerosis.

In many cases, fibromyalgia emerges into muscle pain that is unrelenting and a devastating life experience. The existence of fibromyalgia (and probably myofascial pain syndrome) has been debated for many years, but its existence cannot be denied. The fibromyalgia sufferer has several challenges: to improve their quality of life, to better understand why they hurt, and to help loved ones (and, yes, even their physicians) understand their symptoms and suffering. Fibromyalgia often overlaps other diseases.

Fibromyalgia is more than less of a syndrome. We name syndromes in medicine to associate more than one problem to a specific diagnosis. Fibromyalgia is a diagnosis. Although much maligned and criticized, the official definition established fibromyalgia as a disease entity. Fibromyalgia is primarily pain, but as anybody that suffers from this disease knows, there is so much more, such as fatigue, poor restorative sleep, headaches, irritable bowel, frequent pelvic and bladder pain, and migraine headaches.

The American College of Rheumatology (ACR) in 1990 explained it as the "presence of unexplained widespread pain or aching, persistent fatigue, generalized morning stiffness, poor restorative sleep, and tender points." The ACR defined 11 tender points that had a consistent statistical relationship to patients present with this syndrome in the rheumatology clinic. We now believe that abnormal pain processing mechanisms are at the root of fibromyalgia. Fibromyalgia sufferers have a low pain threshold and a high discrimination of pain.

percent in length during muscle contraction.

Myofilaments are made of two types of protein: **actin** and **myosin**. These proteins are in the form of long filaments. The filaments made of myosin are thicker than the filaments made of actin. These filaments interlock and are able to slide over each other, shortening the length of the muscle. When the muscle is stretched, the filaments tend to be pulled apart. During shortening (contraction), they shorten by sliding past one another. It appears that during contraction several cross-links are made between the actin and myosin filaments. By the process of making and breaking these cross-links, the two filaments move toward one another and the whole muscle shortens. This process is very rapid.

Cardiac muscle has a similar appearance to skeletal muscle. It has striations and is thought to contract in the same manner as the skeletal muscle. Smooth muscle has no striations and is composed of spindle-shaped cells totally lacking in myofibrils. Researchers still do not fully understand the smooth-muscle contraction mechanism.

The Arm: Example of a Fabrica Design

The arm has a wide range of movements. It swing backward and forward in walking and running, and can be folded across the chest or raised above the head. The shoulder forms a base for the arm with most of the upper arm muscles originating from this area. In the upper arm, the **biceps** and **triceps** are arranged to give the forearm power to thrust and bend. The two muscles join at the elbow and allow you to bend and straighten your arm and also rotate your wrist and hand. The forearm muscles transmit power to the wrist, hands, and fingers. A group of **flexors** and **extensors** controls the movements of the wrist, acting in conjunction with other muscles of the fingers, thumb, radius, and ulna. These sets of muscles allow the arm and wrist to bend (flexion) and straighten (extension) as well as move outward away from the body (**abduction**) and inward toward the body (**adduction**). Some of these muscles participate in more than one type of movement.

BICEPS BRACHII

The **biceps brachii** (two-headed arm muscle) consists of the long head and the short head. It extends from the shoulder to the elbow and is the main flexor of the elbow joint. When working with other nearby muscles, it can also move the shoulder, since its upper ends are attached to the **scapula** (shoulder blade). In addition, it can twist the lower arm so that the palm faces outward, a movement called **supination**. At the lower end, the biceps tapers into a flat, strong tendon that is firmly fixed to a bulge on the upper end of the radius. The biceps and the triceps

work together to control the up and down movement of the forearm.

TRICEPS BRACHII

The **triceps brachii** (three-headed muscle) lies at the upper portion of the inside of the arm. It is the main extensor of the arm and is made up of three teardrop shaped heads: the long head, the lateral head, and the medial head. When working with other nearby muscles it can also move the shoulder, since its upper ends are attached to the scapula. The long head, the largest of the three heads, is attached to the scapula (shoulder blade) just below the rounded socket of the shoulder joint and extends almost three-fourths of the way toward the front of the arm. The lateral head lies on the back and side of the upper arm. The medial head curves around the back of the humerus (upper arm bone) and is mostly covered by the long head. The lower end is attached to the flattened end of the ulna. The triceps brachii extends the forearm at the elbow joint. It works with the biceps brachii to control the up and down movement of the forearm.

Form and Function in Skeletal Muscles

Another example of this structure and function theme is the biceps brachii muscle of the upper arm and its control by neurons. Long extensions of the neurons transmit electrochemical impulses, making these cells especially well structured for communication. The movement of our body depends on the structure of muscles and movements of bones. The movement produced by a contracting muscle depends on how it is attached to the bones and how the bones articulate with each other. In such a familiar example, the relation between structure and function is obvious.

The dependence of activity on structure becomes more subtle, but no less real, as we direct our attention to the lower levels of organization, such as tissues, cells, and organelles. Our understanding of how a muscle contracts rests on the ultrastructure of the contractile machinery as well as on its chemical properties.

As an example of functional anatomy at the subcellular level, consider the organelles called mitochondria. **Mitochondria** are quite numerous in skeletal muscles. They are the sites of oxidative metabolism, which powers the cell by a process using oxygen and tapping the energy stored in glucose and triglycerides. An outer membrane surrounds a mitochondrion, but it also has an inner membrane with many infoldings. Molecules embedded in the folds of the inner membrane carry out many of the steps in oxidative metabolism. The infoldings pack a large amount of membrane into a minute space. In exploring life on its different structural levels, we discover operational beauty at every turn.

The way these systems operate remind us of the well-accepted **all-or-none principle** in muscle and nerve physiology. In skeletal muscles, individual fibers contract to their fullest extent or not at all. A minimal threshold must be made in order for any action to take place. It either contracts, or not at all. In neurons, if a stimulus is strong enough to initiate an action potential, a nerve impulse is propagated along the entire neuron at a constant strength.

The Hands and Their Movement

The movement of the hand and fingers of a concert pianist is an awesome sight. The necessity of coordination, timing, and order to play Beethoven's "Fifth Symphony" or Bach's "Jesu — Joy of Man's Desire" is a feat that is not accomplished by chance. There is marvelous skill not only in playing the music, but also in the 70 (35 in each hand) separate muscles contributing to the hand movements on the keyboard. The hand has been described as the most sophisticated "tool" in the body. It looks like it was crafted for maximum dexterity and strength in movement. The hand is capable of 58 distinct movements. These movements allow for dexterity and power for a diversity of actions ranging from piano playing and

threading a needle to holding a jackhammer. This amazing diversity of functions is accomplished with the help of muscles in the forearm and wrist. The fingers have no muscles in themselves; the tendons transfer force from muscles in the forearm and palm.

The forearm muscles (figure 6.3) promote most hand movements. These movements are assisted and made more precise by a number of small **intrinsic** muscles in the hand. These hand muscles include the four **lumbrical** muscles that lie between the metacarpals (visible on the palm surface), and the seven **interosseous** muscles that lie deep beneath the skin and inferior to the lumbricals. Together, the lumbricals and interossei flex the knuckles. They also extend, adduct, and abduct the fingers. There are four thenar muscles that act exclusively to circumduct and oppose the thumb.

Orthopedic surgeons could write many manuals suggesting various ways to repair hands that have been injured. Yet, there has never been a surgical technique that succeeded in improving the movement in a normal healthy hand. It frequently takes over a dozen muscles and tendons working together with the opposable thumb to accomplish one movement. No wonder Sir Isaac Newton was convinced of intelligent action in creation from his study of the thumb alone!

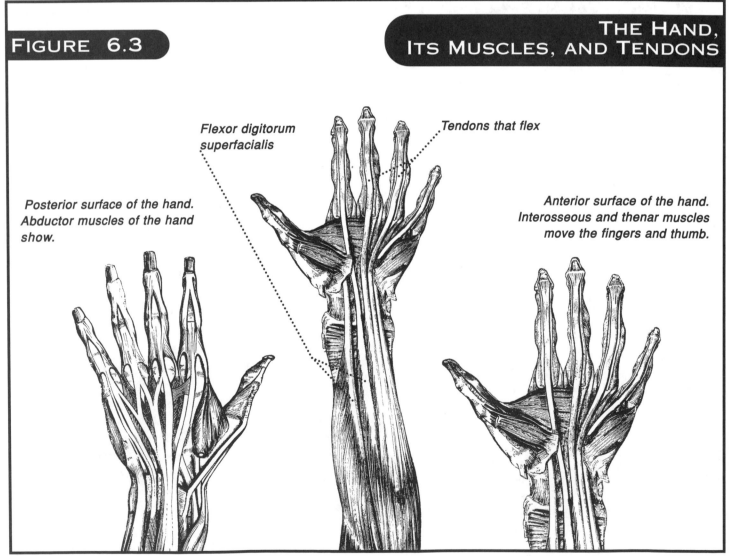

FIGURE 6.3

THE HAND, ITS MUSCLES, AND TENDONS

Flexor digitorum superfacialis

Tendons that flex

Posterior surface of the hand. Abductor muscles of the hand show.

Anterior surface of the hand. Interosseous and thenar muscles move the fingers and thumb.

CHECK YOUR UNDERSTANDING

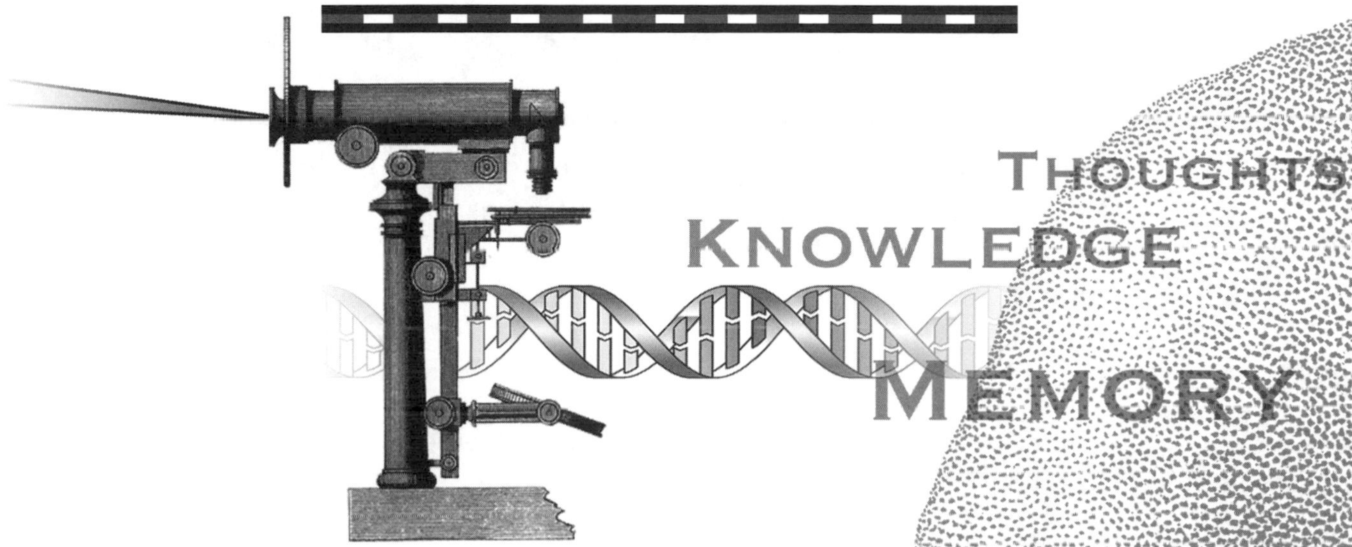

THOUGHTS

KNOWLEDGE

MEMORY

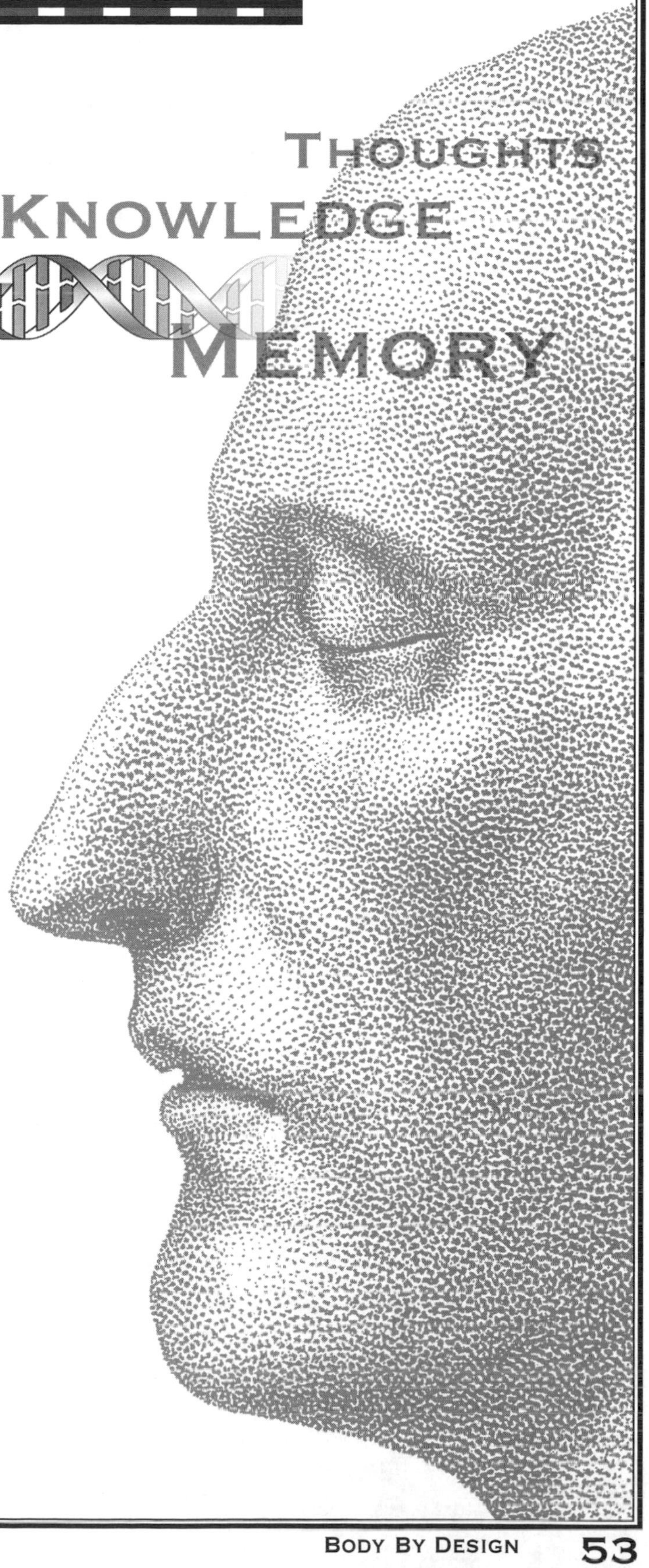

Muscular System

1. What are the main components of the muscular system?

2. What is the overall function of the muscular system?

3. Name and describe an interwoven aspect of the skeletal system.

4. Describe the structure of a skeletal muscle and tell how its design is an evidence for creation.

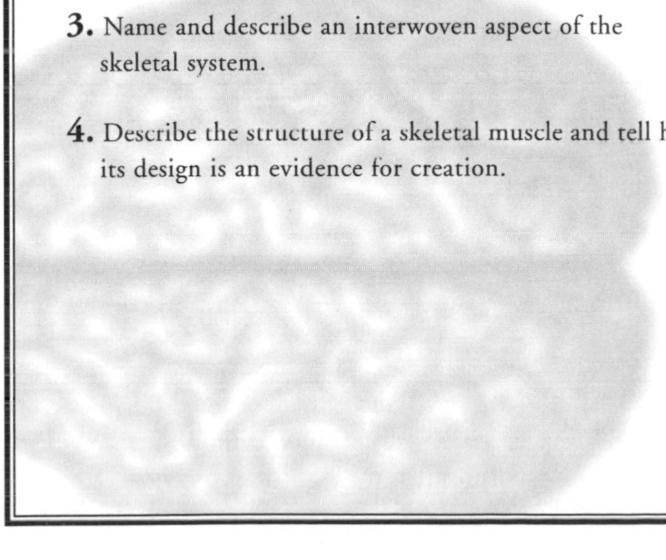

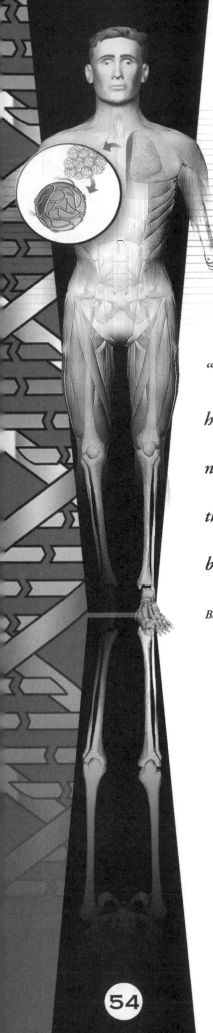

A VOYAGE INTO THE MULTIFACETED DIGESTIVE SYSTEM

CHAPTER 7

"To be a member is to have neither life, being, nor movement, except through the spirit of the body, and for the body."

Blaise Pascal

A human being is more than the sum of its parts" is the major theme of a *Life* magazine article by Alex Tsiaras. In the beautifully illustrated photo essay "A Fantastic Voyage through the Human Body," the dynamic nature and unique properties of the 11 organ body systems are discussed and pictured. Each multi-faceted system illustrates the elaborate design and the inter-dependence of parts in the human body. Any absent part in one of the body's many "adaptation packages" could lead to dysfunction of that system and, sometimes, could even lead to death.

In this chapter we have selected several familiar examples from the human body to illustrate the design argument of irreducible intricacy. Many "molecular and cell teams" are present in the body to illustrate this feature. A question to ponder as you study these particular examples is this: Are the mechanisms proposed in *The Blind Watchmaker* by Dr. Dawkins a sufficient argument to explain this remarkable order and complexity in human anatomy and physiology? Will time and chance produce such wondrous and complex systems by evolution?

The Dynamic Digestive System

The human digestive system (figure 7.1) is a long tube with an opening at each end and many specialized organs in between. If the tube of an adult were fully stretched, it would extend 21 to 30 feet. From beginning to end, a mucous-coated epithelium lines all the surfaces facing the lumen (space in a tube). The thick, moist mucous pro-tects the wall of the tube and enhances the diffusion across its inner lining. Substances advance in one direction from the **oral cavity** (mouth) through the **pharynx** (throat),

| **TABLE 7.1** | Functions of the Liver |

1) It detoxifies otherwise poisonous substances, such as alcohol and harmful drugs. (A body whose liver lacks this function will often develop cirrhosis of the liver.)

2) It produces bile, as well as enzymes in metabolism.

3) It removes glucose from the blood under the influence of insulin and stores it as glycogen. When the glucose level falls, the hormone glucagon causes the liver to break down glycogen-releasing glucose into the blood.

4) Liver cells make many complex blood proteins.

5) Liver cells convert nitrogenous wastes into urea that can be excreted by the kidneys.

6) The liver, along with the kidneys, helps to regulate the contents of the blood.

esophagus, and gastrointestinal tract (gut). The gut starts at the **stomach** and extends through the **small intestine**, **large intestine** (**colon**), and **rectum**, ending at the **anus**. Accessory organs, such as the **salivary glands**, **gall bladder**, **liver**, and **pancreas**, secrete chemicals into various digestive tract regions. Specifically, they secrete digestive enzymes, buffers, and mucus, which help in metabolism, moisturizing, and lubricating the food as it passes through the gut.

Function of the Digestive System

The digestive system is responsible for processing food, breaking it down into usable proteins, carbohydrates, minerals, fats, and other substances and introducing these into the bloodstream so that the body can use them. The digestive, or alimentary, tract begins at the mouth, where the teeth and tongue begin the breakdown of food, aided by saliva secreted by the salivary glands. The chewed food, combined with saliva, is swallowed, carrying it in peristaltic (contractile) waves down the esophagus to the stomach. In the stomach, the food combines with hydrochloric acid that further assists in breaking it down. When the food is thoroughly digested, the fluid remaining, called **chyme**, is passed through the **pyloric sphincter** to the small and large intestines. Within the long, convoluted intestinal canals, the nutrients are absorbed from the chyme into the bloodstream, leaving the unusable residue. This residue passes through the colon (where most of the water is absorbed into the bloodstream) and into the **rectum** where it is stored prior to excretion. This solid waste, called **feces**, is compacted together and, upon excretion, passes through the

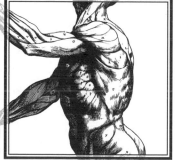

anal canal and the anus. Along the way through the digestive tract, the pancreas, spleen, liver, and gall bladder secrete enzymes that aid in the digestive process.

Villi: An Interwoven Fabric in the Gut

The small intestine is responsible for completing digestion and for absorbing the usable food products into the lymphatic system and bloodstream. The small intestine itself consists of a coiled, narrow tube (1–2 inches in diameter), between 19 and 22 feet (about 6–7 meters) long, in the lower abdomen, below the stomach. The small intestine extends from the **duodenum**, where it accepts the chyme (predigested food), to the iliocecal orifice, where it passes semifluid food byproducts to the large intestine. The food is passed through the intestinal tract in wave-like contractions, called peristaltic waves, in the intestinal wall. The food is further digested by bile and other digestive juices deposited into the duodenum from the gall bladder, pancreas, and liver.

The digesting food passes by the millions of **villi** (projections) on the inside wall of the intestines that absorb proteins and carbohydrates into their capillaries, and lymphatic nodules, which absorb fats. The villi pass the proteins and carbohydrates to the liver for metabolic processing, and the lymphatic nodules pass the fats through the lymphatic system into the bloodstream. The small intestine is anchored to the spinal column by a vascular membrane, the mesentery.

These processes can be clearly observed in the largest internal organ of the body, the **liver**. One of the main functions of the liver is to control the level of vital nutrients in the blood, such as carbohydrates and proteins (table 7.1).

FIGURE 7.1

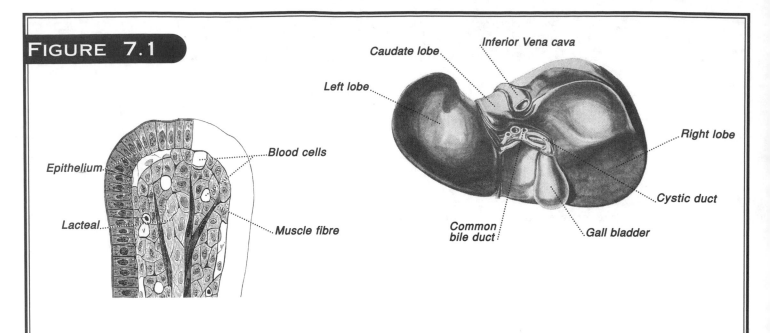

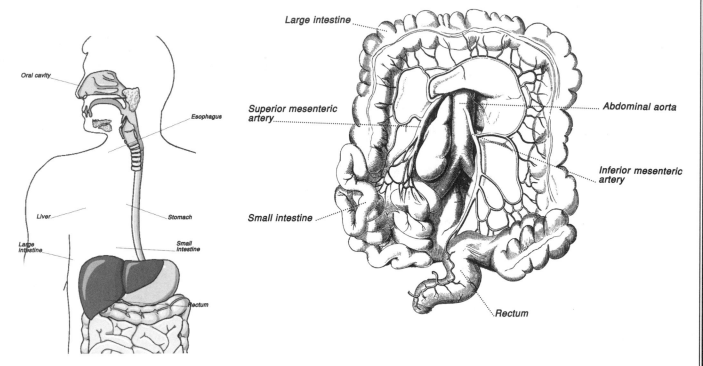

The majority of digestion occurs in the organs of the abdominal cavity. The largest of these is the liver. The liver supplies the gastrointestinal tract with powerful enzymes, such as bile, to break down food. The liver also destroys red blood cells, forms urea for the excretion of nitrogenous wastes, forms fibrinogen, used in blood coagulation, stores glycogen, helps in the metabolism and storage of vitamins, and produces protective and antitoxin substances, among its many functions.

The small intestine is responsible for completing digestion and for absorbing the usable food products into the lymphatic system and bloodstream. It extends from the duodenum, where it accepts the chyme (predigested food), to the iliocecal orifice, where it passes semifluid food byproducts to the large intestine. The large intestine is a broad, corrugated tube which accepts the byproducts of digestion from the small intestine and passes them along to be excreted, continuing to process the material on the way. Any unabsorbed food materials are stored in the large intestine until the body can partially reabsorb water from them, then passing the remains are passed along to the anus for elimination.

OVERVIEW OF THE DIGESTIVE SYSTEM AND ITS DESIGN

The importance of the liver should not be underestimated in the body. Liver transplant patients know their lives hang in the balance until a fully functioning liver replaces a degenerate one. Liver cells provide an example of vesicular transport of proteins and carbohydrates in an organelle, the smooth **endoplasmic reticulum** (ER). On their ribosomes, liver cells make many blood proteins that are transported in vesicles through the ER before release into the bloodstream.

In addition, liver cells store and transport carbohydrates in the form of glycogen. The hydrolysis (splitting) of glycogen leads to the transport and release of glucose subunits from the liver cells, a process that is important in the regulation of blood glucose levels. Movement of glucose within and between cells is facilitated by vesicular transport. In addition, enzymes of the smooth ER of liver cells help detoxify drugs and poisons. **Detoxification** usually involves adding hydroxyl (—OH) groups to drugs, increasing their solubility, and making it easier to flush the compounds from the body. The removal of alcohol, barbiturates, and hazardous drugs in this manner by smooth ER liver cells is also accomplished through vesicular transport.

An Unexpected Design

The news media publishes many articles about microbes that cause disease, but only a few articles report about microbes that are useful. In fact, "microbe phobia" permeates much of our society today. Actually, only about five percent of all bacteria are pathogenic. Many bacteria are beneficial and some are even essential for human life. For example, bacteria are needed to make yogurt from milk. Yogurt helps your body synthesize vitamins more efficiently. Bacteria in yogurt also help us by temporarily occupying an empty niche during antibiotic treatment and preventing germs from growing . This relationship between microbe and man could be called an "adaptation package."

An adaptation package is a biological relationship in which the whole is functionally more than the sum of its individual components. *Escherichia coli* (figure 7.3) are the predominant bacteria in the lower intestine, and they constitute about 75 percent of all the living bacteria in feces. Biologists refer to this cooperation between *E. coli* and the colon as mutualism, a relationship where both species benefit from living together. More simply stated, *E. coli* provides us with vitamins as its "rent money." Humans, in return, provide a home for these beneficial bacteria.

The majority of microorganisms in the intestines under normal conditions do no harm. Indeed, the intestinal bacteria contribute to the general well-being of both microbes and people by synthesizing a number of the vitamins essential for good nutrition and breaking down various macronutrients. The human body cannot synthesize niacin

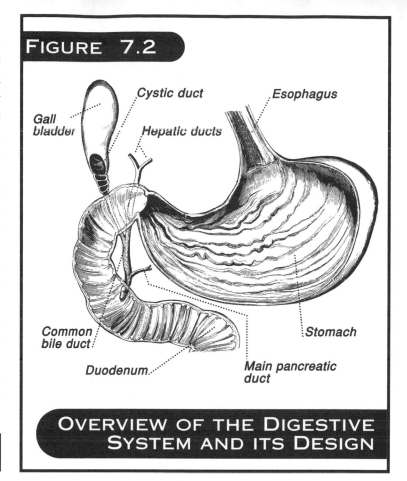

FIGURE 7.2

Cystic duct

Esophagus

Gall bladder

Hepatic ducts

Common bile duct

Stomach

Duodenum

Main pancreatic duct

OVERVIEW OF THE DIGESTIVE SYSTEM AND ITS DESIGN

to make **nicotinamide adenine dinucleotide** (NAD) which is necessary for energy conversion in the cell's mitochondria. Bacteria in significant amounts in the colon form vitamin K, niacin, NAD, and B-complex vitamins.

The B vitamins, including niacin, cobalamin (B_{12}) biotin, thiamine, and riboflavin, are necessary for normal energy levels, freedom from fatigue, and proper functioning of nerves. A prolonged deficiency in any one of these vitamins may lead to chronic fatigue and inability to lead a normal life. As for the benefit to *E. coli* (and other enteric bacteria), man's colon provides them a stable nutritional home. In short, both parties benefit from this mutualistic relationship.

The mutualistic relationship between our digestive cells and these helpful microbes shows amazing cooperation and is another example of emergent properties in living things. The large intestine contains the highest numbers of resident flora because of the available moisture and nutrients in the colon. If you take away *E. coli* and other bacteria, the function of the digestive system is severely impaired. This cooperation among cells is similar to the interdependent parts of a mousetrap and summarized in table 7.2.

Mutualism is, therefore, evidence for creation. In mutualism there is a marvelous fit between two radically different organisms. Mutualism poses a problem for macroevolution because it requires that the complementary traits in two different organisms evolved at the same time.

Simultaneous mutations must have occurred during natural selection in two very different organisms, although we have already pointed out the difficulty of just one successful trait evolving from random mutations. Another problem is the tendency for mutualism to degenerate into parasitism by a mutation.

We must, therefore, ask if there is any evidence for mutualism having arisen by evolution. There appears to be no record of new mutualism emerging in the last century. It is clear that mutualism could not have simply evolved by chance alone because of the incredibly low probability that both traits would have arisen simultaneously. We must conclude that the most plausible explanation is that human intestinal cells and these bacteria were created to function together.

In conclusion, the relationship between intestinal bacteria and humans is optimal for survival because of the ability for cooperation within this entire "package of parts." In this case, it is a mutualistic, coordinated system of microbes working together with man's gastrointestinal tract. It is adaptive in that it increases the survival of both human and microbe. In fact, this remarkable unity between these magnificent microbes and our intestines can be logically derived as having its origin in an intelligent designer. This remarkable cooperation is strong evidence for creation because it defies the laws of probability that two very different organisms can live together in such remarkable harmony.

This dynamic digestive system with its interwoven parts, the villi and its mutualistic bacteria, are part of the Creator's wise design for the human body. Without these friendly bacteria in the digestive system, many vitamins and other health benefits would be missed. The majority of microorganisms are there for our benefit. No doubt these organisms were a part of the original blueprint for the human body. Since the fall of man, however, there are a number of pathogens that invade these same niches normally occupied by harmless bacteria. Invading pathogens cause havoc in our body and may cause death.

Microbial diseases of the digestive system are second only to respiratory diseases as causes of illness in the United States. Most likely, infectious diseases of the digestive tract rank first in the entire world, but accurate statistics are not available. Most such diseases result from the ingestion of water or food contaminated with pathogenic microorganisms, or their toxins. These pathogens usually enter the food or water supply after being shed in the feces of people or animals infected with them. Therefore, microbial diseases of the digestive system are typically transmitted by a fecal-oral cycle. This cycle is interrupted by effective, responsible sanitation practices in food handling, by modern methods of sewage treatment, and disinfection of drinking water. Moreover, as more of our food, especially fruits and vegetables, are grown in countries with poor sanitation, outbreaks of food-borne disease from imported pathogens will increase. Several examples of diseases transferred in this way are given in table 7.4.

Be Ye Clean: Principle for Cleanliness

Although man is faced with many diseases of the digestive tract, the Creator was not unaware. Ever since ancient times God has provided a solution to the spread of infectious disease. This solution included the use of disinfection and antiseptic practices. Recall that Moses and his fellow Israelites had over 40 years of camping experience when he wrote this law. The Israelites learned to be careful about what they ate and drank during their time in the wilderness.

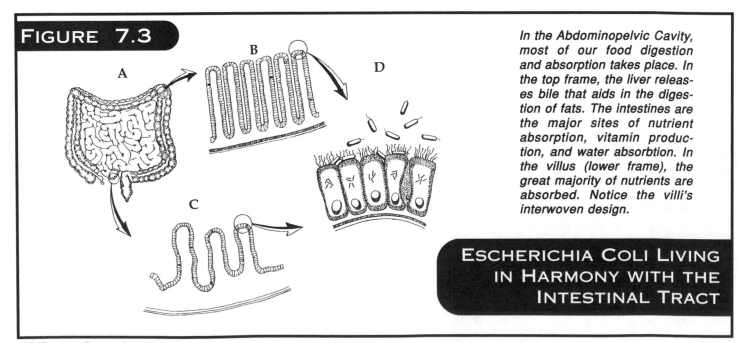

FIGURE 7.3

A B C D

In the Abdominopelvic Cavity, most of our food digestion and absorption takes place. In the top frame, the liver releases bile that aids in the digestion of fats. The intestines are the major sites of nutrient absorption, vitamin production, and water absorbtion. In the villus (lower frame), the great majority of nutrients are absorbed. Notice the villi's interwoven design.

ESCHERICHIA COLI LIVING IN HARMONY WITH THE INTESTINAL TRACT

TABLE 7.2	An Adaptation Package
	Escherichia coli living within the digestive system

Vitamins and Enzymes	Metabolic Role	Disease if Deficient
1. Vitamin K	Needed in blood clotting	Hemorrhage in newborns who lack gut bacteria
2. Vitamin B_{12}	Coenzyme needed in protein formation	Pernicious anemia; lack of energy
3. Niacin (Vitamin B_3)	Part of coenzymes in energy metabolism	Pellagra; lack of energy; fatigue
4. Vitamin B-Complex (thiamine, biotin, and riboflavin)	Carbohydrate metabolism Coenzymes in cell respiration	Beriberi, loss of appetite, fatigue, inflammation and breakdown of skin
5. Lactase	Breaks down lactose (milk sugar)	Lactose intolerance (cannot digest dairy products)

The principles laid down in the Levitical laws were given to the Jews, in part to make them a distinct people obedient unto God. However, the laws were given to the Israelites for their own good and protection against disease, as well. God was (and still is) interested in His people's health. Although Moses may have not understood **the germ theory of disease**, he did desire to please God and protect his people. Consequently, Moses wrote down God's detailed laws for "cleansing" food, water, and utensils, thereby establishing the principles for modern sanitation.

The Egyptians had many treatments that were very ineffective in treating common infectious diseases, from historical records. In contrast, the Jewish people had many effective sanitation and eating practices, such as eating only "clean" foods. Moses' instructions to the Israelites were among the first to stipulate the isolation of people with infectious diseases, stressing that precautions to contain people with disease be taken. God's chosen ones were the first people to implement the principle of quarantine. The result was an effective containment of microbial diseases. In addition, the Israelites were required to keep sewage "out of the camp" (Lev. 13), and this practice would have greatly reduced water-borne and enteric diseases caused by *Escherichia coli* and other intestinal parasites. Even before Semmelweis, Pasteur, Tyndall, and Lister, God gave Israel medical success with a prescription for protection against infectious disease!

TABLE 7.3	Diseases of the Digestive System and the "Be Ye Clean" Principle	

Bible Passage	Disease Principle	Microbiological Comments
Exod. 15:26	Obedience leads to fewer diseases	Promise given that people who follow the Creator's prevention principles will live healthier lives.
Lev. 13:46	Quarantine	Isolation of individuals with infectious disease from general population will reduce and contain diseases.
Lev 13	Cleanliness (Clean vs. Unclean)	Some food and water contain microscopic viruses, bacteria, protozoans, and multicellular parasites.
Lev. 13:52	Sterilization	The process by which all living organisms in an Tyndallization object/utensil is killed or removed by heat.
Lev. 14:6	Use of hyssop soap	This soap had antiseptic properties (having substances used for killing or limiting the growth of microorganisms and parasites).
Num. 19:7, 8, 19	Handwashing	Reduces the number of microbes and parasites so (w/running water) as to prevent likelihood of diseases.
Deut. 23:10-14	Sanitation	Keeping waste out of the "camp" reduces the chance of having contaminated food and water microbes and parasites. Removal of waste keeps enteric viruses, bacteria, protozoans, tape worms, and other helminth worms down in number.

TABLE 7.4   Disease and Disorders of the Digestive System

Organ	Disease	Pathogen (Germ Type)
1. Mouth	Dental caries	*Streptococcus mutans*
2. Stomach	Ulcers	*Helicobacter pylori* (bacterium)
3. Small intestine	Helminth infestation	Tapeworms
4. Small intestine	Cryptosporidiosis	*Cryptosporidium parvum* (protozoan)
5. Large intestine	Giardiasis	*Giardia* (protozoan)
6. Intestines	Gastroenteritis	*E. coli 0157H7*
7. Liver	Hepatitis	Hepatitis B virus

DISEASE FOCUS 7.1 Dental Caries

The Teeth

A tooth consists of an exposed crown supported by a neck anchored firmly to the jaw by one or more roots. The roots of teeth fit into sockets. Each socket is lined with a connective tissue **periosteum**, called the periodontal membrane. The root of a tooth is covered with a bone-like material called the **cementum**. Fibers in the periodontal membrane insert into the cementum and fasten the tooth in its socket. The **gingiva**, or gum, is the mucous membrane surrounding the alveolar processes in the oral cavity. The bulk of a tooth consists of dentin that is a substance similar to bone, but harder. Covering the dentin on the outside and forming the crown is a tough durable layer of enamel. **Enamel** is composed primarily of calcium phosphate and is the hardest substance in the body. The central region of the tooth contains the pulp cavity. The **pulp** is composed of connective tissue with blood vessels, lymph vessels, and nerves. A root canal is continuous with the pulp cavity and opens into the connective tissue surrounding the root through an apical foramen at the root tip.

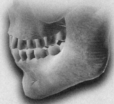
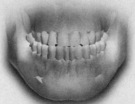
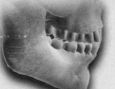

Broken Boundaries and Tooth Decays

Although enamel is the hardest substance in the body, it can be weakened by acidic conditions produced by bacterial activity, resulting in dental caries. These caries must be artificially filled because new enamel is not produced after a tooth erupts. The rate of tooth decay decreases after age 35, but then periodontal diseases may develop. Periodontal diseases result from plaque or tartar buildup at the gum line. This buildup wedges the gum away from the teeth, allowing bacterial infections to develop.

Saliva contains antimicrobial substances, such as **lysozymes**, that help protect exposed tooth surfaces. Some protection is also provided by crevicular fluid, a tissue exudate that flows into the gingival crevice and is closer in composition to serum than saliva. It protects teeth by virtue of both its flushing action and its phagocytic cells and immunoglobulin. Localized acid production within deposits of dental plaque results in a gradual softening of the external enamel. Enamel low in **fluoride** is more susceptible to the effects of acid.

The dominant microorganisms present are Gram-positive rods and filamentous bacteria. *Streptococcus mutans* is present in small numbers only. *S. mutans* grows well in glucose broth and grows prolifically when sucrose is high in the diet. *S. mutans* is the prime cause of dental caries and broken barriers as they grow in numbers in plaque. Although once considered the cause of dental caries, *Lactobacillus* organisms actually play no role in initiating the process. These very prolific lactic acid producers, however, are important in advancing the front of decay once it is established. A tooth with plaque accumulation is difficult to clean. **Decay** begins as acids formed by bacteria attack enamel. Decay advances through the enamel and then the dentin. Decay enters the pulp and may form abscesses in the tissues surrounding the root.

There is historical evidence that dental caries were not as common in people of previous generations as they are today. Most likely this is due to a change in dietary habits of man, such as eating foods rich in sugar. Before processed sugar become common in foods, teeth lasted longer. Although teeth from fossil men do show some cavities, "early" men seemed to have kept their teeth fully intact until old age. This is one more evidence demonstrating that man may have once lived to great ages with good health.

CHECK YOUR UNDERSTANDING

THOUGHTS
KNOWLEDGE
MEMORY

Digestive System

1. List at least three of the organs of the digestive system.

2. What is the overall function of the digestive system?

3. Give examples of and describe the intertwining parts of the digestive system.

4. Discuss how the villi are an interwoven component in the digestive system. Why could it not have evolved as evolutionists say? Make a diagram illustrating the interwoven villi.

5. Explain why some bacteria are not classified as "germs" and are considered beneficial for living. Why are some bacteria even considered essential for healthy living?

6. What causes dental caries?

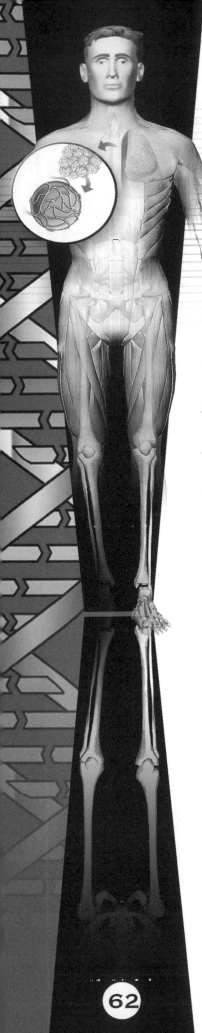

INFERRING DESIGNS
IN THE
EXCRETORY SYSTEM

CHAPTER 8

"The kidneys show clear

evidence of being divinely

designed filters."

(Frank Sherwin)

Extraordinary Excretory System

All organisms produce waste. These waste materials must be removed so that the organism is not poisoned by its own metabolic byproducts. In humans, the removal of these wastes is handled by the lymphatic system, the circulatory system, and the excretory system. Many body parts and systems indeed work together to accomplish the work of body "janitoring." The excretory system has extraordinary capabilities to remove nitrogenous wastes from the body through the processes of filtration, reabsorption, and secretion of urine.

Removing liquid waste is the task of the urinary tract, which regulates the content of our body's fluids. The key organs of the excretory system are the **kidneys**, the **ureters**, the **urinary bladder**, and the **urethra**. The kidneys are two reddish-brown, bean-shaped organs that sit in the back of the abdominal cavity. They are the body's sanitary engineers. The kidneys essentially filter and condition the blood, eliminating waste materials, balancing the salts and liquidity of bodily fluids, and keeping the acid-base level just right.

Fortunately, we have two kidneys. If you lose one, life still goes on. Its mate enlarges to assume the function of both organs. Lose function in both kidneys, and you need a dialysis machine or a transplant to survive. **Dialysis** machines filter the blood through a membrane that takes out larger molecules, such as proteins.

Urine is the fluid produced by the kidneys as they remove waste chemicals from the blood. Urine is made up primarily of water together with some electrolytes and organic materials dissolved in it. The concentration of each of these substances varies with a person's health, diet, and degree of activity. By testing the chemical composition of urine, doctors can learn much about the general health of an individual.

Urinary tract infections, kidney malfunction, diabetes, and liver disease are just a few of the medical problems that can be diagnosed through urinalysis.

Boundaries to Pathogens

The human body is constructed to prevent microbial invasion, a fact particularly evident in studying the anatomy of the **genitourinary tract**. Under certain circumstances, however, the genitourinary tract can be invaded by a variety of **opportunistic pathogens** from the normal flora as well as by other species. The urinary tract consists of the kidneys (in the upper urinary tract), the bladder (in the lower urinary tract), and accessory structures. The kidneys act as a specialized janitory (filter) system to clean the blood of many waste materials, and selectively reabsorbing substances that can be reused. Materials are excreted in the urine, which is usually about pH 6 because of excess hydrogen ions from foods and metabolism. The normal pH can range from about 4.4 to 7.5, but consistently alkaline urine suggests bacteria that converts the hydrogen in urine to ammonia. A tube called the ureter connects each kidney to the urinary bladder where it drains. The bladder acts as a holding tank, which, when filled, empties through the urethra.

The urinary tract is generally well protected from infection. Infections of the urinary tract occur far more often in women than in men because the female urethra is about 1.5 inches, compared to about 8 inches in the male, and is adjacent to the genital and intestinal tracts. Groups of muscles near the urethra keep the system shut most of the time and help prevent infection. The outward and downward flow of urine also helps clean the system by flushing out microorganisms before they have a chance to multiply and cause infection.

The urinary tract has built-in "barriers" to minimize an infection through a number of ways besides its anatomy. Normal urine contains antimicrobial substances such as organic acids and small quantities of antibodies. During urinary tract infections, larger quantities of specific antibodies can be found in the urine. There is also evidence that lymphoid cells infiltrate the infected kidneys and form protective antibodies locally at the site where they are needed. Also, during an infection, an inflammatory response occurs in which phagocytes are very important in engulfing and destroying the invading microorganisms.

Urinary tract infections are possible (Disease Focus 8.1), however, in spite of the many protective mechanisms. Many kidney and urinary tract infections are difficult to eradicate, are often chronic, and can destroy the normal kidney. Failure of both kidneys results in death unless the person is fortunate enough to be able to use a dialysis machine or to receive a kidney transplant.

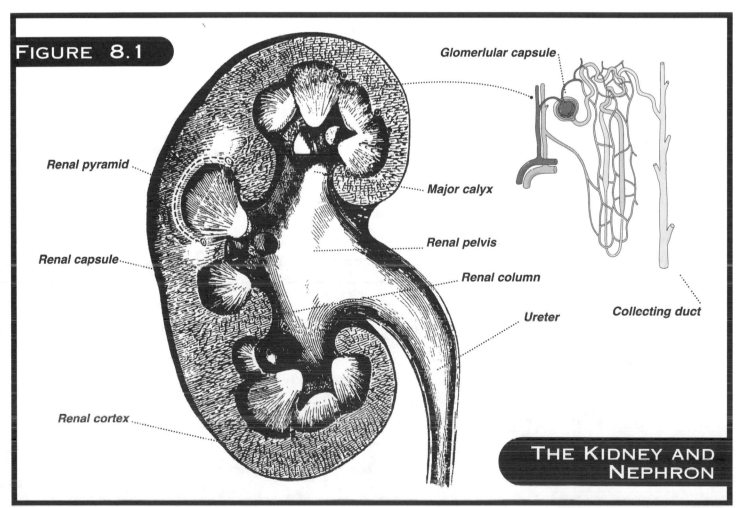

FIGURE 8.1

Glomerlular capsule

Renal pyramid

Major calyx

Renal capsule

Renal pelvis

Renal column

Ureter

Collecting duct

Renal cortex

THE KIDNEY AND NEPHRON

Urinary Tract Infections

The anatomical structure of the human excretory system is such that the external genitalia and the lower aspects of the **urethra** are normally contaminated with diverse microbes. The tissues and organs that compose the remainder of the urinary system, the bladder, ureters, and kidneys, are sterile, and therefore urine that passes through these structures is also sterile. When pathogens gain access to this system, they can establish infection. Some pathogens of urinary tract diseases include: viruses (e.g., *Herpes hominus*), Gram-positive and Gram-negative bacteria, fungi, helminth worms, and protozoans.

Urinary tract infections may be limited to a single tissue or organ, or they may spread upward and involve the entire system. Infections such as **cystitis** involve the bladder and may spread through the ureters to the kidneys.

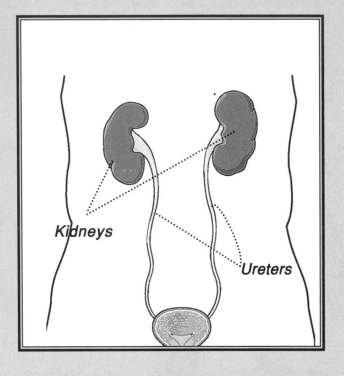

Kidneys

Ureters

Under normal conditions, the urinary tract is protected from infection by a number of molecular mechanisms along with its anatomy. Normal urine contains antimicrobial substances such as organic acids and small quantities of antibodies. During urinary tract infections, larger quantities of specific antibodies can be in the urine. There is also evidence that lymphoid cells infiltrate the infected kidneys and form protective antibodies locally at the site as they are needed. In addition, during infection an inflammatory response occurs in which phagocytes are of importance in engulfing and destroying invading microorganisms. However, in spite of many protective mechanisms, urinary tract infections are possible. When they occur you should seek the advice and treatment of a physician. Most infec-

Glomerulonephritis is an inflammation that results in the destruction of renal corpuscles. Organisms other than bacteria may also act as etiological agents of urogenital infections. *Trichomonas vaginalis*, a pathogenic flagellated protozoan, is commonly found in the vagina, and under appropriate conditions it is responsible for severe inflammatory infections. *Candida albicans*, a pathogenic yeast, is normally found in low numbers in the intestines, but may cause problems in the urinary tract when their numbers grow exponentially.

tions will clear in a couple of weeks under their care. Sometimes people allow urinary tract infections to develop into kidney infections. These are difficult to eradicate, often chronic, and can destroy the normal kidney. Failure of both kidneys results in death unless one is fortunate enough to receive a kidney transplant. Fortunately, the wise Creator gave us two kidneys and generally this is sufficient to last us a lifetime.

The Nephron, an Intertwining Unit

The **nephron** is the functional unit of the kidney, responsible for the actual purification and filtration of the blood (figure 8.1). About one million nephrons are in the cortex of each kidney, and each one consists of a **renal corpuscle** and a **renal tubule**, which carry out the functions of the nephron. The renal tubule consists of the **convoluted tubule** and the **loop of Henle**.

The **Bowman's capsule** contains the primary filtering device of the nephron, the **glomerulus**. Blood is transported into the Bowman's capsule from the **afferent arteriole** (branching off of the **interlobular artery**). Within the capsule, the blood is filtered through the glomerulus and then passes out via the efferent arteriole. Meanwhile, the filtered water and aqueous wastes are passed out of the Bowman's capsule into the **proximal convoluted tubule**.

The **glomerulus** is the main filter of the nephron and is located within the Bowman's capsule. The glomerulus resembles a twisted mass of tiny tubes through which the blood passes. The glomerulus is semipermeable, allowing water and soluble wastes to pass through and be excreted out of the Bowman's capsule as urine. The filtered blood passes out of the glomerulus into the efferent arteriole to be returned through the medullary plexus to the intralobular vein.

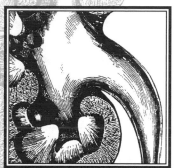

Once the waste liquid passes through the opening in the Bowman's capsule, it goes into the convoluted tubule, where it is passed through the loop of Henle and into the distal convoluted tubule. From there the urine passes to the calyces and into the renal pelvis. The loop of Henle is a U-turn in the tubule responsible for carrying urine out of the nephron and into the calyces. It is bordered by the proximal and **distal** parts of the **convoluted tubule** and features the **ascending and descending limb** flanking the U-turn.

The functional unit in the kidney that produces urine is called a nephron. Urine formation results from glomerular filtration, tubular reabsorption, and tubular secretion. Filtration takes place in the glomerulus where water and solutes, smaller than proteins, pass through the glomerular capsule from the blood. Red blood cells are screened and do not enter the nephron in a healthy kidney, but remain in the bloodstream or capillary. Tubular reabsorption takes place in the proximal renal tubule, where water, glucose, amino acids, and needed ions are transported out of the filtrate through cells. They return to the bloodstream in the **peritubular capillaries** from the nephron.

Tubular secretion is the process in which protons ($H+$), ammonia ($NH4+$), potassium ($K+$) certain drugs, and creatine are removed from the peritubular capillaries and secreted by renal tubule cells into the filtrate. Eventually some water, urea, and uric acid accumulate in the collecting ducts to form the urine. The urine is removed by way of the ureters, the urinary bladder, and the urethra. After the urinary bladder is partially filled and pressure is exerted, the urine finally exits the body through the urethra channel.

What Makes it Extraordinary?

Essentially, three characteristics make the excretory (urinary) system amazing. First, its basic unit, the nephron, is a multifaceted system in itself in that it performs the functions of filtration, **reabsorption**, and **secretion** simultaneously. In addition, the total volume that our kidneys filter in a lifetime, usually without failure, is staggering. Finally, its structure and function precludes its emerging by chance.

All body cells are metabolic furnaces, burning glucose and producing waste. Throughout the daily routines, as cells metabolize sugars, they produce waste and release it into the blood. Five to six liters of blood pass through the nephrons at a rate of 1,200 ml/min. This translates into all the blood filtering through the kidneys about 20 times every hour. Our blood passes through 60,000 miles of vessels and picks up waste from the hardworking cells. Then the kidneys use water to remove the toxins that would otherwise poison the blood. In a normal adult, the excreted rate is about 125 ml/min., or about 180 liters (48 gallons)/day. This amounts to about 17,520 gallons/year or 1,401,600 gallons in an 80-year lifetime. This is an extraordinary amount for a machine to filter. The role of the kidneys in your body is to filter and chemically balance the blood. The kidneys excrete waste products, but also recycle useful elements for body tissues through the circulatory system.

If the kidneys fail, dialysis machines can take over the job. Dialysis refers to the process of separating molecules of different sizes using a semipermeable membrane. Dialyzers permit patients to get their dialysis treatment three times a week. From a vein in the arm, blood flows into the unit where it passes by a semipermeable membrane that allows wastes but not blood cells to pass through it. A second filter removes air bubbles before the machine pumps the cleansed blood back into the body.

The dialysis machine can temporarily help people overcome their kidney deficiency. The dialysis machine made by bioengineers can substitute for our kidneys for several months. However, newer dialysis machines may help some patients with minimal kidney function for periods up to four years. Eventually, however, the patient will want to obtain a kidney transplant. Few people would want to be on dialysis for a lifetime. Yet, everyone would agree that dialysis machines are engineered with preplanned design. How, then, could anyone say the kidney happened by accident?

CHECK YOUR UNDERSTANDING

THOUGHTS
KNOWLEDGE
MEMORY

Excretory System

1. List at least three organs or components of the excretory system.

2. What is the overall function of the excretory system?

3. Describe and make an illustration of an intertwining part of the excretory system.

4. Discuss how a kidney is irreducibly complex.

5. What causes a urinary tract infection?

A Case Study

A lab technician forgets to label three patients' recent urine samples and a distilled water sample. She performs various tests on these samples to try to determine which urine belongs to which patient. One patient was on a high-salt diet; one was on a high-protein diet; one was diagnosed as hypoglycemic; and one had uncontrolled diabetes mellitus. The test results for the three urine and the distilled water samples are given below.

Chemical Test	Sample A	Sample B	Sample C	Sample D
Glucose in Urine	trace	abundant	none	none
Blood Glucose	90 mg/dL	250 mg/dL	50 mg/dL	90 mg/dL
Urine Odor	aromatic	sweet	aromatic	none
pH of Urine	6.3	5.2	4.0	7.0
Specify Gravity*	1.030	1.029	1.010	1.000
Volume of Urine	140 mL	170 mL	87 mL	100 mL

*Specific Gravity is a density measure used to describe the weight of urine to the weight of distilled water (D =1.000).

6. The urine sample from the diabetic (high blood sugar) patient is in which test tube?
A) Tube A   B) Tube C   C) Answer cannot be determined   D) Tube B   E) Tube D

7. The urine sample from the hypoglycemic (low blood sugar) patient is in which test tube?
A) Tube A B)   Tube C   C) Answer cannot be determined   D) Tube B   E) Tube D

8. Tube D must contain the distilled water because:
    A) by definition, the specific gravity of distilled water = 1.000.
    B) by definition, the pH of distilled water is 7;
    C) process of elimination leaves only Tube D for water;
    D) specific gravity is the water volume weight divided by the substance volume weight.
    E) there is no glucose in it.

9. The effect of a diuretic drug would most directly affect which variable?
A) specific gravity   B) pH   C) volume   D) glucose   E) odor

10. The tube with the highest concentration of hydrogen ions is
A) Tube A   B) Tube C   C) Tube D   D) Tube B   E) Cannot be determined

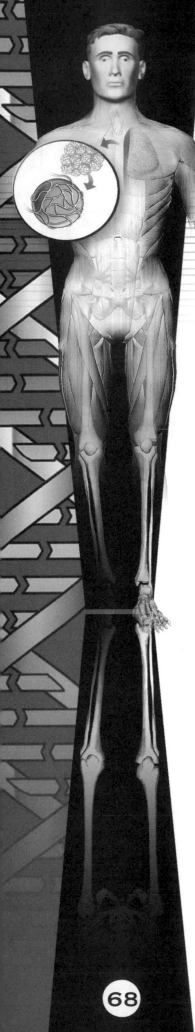

Thus, by ocular observations and dissections, by experiments and measurements, and by calculations and inductive reasoning, it is absolutely necessary to conclude that the blood is propelled by the heart in a circle and this is the only end of the heart.

(William Harvey, 1628)

In order for the body to stay alive, each of its cells must receive a continuous supply of nutrients and oxygen. At the same time, carbon dioxide and other byproducts of cellular metabolism must be collected for removal from the body. This process is continually maintained by the body's 60,000-mile network of vessels collectively known as the circulatory system. The primary circulatory system consists of the **heart** and **blood vessels**. Together, they maintain a continuous flow of blood through the body, delivering oxygen and nutrients to and removing carbon dioxide and waste products from peripheral tissues. The heart, a marvel of design and precision engineering, is the main component of the circulatory system. At the rate of about 70 beats per minute, the heart pumps oxygen-rich blood from the lungs to all parts of the body through a network of blood vessels that consists of major types. Throughout the entire scheme, intelligent design and irreducible complexity are not only observable but are the only solutions for the circulatory system's very existence.

Two organs that man depends upon most for daily living are the heart and the lung. Both of these vital organs clearly show evidence of a planned relationship between their structure and function. In the early days of science, perception of how these organs functioned was inadequate in terms of the knowledge we have today. Before the days of William Harvey and other Renaissance scientists, the form and function of these vital organs was merely hypothesized. Experimentation later corrected early misconceptions.

Harvey and the Heart

"The heart of creatures is the foundation of life, the Prince of all, the Sun of their microcosm, on which all vegetation does depend, from whence all vigor and strength flow."
(William Harvey, M.D., 1628,
letter to Charles I of England)

According to **Galen** (A.D. 131-210), the blood was formed in the intestines, and then in the liver was charged with natural spirits, and finally carried to the right side of the heart by the veins. Contractions of the right atrium and ventricle were thought to cause the blood with natural spirits to ebb and flow throughout the veins to all parts of the body. Some of the blood was supposed to ooze by invisible pores into the septum of the heart and into the left ventricle where it mixed with a certain quantity of air. Last, the blood was thought to be drawn from the lungs though the pulmonary veins and stuffed with vital spirits. (Galen thought that all living things were controlled by a mystical influence that he called "vital force.") Pulsations of the left ventricle then were thought to move the vital spirits back and forth in the arteries to the heart, and quicken and restore all body tissues (figures 9.2). In contrast to Galen, William Harvey's view of the heart and circulation rested neither on books nor opinions of his predecessors, but on direct ocular observations, dissections, and experimentation. Note that Harvey summarized that the reason for the heart's design was to accomplish a purposeful function. With this, he no doubt meant to lay to rest the misguided confidence of his readers in those mystical attributes of the heart so dearly cherished by church people, kings, and commoners alike. Harvey said:

"The blood is propelled by a muscular pump, the heart. Blood flows into a chamber of the heart. Then, the entrance is closed by a valve and the chamber is contracted, forcing the blood into a second chamber and then into an artery."

In 1628 Harvey published a small book written in Latin called *Exercito Anatomica de Motu Cordis et Sanguinis in Animalibus*, which is translated as *An Anatomical Dissertation on the Movement of the Heart and Blood in Animals*. Harvey's idea had been, by far, the most widely accepted of several competing theories of blood flow, but *De Motu Cordis* (as it is usually called) would in time bring the death blow for all of them. Harvey used a combination of quantitative and qualitative methods to make a series of easily conformable observations and measurements that led him to his conclusion. Like the neo-Darwinism of today, many people in Harvey's day refused to accept his explanation, especially those who favored the established ideas of Galen. Marcello Malpighi later demonstrated capillaries by means of a light microscope in 1632 and this vindicated Harvey. Harvey's list of credits and accomplishments include being the personal physician to **King Charles I**. The work of Harvey revolutionized the field of physiology and laid the foundation for a new way of scientific approach, which we now call the scientific method.

The Heart: A General Anatomy

The heart is located in the chest or thorax region just behind the **sternum** (breastbone), and it is nestled in a small cavity between the lungs. The average human heart is approximately the size of the individual's fist. A tough sac called the **pericardium** sheaths the heart. Membranes within the pericardium secrete a lubricating fluid that permits the pericardium to slide smoothly against the heart surface as the cardiac muscles contract. Several large, tube-like blood vessels branch off of the top of the heart, which bring blood to and from the heart. The heart itself has a network of blood vessels called the **coronary** "of the heart" that supplies oxygen and nutrients to the hard-working cardiac muscles.

Within the heart, there are four main sections or chambers. The chambers are divided into two kinds: the thin-walled upper chambers called the **atria** and thick-walled lower chambers called the **ventricles**. The ventricles and atria are divided into left and right by a thick wall called the **septum**. It is through the rhythmic action of the muscles in the walls of these chambers that blood is pushed throughout the entire circulatory system. The atria serve as the blood-receiving chambers of the heart, and the ventricles serve as the blood-pumping chambers that force blood through the blood vessels.

Overlooked Anatomy

It is not unusual for diagrams in beginning anatomy and physiology texts to overlook some not-so-glamorous structures in the body. This is often the case because artists tend to copy diagrams from other books that are copies themselves. Instead of making figures from

FIGURE 9.1

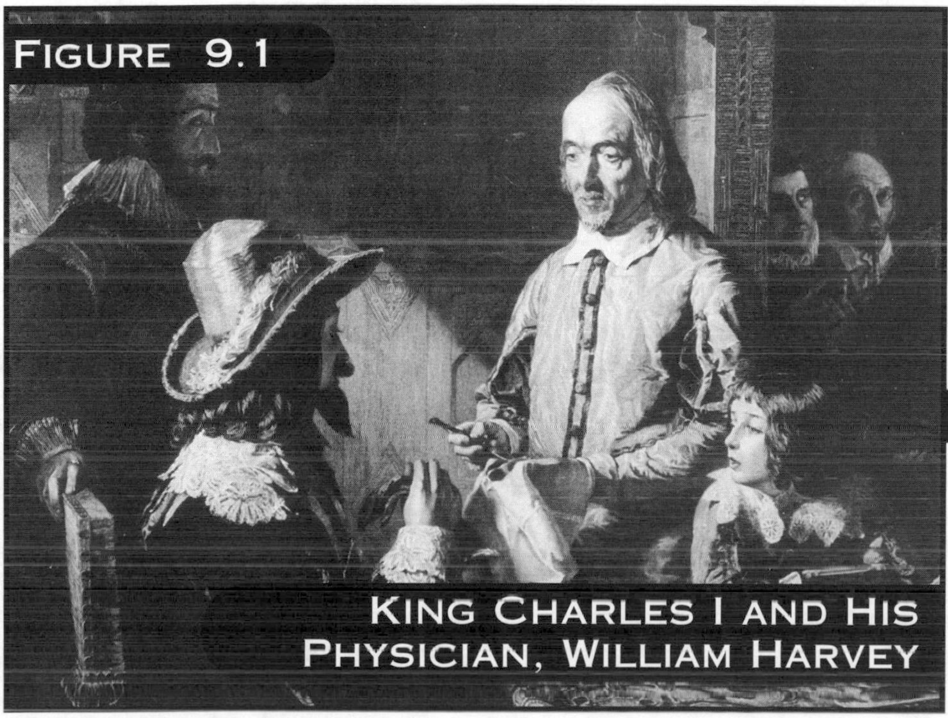

KING CHARLES I AND HIS PHYSICIAN, WILLIAM HARVEY

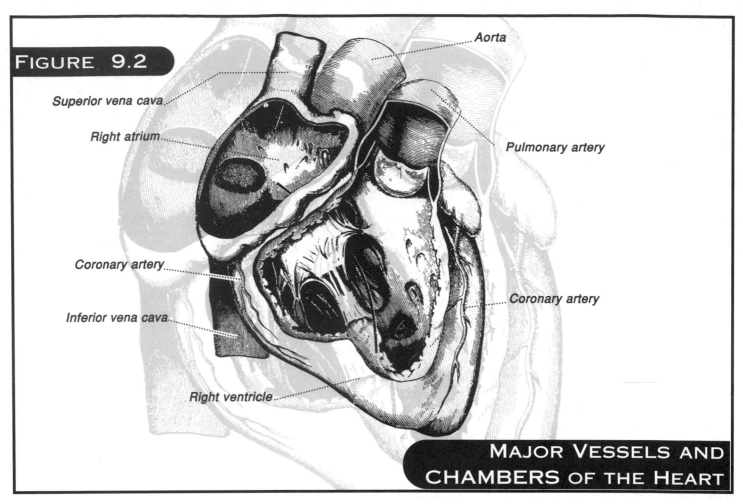

FIGURE 9.2

Aorta

Superior vena cava

Right atrium

Pulmonary artery

Coronary artery

Coronary artery

Inferior vena cava

Right ventricle

MAJOR VESSELS AND CHAMBERS OF THE HEART

cadavers, they copy or modify "accepted" figures of anatomy. Frequently, one error reproduces itself for many generations of diagrams. Historically, this was the case for over a thousand years. Things did not change until Vesalius and Harvey relied upon observation alone. Today, the same types of errors take place. Therefore, it is always important to remember that nothing takes the place of firsthand observation and thinking. Don't merely believe it because the text says so. For example, few textbooks depict the **right auricle** sometimes affectionately referred to as the "*ear of the heart*" by medical students. The right auricle protects the aorta and the right coronary cuspid arteries. The **appendix aurculae** is so-named due to its fancied resemblance to a dog's ear. It is a small conical, muscular pouch, the margins of which present a dentate edge. It projects from the sinus forward and to the left side, overlapping with the aorta.

To prevent back-flow of blood in the heart, the Creator integrated a series of valves into the heart that work flawlessly together to keep blood moving in the right direction. The two main valves within the heart are the **bicuspid valve** (or **mitral valve**) and the **tricuspid valve**. These valves, known collectively as the A-V valves (**atrioventricular valves**), separate the atria and the ventricles. The tricuspid valve connects the right atrium and right ventricle, and the bicuspid valve (mitral valve) connects the left atrium and the left ventricle. The **aortic and pulmonary semilunar valves** are the two valves that allow blood to flow to the body from the ventricles. Each cusp of the bicuspid and tricuspid valves is held in position by strong tendinous

cords called **chordae tendinae**, which are held to the ventricle walls by cone-shaped papillary muscles. These keep the cuspid valves from everting, like an umbrella in a strong gust of wind, when the ventricles contract. The **pulmonary semilunar valve** allows blood to exit the right ventricle and enter the pulmonary arteries that carry the blood to the lungs to become oxygenated. The **aortic semilunar valve** allows blood to exit the left ventricle and enter the aorta. The **aorta** is the largest blood vessel in the body and is the main artery that brings blood to all body tissues (figure 9.2).

Interwoven Designs in the Heart

When one looks at the heart, it is easy to see an interwoven or interconnecting design. Anyone can see that the intricate networks of blood vessels that enter and exit the heart are of intelligent contrivance. There are two interwoven properties of the heart, however, that often go unnoticed to the untrained eye. These properties are the autonomic control of the rhythmic pulsation of the heart as it pumps and the centrifugal flow of blood through the heart and blood vessels.

The heart pumps approximately 2,000 gallons of blood each day for a total of about 680,000 gallons each year. To accomplish this unending, seemingly impossible task, the atria and ventricles must contract and relax on a highly coordinated series of actions which is known generally as the cardiac cycle. Nerves stemming from the **medulla oblongata** autonomically control the cardiac cycle. The stage of this cycle when the heart relaxes and fills with blood is the phase known as **diastole**, while the pumping and contracting stage is known as **systole**. Each **cardiac cycle** is perceived as a heartbeat. The heartbeat is an important diagnostic tool for physicians. A difference in pitch or quality of the heartbeat can be interpreted as a number of heart defects and dysfunctions. Often an abnormal sound in a heartbeat, a heart murmur, is caused by a damaged valve. Valve problems may arise from a bacterial disease of the heart called **rheumatic fever**, from inherited genetic defects, or from anomalies of fetal development.

The heart is regulated by **autonomic** or involuntary control. The blood requirements of the body tissues and organs are not constant. They depend on present activity level, overall health, stress level, and state of consciousness (awake or sleeping). The brain increases the heart rate by means of the body's autonomic nervous system. Accelerator nerves link the heart to the central nervous system. These nerves transmit signals to the heart's **pacemaker**, or the **sinoatrial (S-A) node**, thereby, increasing the heart rate.

Signals that are refractory and opposite of those of the accelerator nerves are the signals from the vagus nerves. Both the **accelerator** and **vagus nerves** are part of the autonomic nervous system, but the accelerator nerves belong to the **sympathetic division**, and the vagus nerves belong to the **parasympathetic division**. These two nerve types accurately and efficiently control the heart rate from the 120–170 beats per minute during a strenuous workout, to the 50–60 beats per minute during sleep. The whole system is very interdependent and precisely tuned. If it fails in one part, the whole system falters. Another important, often ignored, example of intelligent engineering in the body is the centrifugal flow of blood within the blood vessels. As the blood flows through the heart, the arteries, the capillaries, and back to the heart through the veins, a potential for friction to build up is evident. The Creator, in His divine wisdom, took care of this situation.

A scientist at Imperial College, London, discovered that the blood vessels pathways were helical and that they were designed with a spiraling effect built in. The gentle spiraling makes the blood flow more evenly compared to straight vessels. Also, it was found that damage from turbulent flow was much less likely with helical vessels, especially at **T-junctions**. This effect could be important in heart bypass surgery where veins in the leg are used to replace the sections of clogged cardiac arteries around the heart. If the replacement vessels were given

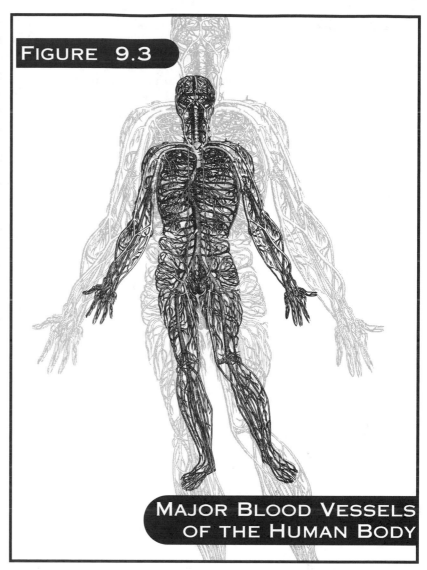

FIGURE 9.3

MAJOR BLOOD VESSELS OF THE HUMAN BODY

a slight twist, the time it would take for the vessels to become clogged again would increase.

This effect of swirling has been proven to significantly reduce friction between blood and the blood vessels. Any mechanic will tell you that less friction in a machine is always better. Our bodies are the most perfect machines ever built. God designed and thought through every minute aspect of structure and function of the human body, so that everything would work perfectly and flawlessly together. Could these properties of blood flow and heart regulation have evolved over millions of years by numerous, random, and slight mutations and natural selection? This is a logical impossibility. Our Creator's attention to detail in the design of every body part is extraordinary. Man is God's masterpiece — the crown of creation.

The Blood Vessels

Blood vessels are multi-layered, muscular tubes that carry blood to and from all parts of the body. The human circulatory system is made up of three main types of blood vessels.

Arteries are thick-walled, muscular blood vessels that carry blood away from the heart to the organs and tissues of the body. These vessels must be very durable because of the high pressure that the pumping action of the heart places on them. The walls of arteries consist of three layers. The outer layer is very fibrous and tough, giving elasticity and shape. The middle layer, the thickest layer, is made up of circular layers of smooth muscle. The brain makes adjustments in blood pressure by changing the diameter of arteries using this middle layer of muscle. The inner layer is merely a sheet of cells smooth enough to let blood flow. **Arterioles** are small branches of the artery that are about 0.2 mm in diameter. The arterioles branch into metarterioles that further branch into capillaries.

Capillaries, the smallest of the three blood vessel types, are microscopic in size. They link the arterioles and venules and are the functional units of the circulatory system. Some ten billion capillaries lace all body tissues, bringing blood within reach of every cell. They are the smallest blood vessels and contain less than 5 percent of the total circulating blood volume at any one time. Capillaries branch off from the metarterioles that connect arterioles with venules. The capillaries have thin walls, a mere one cell thick, across which gas and wastes are exchanged. As blood flows through the capillaries in the lungs, it changes from venous blood to arterial blood by diffusing carbon dioxide out and oxygen in. The color of blood changes in the process from a deep crimson to a bright scarlet. As blood flows through tissue capillaries, it changes back from arterial blood to venous blood. The oxygen leaves the blood to enter cells, and carbon dioxide and other wastes leave the cells and enter the blood. Capillaries converge to form **venules** and then further converge to form veins.

Veins are vessels that carry blood from the capillaries of the organs and tissues toward the heart. They have small **valves** that open to let blood through and close to prevent it from flowing backwards. These valves are designed to allow the skeletal muscles to abet the return of blood to the heart. During movement or exercise, muscular contractions squeeze the veins, forcing blood through them — the valves control the blood, only allowing it to flow toward the heart. The structure of veins is similar to that of arteries, but their walls are not as thick nor as elastic as arteries because less force is exerted on their walls from blood.

Blood Circulation

Blood follows two major and two minor pathways or circuits throughout the body. The two major pathways are known as the systemic and pulmonary circuits, and the two minor pathways are known as the portal and renal circuits. Within these circuits, there are characteristic blood vessels and organs that give them their name and separate them from the others (table 9.1).

Systemic circulation is the movement of the blood through all parts of the body except the lungs. The aorta, the main blood vessel of the systemic circuit, leaves the left ventricle of the heart and branches out and enters every organ in the body. As the aorta leaves the heart, it forms an arch as it turns toward the lower body. This arch is known as the aortic arch. From the top of the aortic arch, two arteries, called the

---

DESIGN FOCUS 9.1

Layers of the Blood Vessels

Tunic is a Latin word that means covering or coat. Tunic was originally used to describe ornamental coats in Roman soldiers. In anatomy, the word *tunica** is used to describe layers, or coats, in the walls of the circulatory blood vessels: arteries, veins, and capillaries. These layers wrapping blood vessels reminds us of sleeves, coats, and layers of clothing. Just like the ornamental coats of the Roman soldiers were not there by chance, neither are the tunics inside the body. Good tunics are seamlessly inter-woven, like tapestries, where one cannot see the stitching. This is still another piece of evidence for intelligent design of the body. If tunics evolved by some random, physio-chemical force, then one should observe "stitches" in these layers. We do not, however, observe any intermediate form in blood vessels. Each layer in a blood vessel is fully formed and complete. The easiest example of tunics to observe in the body are those lining the arteries and veins. You may observe the following in a cross section:

1. *Tunica externa*, the outermost layer, composed of connective tissue.
2. *Tunica media*, the middle layer, composed of smooth muscle. The tunica media of arteries has variable amounts of elastic fibers.
3. *Tunica interna*, the innermost layer, composed of simple squamous epithelium and fibers composed of elastic.

(*This term is also used to describe the walls of the gastrointestinal tract, the lining of genital organs, and the linings of organs where smooth muscles occur.)

carotid arteries, carry blood to the brain and head. Also, two more arteries, the subclavian arteries, branch off of the aorta and supply blood to the arms. As the aorta continues down it is known as the descending aorta. The descending aorta feeds the organs within the abdominal cavity and continues toward the legs. As it approaches the legs, it separates into two common iliac arteries. The common iliac arteries become the femoral arteries as they enter the leg. The blood flows through the tissue capillaries where cells are rejuvenated. The capillaries converge to form veins. There are several major veins that drain large sections of the body into the superior and inferior vena cava. The **jugular veins** drain the head and brain, the subclavian veins drain the arms, and the femoral veins drain the legs. The superior and inferior vena cava converge at the right atrium where blood undergoes pulmonary circulation.

Pulmonary circulation

Pulmonary circulation is the movement of blood between the heart and the lungs. Pulmonary circulation begins as the blood passes through the pulmonary semilunar valve and enters the pulmonary artery. (Note: the pulmonary artery is the only artery that carries deoxygenated blood and the pulmonary vein is the only vein that carries oxygenated blood.) The blood travels to the lungs where carbon dioxide is released and oxygen is picked up. The blood then returns to the left atrium via the pulmonary veins.

Portal circulation

Portal circulation, a subsystem of **systemic** circulation, is the movement of blood from the digestive organs to the liver. Digested nutrients are picked up in the digestive organs by the blood. A substantial amount of the carbohydrates in the blood are deposited in the liver and stored in the form of glycogen. The liver also recycles old red blood cells and removes toxins and other unwanted substances from the blood. Certain substances, such as lipoprotein and urea that are produced in the liver, enter the blood and are brought to other parts of the body. The liver is supplied with blood by the **hepatic portal vein** and is drained by the **hepatic vein** into the inferior vena cava.

Renal circulation

Renal circulation, also a subsystem of systemic circulation, is the movement of blood from the body organs through the kidneys. The kidneys are supplied with blood through a branch of the aorta called the renal artery. The blood is then filtered through a very intricate and multi-step process as discussed in chapter 8. The newly filtered blood then exits the kidneys through the renal veins and heads back to the heart through the inferior vena cava.

Exploring the Bloodstream

"When Charles Darwin was climbing the rocks of the Galapagos Island, he must have cut his finger occasionally or scraped his knee. Young adventurer that he was, he probably paid no attention to the blood trickling out."

If Charles Darwin had paid attention to his cuts and bruises and had known the biochemistry of blood the way Michael Behe or Dean Kenyon does today, he might have reached a different conclusion about body systems in his *Origin of Species*. Like the multifaceted systems discussed in chapters 7 and 8, the biochemical components involved in blood clotting and wound restoration will function only as an entire unit or not at all.

Clotting involves various chemicals known as **coagulation factors**. Clotting is a complex process in which coagulation

TABLE 9.1	Major Blood Vessels in the Human Body
DESIGNED STRUCTURE	**PURPOSEFUL FUNCTION**
Jugular veins	Receive blood from brain and tissues of head
Superior vena cava	Receives blood from veins of upper body
Pulmonary veins	Deliver oxygenated blood from the lungs to the heart
Hepatic portal vein	Delivers nutrient-rich blood from small intestine to liver for processing
Renal vein	Carries processed blood away from kidneys
Inferior vena cava	Receives blood from all veins below diaphragm
Iliac veins	Carry blood away from the pelvic organs and lower abdominal wall
Femoral vein	Carries blood away from the thigh and inner knee
Carotid arteries	Deliver blood to neck, head, brain
Ascending aorta	Carries oxygenated blood away from heart; the largest artery
Pulmonary arteries	Deliver oxygen-poor blood from the heart to the lungs
Coronary arteries	Service the incessantly active cardiac muscle cells of the heart
Brachial artery	Delivers blood to upper extremities; blood pressure measured here
Renal artery	Delivers blood to kidneys, where its volume, composition are adjusted
Abdominal aorta	Delivers blood to arteries leading to the digestive tract, kidneys, pelvic organs, and lower extremities
Iliac arteries	Deliver blood to pelvic organs and lower abdominal wall
Femoral artery	Delivers blood to the thigh and inner knee

The One-Way Circulation Of Blood

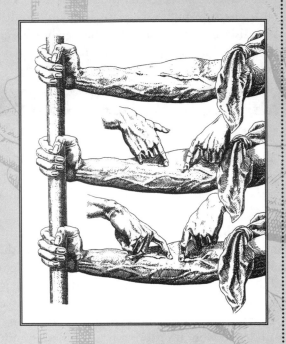

These experiments demonstrate the existence of one-way valves in the arms. In a paraphrase (translated from Latin) of Harvey's words: With the arm bound as before and the veins swollen, if you will press on the vein a little below a swelling or valve and then squeeze blood upward beyond the valve with another finder, you will see that this part of the vein stays empty and that no back flow can occur through the valve. But as soon as the finger is removed, the vein is filled from below (blood comes from the lower arm and hand toward the upper arm).

In the figure, the experimenter has pressed on a vein at a point to block the flow from the wrist toward the elbow. With another finger, he has milked the blood out of it unto a point, the first valve proximal to it when he tries to force blood onward, it stops at valve. It can go no farther, and it causes the vein to swell at that point. Blood can flow from right to left through that valve but not from left to right. You can easily demonstrate the action of these valves in your own hand. Hold your hand still, below waist level until veins stand up on the back of it. Do not use a turniquet! Press on a vein close to your knuckles, and while holding it down, use another finger to milk that vein toward the wrist. It collapses as you force the blood out of it, and if you move the second finger, it will not refill. The valves prevent blood from flowing back into it from above. When you remove the first finger (on your left), however, the vein fills from the lower arm toward the elbow. In summary, Harvey deduced the design on the one-way valves in veins throughout the body. His conclusion, "Blood circulates in a one-way direction."

factors activate each other. That is, the first coagulation factor activates the second, the second activates the third, and so on. There are about a dozen factors involved in the 30-plus reactions that involve clotting and wound restoration. This is why the blood clotting system is called a **cascade,** a system where one component activates another component. In this chapter, you will explore the complex mechanism behind blood clotting.

About two to three percent of the protein in blood plasma consists of a protein complex called **fibrinogen**, a protein waiting to react. Normal fibrinogen is dissolved in plasma, like salt is dissolved in the Gulf of Mexico. Another protein called **thrombin** slices several small pieces from two of the three pairs of protein chains in fibrinogen. The trimmed

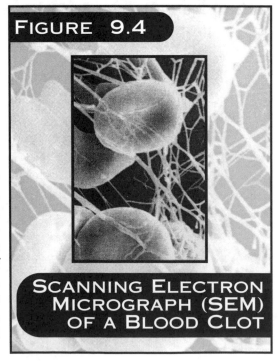

FIGURE 9.4

SCANNING ELECTRON MICROGRAPH (SEM) OF A BLOOD CLOT

protein is now called fibrin. It has sticky patches exposed on its surface that have been covered by the pieces that were cut off. The sticky patches are precisely complementary to portions of other fibrin molecules. Long threads form, cross over each other, and (much as a fisherman's net traps fish) make an intricate protein meshwork that entraps blood cells. This is the initial clot (figure 9.4).

One way of understanding blood clotting is by comparing it with a car engine. Most biochemical systems are composed of interrelated parts and components that must act simultaneously for the necessary functions in the system to work. These complex physiological systems in our body operate much like a car engine in which the spark plugs, pistons, radiator, fan belt, and other parts must operate simultaneously.

The formation, limitation, strengthening, and removal of the blood clot is an integrated biological mechanism. Problems with any single component can cause the entire mechanism to fail. This is analogous to the car engine, which fails to operate if the fan belt is missing, the distributor cap is cracked, or the spark plugs are clogged. The lack of certain blood clotting factors, or the production of defective factors, often results in serious health problems or death. The most common form of **hemophilia** occurs because one of these blood factors is missing. How could the blood clotting mechanism in humans evolve step by step over millions of years under the action of nothing more than random physiochemical forces?

Another way to understand the irreducible complexity of biochemical systems is to consider the interlocking components of a mousetrap. The mechanism of blood clotting is much like a mousetrap that has five parts: a catch, a platform, a holding bar, a hammer, and a spring. When assembled there is no gradual improvement of function. It does not work until every part is in place. The same thing is true inside a living cell and in each organ of the human body. Many body systems just will not work unless every part is present at the same time.

Furthermore, the success of blood clotting depends critically on the rate at which the different reactions occur. An organism would not long survive if the protein activated by **thrombin** formed at a significantly faster rate than **proaccelerin**. Blood clotting depends not only upon the occurrence of these reactions, but also on the correct timing and rates of their actions. If these interrelated mechanisms began to originate in a slow, creeping fashion by microevolutionary changes, the result would be disastrous. Any member missing in the "**molecular team**" would have prevented the final mechanisms from working and most likely would have proved lethal before the end result was achieved by natural selection. It is more logical to believe that this irreducibly complex set of biochemical reactions was put there by the actions of the Master Planner.

Remember, the Creator formulated not only the plan for the blood cascade but also produced the first working organisms. He is not only the chief architect of the blood cells, proteins, and platelets, but also the manufacturer of the components. He keeps everything going because He is the maintainer. The predictable order of the coagulation cascade exists because the order of a precise plan was produced by intelligent cause. These finely tuned and interdependent biochemical interactions are examples of what biochemist Behe calls irreducible complexity. Most creation scientists would go a step further and say this is clear, physical evidence of fingerprints from the Master's hand.

Uniform Experience

Dr. Charles Thaxton argues for the "**principle of uniform experience**" to support the idea that there is an intelligent cause for life. (This principle was previously discussed in the Mount Rushmore "rock formation" of chapter 2.) Even though we do not see the construction process, we logically conclude from our experience that workmen following a blueprint when they carved these stones. This plan was devised in the mind of an architect ahead of its actual construction.

The idea starts on the table of an architect. From there a blueprint is taken to the field to see if the plan is practical. Once adjustments are made, construction begins on the monument (figure 9.6). We recognize intelligence at Mount Rushmore, because of the symmetry in the stones as we see the heads of U.S. presidents, the overall interdependence of the forms that compose the entire surface, and the obvious purpose revealed by the sculpture. We reject the notion that the shapes of these rocks are the products of wind and water erosion. It is the action of human hands. Likewise, according to our "experience," we can logically conclude that living systems with order, organization, complexity, symmetry, interdependence, and purpose are also products of intelligent design. From this principle of common or uniform experience, we may deduce that human DNA, like the Mt. Rushmore blueprint, is a predestined plan conceived by an architect before its construction (figure 9.6). As we consider the common experience of blood drawn from our body, we may also deduce that DNA provided genetic instructions for the manufacture of red blood cells. Each of these was devised by an intelligent cause.

Our best judgment tells us that information, a code, or a message takes an intelligent agent to generate it. We never see functional complexity derived from disorder, by chance, or by chaos. We must logically conclude that patterns observed in the components of blood are by the action of God's unseen hand!

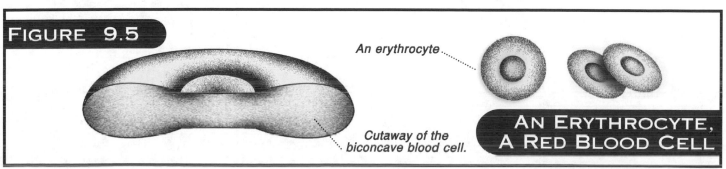

FIGURE 9.5

An erythrocyte

Cutaway of the biconcave blood cell.

AN ERYTHROCYTE, A RED BLOOD CELL

FIGURE 9.6

THE PRINCIPLE OF UNIFORM EXPERIENCE
1. CONCEPTION OF A PLAN 2. BLUEPRINT OF A PLAN
3. PRODUCTION OF A PLAN 4. PRODUCT OF A PLAN

DESIGN FOCUS 9.3

The Importance of the Biconcavity of Red Blood Cells

Normal erythrocytes are nearly uniform in size, with diameters of 7.2–7.9 μm (μm, microns, or 10^{-6} m). The average red blood cell is about 2 μm thick at its thickest part. However, erythrocytes with much larger and much smaller sizes may be found in certain disease states. The shape of the normal erythrocyte is a biconcave disc (figure 9.5). This configuration allows for maximum surface contact of hemoglobin with the cell, thus greatly facilitating the exchange of blood gases. In fact, IBM did a study on the ideal shape of a solid object (3-D) that would maximize oxygen diffusion. After running numerous simulations on an IBM mainframe computer, the biconcave disc or "lifesaver" shape was determined optimal. Furthermore, this shape gives the red blood cell great flexibility and elasticity. This shape also allows it to be folded when it has to move through very narrow blood capillaries. The smooth, round edges reduce the amount of friction the cell may encounter in microcirculation.

Oxygen molecules attach to hemoglobin molecules within erythrocytes to give blood its red color. A hemoglobin molecule consists of four protein chains called globins, each of which is bound to one heme, a red-pigmented molecule. Each heme contains an atom of iron that can combine with one molecule of oxygen. Thus, the hemoglobin can transport up to four molecules of oxygen. Considering that each erythrocyte contains about 280 million hemoglobin molecules, a single erythrocyte can transport over a billion molecules of oxygen. It is within the lungs that oxygen molecules contained in inhaled air attach to the hemoglobin molecules and are transported via erythrocytes to trillions of body cells.

Check Your UNDERSTANDING

THOUGHTS
KNOWLEDGE
MEMORY

Circulatory System

1. List at least three organs (components) of the circulatory system.

2. What is sickle cell anemia? How do you identify sickle cell anemia in the lab?

3. Describe the job and makeup of the blood.

4. Discuss how a vein is an interwoven component in the circulatory system.

5. Is sickle cell anemia a beneficial trait? Explain why or why not.

6. Explain how homeostasis (and feedback) relates to blood clotting. Explain a positive feedback mechanism.

INVESTIGATING THE RESPIRATORY SYSTEM AND THE LUNGS

CHAPTER 10

The nose acts as a conditioner for the respiratory system. Every day, it treats approximately 50 cubic feet of air, the amount enclosed in a small room.

(Jackson, 1993, p. 65)

Oxygen Is Essential

Oxygen is essential — without oxygen, under normal circumstances, we would have brain damage in four minutes and within five to six minutes, we would die. Every cell in the body needs oxygen to do its metabolic processes. The exchange takes place in the lungs, and at top performance an athlete may process over 300 liters of air each minute, whereas a couch potato will use only 8 liters in order to extract precious oxygen.

Respiratory System Overview

The respiratory system (the **lungs** and connecting tubes) brings oxygen into the body. Our lungs alternately inflate and deflate, usually between 12 and 20 times a minute. When we exercise, we breathe more rapidly because our muscles are using more oxygen that must be replaced. The respiratory system starts processing air as soon as we inhale it. The nasal passages immediately filter, warm, and humidify it. The entire nasal cavity is lined with mucous membranes full of blood vessels; heat from the blood acts as a humidifier, moistening the air. The surface layers of the mucous membranes contain **cilia**, tiny hair-like structures that literally wave in the wind, creating a flow of mucus down the throat, or pharynx. Small particles such as bacteria and dust become trapped in the sticky mucus and can then be swallowed.

The respiratory system is responsible for supplying oxygen to the blood and expelling waste gases, of which carbon dioxide is the primary constituent, from the body. The upper structures of the respiratory system are combined with the sensory organs of smell and taste (in the nasal cavity and the mouth) and the digestive system (from the oral cavity to the pharynx). At the **pharynx,** the specialized respiratory organs diverge into the airway. The **larynx,** or voice box, is located at the head of the **trachea,** or windpipe. The trachea extends down to the **bronchi** that branch off at the tracheal bifurcation to enter the **hilus** of the left or right lung (figure 10.1).

The lungs contain the narrower passageways, or **bronchioles,** which carry air to the functional unit of the lungs, the **alveoli.** There, in the thousands of tiny alveolar chambers, oxygen is transferred through the membrane of the alveolar walls to the blood cells in the capillaries within. Likewise, waste gases diffuse out of the blood cells into the air in the alveoli, to be expelled upon exhalation. The **diaphragm,** a large, thin muscle below the lungs, and the **intercostal** and **abdominal muscles** are responsible for contracting and expanding the thoracic cavity to effect respiration. The ribs serve as a structural support for the whole thoracic arrangement, and pleural membranes help provide lubrication for the respiratory

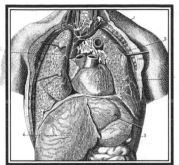

organs so that they are not chafed during respiration.

After air passes through the trachea, it is passed through the bronchial tree network, first to the primary bronchi, then to the secondary bronchi, to the tertiary bronchi, then to the **bronchioles,** and finally the terminal **bronchioles** which pass the air into the alveolus of the lung. In the alveolus we find the interwoven part.

Interwoven Parts of the Lung

The alveoli are the tiny sacs at the ends (or "leaves") of the bronchial tree. Each small bronchiole divides into half a dozen or so alveolar ducts, which are the narrow inlets into **alveolar sacs.** Each **alveolar duct** subdivides, leading to the three or more alveolar sacs. Each large alveolar sac is like a grape cluster that contains ten or more alveoli. Because the membrane separating the alveolus and the capillary network that carries blood over them is very thin and semipermeable,

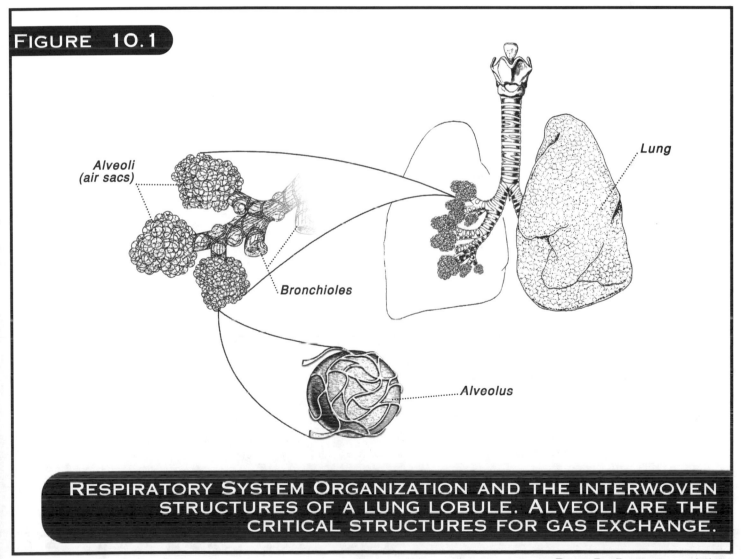

FIGURE 10.1

Alveoli (air sacs)

Bronchioles

Lung

Alveolus

RESPIRATORY SYSTEM ORGANIZATION AND THE INTERWOVEN STRUCTURES OF A LUNG LOBULE. ALVEOLI ARE THE CRITICAL STRUCTURES FOR GAS EXCHANGE.

oxygen can transfer from the air into the blood cells within the capillaries. Likewise, carbon dioxide and other waste gases can transfer out of the blood and into the air to be exhaled from the lungs. The alveoli are particularly susceptible to infection, as they provide bacteria and viruses a perfect place to grow. This accounts for the tendency for a chest cold or other lung problem to advance into **pneumonia**, a potentially dangerous condition in which the innermost parts of the lungs become infected and inflamed, diminishing airflow and oxygen transport due to the dangerous accumulation of fluid.

The Lung

The other vital organ that we depend upon each moment of life is the lung. People can hold their breath for a maximum of five or six minutes, denying the body gas exchange from the lung. If it were not for an automatic feedback mechanism in which the body starts breathing again during our unconscious state, the action of holding one's breath would ultimately lead to death. The basic unit of the human lung is the alveolus, which is a cluster of lung cells. The functional significance of the alveolus provides:

1) increased surface area for gas contact,
2) moisture that aids in exchange and transport of oxygen,

3) a one-cell-thick basement membrane for easy gas exchange.
4) a site of oxygen and carbon dioxide exchange, and
5) close proximity of the capillary to air surface, promoting absorption of gases.

In addition to structural adaptation of the alveolus in the lung, the diaphragm and intercostal muscles (below the ribs) rhythmically contract to promote bulk inflow and outflow of air. Hair-like organelles called cilia in the respiratory tract remove mucous and harmful residues from the system. Once again, structure and function are highly correlated, demonstrating the optimal body plan for survival and adaptation in a changing world.

"Tongue" of the Lung

Like the "ear" of the heart, another overlooked anatomical structure is the anteroinferior part of the superior lobe in the left lung. It forms a small tongue-like projection called the **lingula** (Latin for "tongue"). This structure, during cadaver dissections by medical students, is frequently referred to as the "*tongue*" of the lung (figure 10.2). As a project, you might search for photographs of actual human lungs and see if you can find its "tongue." It is best seen in **transverse (coronal)** sections.

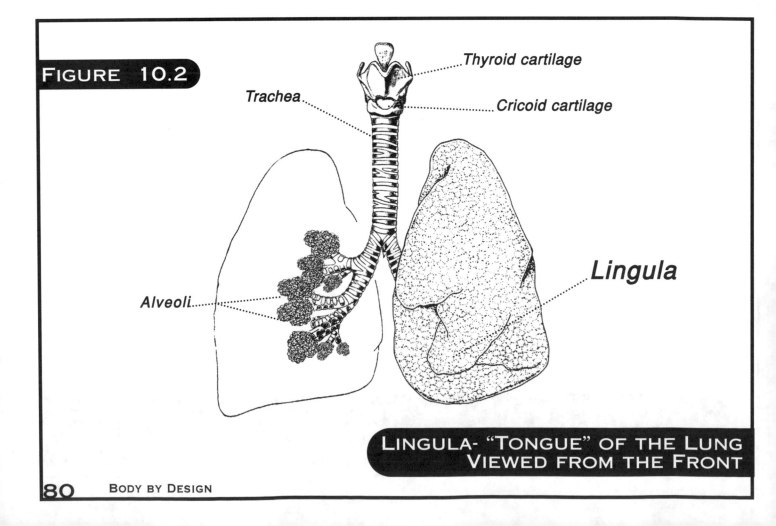

FIGURE 10.2

Thyroid cartilage

Trachea

Cricoid cartilage

Alveoli

Lingula

LINGULA- "TONGUE" OF THE LUNG
VIEWED FROM THE FRONT

SUMMARY

The lingula appears to shield the vital organs from trauma. The lingula protects lung tissue below and also covers part of the heart and blood vessels, including the **pulmonary artery anterior cuspid**, and **left coronary cuspid**.

There are dozens of examples that demonstrate the relationship of human structure to function. We have considered only a few of them. Table 10.1 portrays three basic designed structures from the respiratory system. Hundreds of other examples of formfitting functions in the human body could be given. Various designs of structures in the skeletal, skin, respiratory, circulatory, immune, and digestive systems attest to their remarkable, purposeful functioning. Could any of these precise interrelationships have originated by non-directed, physiochemical forces? Would chemical molecules fall together by chance to produce such intricate systems? To reproduce order out of disorder, code from non-code, and program from non-program, life forms need energy that is precisely directed. Only when energy is directed and transformed can chaos of chemicals produce order. Codes and designs with precise functioning presuppose an intelligent cause behind them. The wonderful patterns, adaptations, and precise functions of the human body parts are clear indications of an Intelligent Designer, a Maker behind it.

Automotive engineers try each year to improve new automobiles. The engineers' blueprints take sport, durability, cost effectiveness, safety, and personal preferences into consideration. If you ever study the features of cars like Cadillac, Lincoln, Mercedes Benz, Volvo, or BMW, you will see similar trademark signs. Each company has its own impressive logo or a quality "landmark."

Although cars keep improving each year by running faster, becoming more energy efficient, looking sportier, containing more electronic gadgets, and in general, getting better, they will never approach what is really the "ultimate machine." It functions with such precision that human physiologists will never fully understand its superlative qualities. Each year, it seems, anatomists, physiologists, and biochemists discover new mechanisms that more fully explain its construction.

One highly praised anatomy and physiology textbook states: "Anatomical structures seem designed to perform specific functions. Each body structure has a particular size, shape, form, or position in the body related directly to its ability to perform a unique and specialized activity. The most logical explanation for such a high correlation between structure and function is a planned origin. In the same way a specific key fits into a lock to unlock a door, many body parts are fitted to perform a specific function." In table 10.1, I present two planned forms with their purposeful functions.

In the same way that an architect plans a house, the master bioengineer produced precisely functioning body parts. Let's visualize a skilled cabinetmaker selecting tools from a box to build a fine cabinet. The worker uses a pencil to draw a blueprint, a ruler to measure the length of a door, a hammer to pound a nail, a screwdriver to remove a screw, a saw to cut

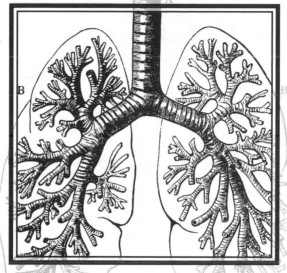

TABLE 10.1	Relationship of Designed Structure to Purposeful Function in the Respiratory System	
SYSTEM	**DESIGNED STRUCTURES**	**PURPOSEFUL FUNCTION**
Respiratory	Lungs are made of connective tissues and elastic fibers; interwoven alveoli inside	Allows for the expansion and contraction of the lungs and this provides a greater exchange of gases with the blood.
Respiratory	Right bronchus is wider and shorter than the left bronchus	The right lung is larger than the left, therefore it needs more inflow and outflow of air for systemic circulation.
Respiratory	Lingula of left lung	Protects lung tissue below and covers part of the heart and blood vessels, including the pulmonary artery anterior cuspid, and left coronary cuspid.

the lumber, and hinges to attach the door to the cabinet. In all, the carpenter may use a dozen distinctly different tools, each with its own role to play. In order to use these tools effectively to build a cabinet there must be a plan before its construction.

According to Behe, "In order to reach a conclusion of design for something that is not an artificial object, or to reach a conclusion for a system composed of a number of artificial objects, there must be an identifiable function of the system."

DISEASE FOCUS 10.1

THE COMMON COLD

Why should you study the common cold and viruses? Nine out of ten Americans catch the common cold each year. Many of those suffering from colds are teenagers, who catch up to six colds per year. According to recent statistics, this translates into about 26 million school days missed by students each year. The study of rhinoviruses is relevant to high school students because they catch between two and three colds per school year on the average.

Students are especially susceptible to catching colds when they are around others who are coughing and sneezing. Symptoms of the common cold include sneezing, coughing, nasal congestion, and/or the sniffles. Viruses cause most colds; however, bacteria such as *Haemophilus influenzae* cause some. Rhinoviruses, coronaviruses, Coxsackie viruses, respiratory syncytial viruses, adenoviruses, reoviruses, echoviruses, and influenza viruses have all been linked with the common cold. Younger students are especially susceptible to colds because they frequently congregate together and touch each other's hands.

In order for a common cold virus (**rhinovirus**) to infect our body, it must pass beyond the nasal passages and reach the nasopharnyx or beyond. Rhinoviruses must attach themselves to the nasal epithelial cells of the throat before infection and multiplication. These throat cells are called ciliated (haired) **pseudostratified epithelial cells**. Some common cold treatments are designed to prevent the cold virus from attaching to these cells.

The common cold is generally caused by rhinoviruses during the fall and winter. Rhinoviruses disturb the upper respiratory system and grow in the nose, where the temperature is a few degrees cooler than the rest of the body. Hence, we use the Greek term *rhinos*, meaning nose, to describe these viruses. We keep catching the common cold because there are so many different rhinoviruses. It is postulated that there are so many cold viruses because these simple life forms (RNA virus) are subject to mutation and their outer proteins change. This diversity of cold viruses is known as antigenic variation. Our body can build immunity against one virus at a time; unfortunately, there may be another hundred that it will eventually have to defend against. Senior adults eventually develop antibodies to about 55 percent of rhinovirus serotypes. It takes a lifetime to build immunity to the majority of cold viruses in one's environment. Just think of it — old age does bring some benefits: great wisdom, and very few colds!

DESIGN FOCUS 10.2

CILIA, MOLECULAR MACHINES IN THE RESPIRATORY SYSTEM

Cilia and flagella are molecular machines in the respiratory system. Bacteria and *Euglena* are single-celled creatures that move about by means of flagella, whereas *Paramecium* moves by means of cilia. Cilia are tiny hairlike projections that extend from the cell membrane and are also found in human cells that line the respiratory passageways. These ciliated cells secrete mucus that traps heavy particles and microbes. The cilia of mucus membrane cells is referred to as the **mucociliary escalator**.

In humans, cilia are also found in stationary cells in the linings of our lungs and respiratory tract, where their continual back-and-forth motion sweeps foreign particles out of the lungs and up the windpipe to be either swallowed or expelled. A human cilium is a structure that looks like a hair and moves like a whip. In contrast, the cilium in *Paramecium* moves the cell much as an oar moves a boat. If the cell is stuck in the middle of a sheet of other cells, the beating cilium moves liquid over the surface of the stationary cell. The Creator used cilia for both jobs. The stationary cells that line the respiratory tract each have several hundred cilia. The large number of cilia beat in symphony, much like the oars handled by slaves on a Roman galley ship, to push mucus up to the throat for expulsion. The action removes air pollutants, cigarette particles, and pathogenic bacteria that may be inhaled and stick in the mucus.

Both cilia and flagella are complex molecular machines consisting of a bundle of several microtubules and motor proteins encased in a flexible membrane. The pull of the motor proteins slides the microtubules past each other, causing the entire assembly to bend. They have both power strokes and recovery strokes that propel *paramecium* in the water. By beating rapidly back and forth like a fish's tail or a row of oars, a cell can swim rapidly through the water. Light microscopes have revealed thin hairs on some cells for over two hundred

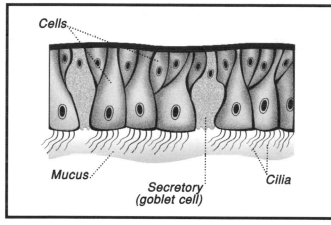

Cells

Mucus

Secretory
(goblet cell)

Cilia

years. The discovery of the intricate, interlacing details of cilia, however, was not noticed until the advent of the scanning electron microscopes. Micrographs revealed that the cilium is a complex structure of motor proteins and microtubules. Microtubules lie stiff and motionless without motor proteins, such as **nexin** and **dynein**. Furthermore, it requires linkers to tug on neighboring strands, converting the sliding motion into a bending motion, and preventing the structure from falling apart. All of these parts are required to perform one function: ciliary motion. Just as a mousetrap does not work unless all of its constituent parts are present, ciliary motion simply does not exist in the absence of microtubules, connectors, and motors. Therefore, we can conclude that the highly interdependent system makes it difficult for a gradual, Darwinian evolution to have taken place.

The cilium molecular machine is a highly intricate system that gives evidence of creation in its interwoven system of proteins. A swimming system requires a paddle to contact the water, a motor or source of energy, and a connector to link the two. All systems that move by paddling, from protozoans to propellers in ships, will not work if any one of the interdependent parts is missing. The cilium is a member of this class of swimming systems. The microtubules are the paddles, whose surface contacts the water and pushes against it. The protein arms are the motors, supplying the force to move the system. The protein arms are the interlacing connectors, transmitting the force of the motor from one microtubule to its neighbor. The complexity and apparent design of the cilium is inherent in the task itself. It does not depend on how large or small the system is, whether it has to move a cell or move a ship: in order to paddle it must have several common parts. Now that is strong evidence for intelligent design and an omniscient Creator as we examine the wisdom in the inward parts of the cilium.

CHECK YOUR UNDERSTANDING

THOUGHTS

KNOWLEDGE

MEMORY

Respiratory System

1. List at least three organs or components of the respiratory system.

2. What is the overall function of the respiratory system?

3. Describe and make an illustration of an interwoven aspect of the respiratory system.

4. Discuss how the alveoli are an interwoven component in the respiratory system. Describe the interlacing complexity of the alveoli.

5. Explain the Genesis 2:7 passage: "*And the Lord God formed man of the dust of the ground, and breathed into his nostrils the breath of life; and man became a living soul.*"

6. Why is it difficult to find a cure for the common cold?

Testing Critical Thinking Skills and the Common Cold

During 1999, 21 percent of the patients in a large hospital acquired severe respiratory infections during their hospital stay. The patients required longer hospital stays than uninfected patients. Medical technologists provided this data:

Rate of environmental isolation for adenovirus on:

Bedroll	10%
Coffee Cups	5%
Toilet/Commode	1%
Door Knobs	18%
Call Button	6%
Handkerchiefs/Hand towels	30%

7. What is the most likely mode of transmission of the adenovirus in hospitals?

a. The disease was caught each time patients left their beds.

b. Nurses and visitors brought in the disease.

c. Infected handkerchiefs and hand towels were stockpiled, then distributed to patients.

d. Patients were sneezing on each other.

Hospital personnel hands after patient contact that was positive for adenovirus

Used gloves	0%
Washed with non-disinfectant soap	40%
Did not use gloves	59%
Washed with disinfectant soap	3%
Had before patient contact	3%
Did not wash hands	20%

8. Given this data, how do you slow the spread of a disease?

a. Have all hospital personnel and patients take megadoses of vitamin C.

b. Quarantine all patients with respiratory disease in a separate wing of the hospital.

c. Have all hospital personnel be required to wear masks and sterile "space-suits," like the video *Outbreak*.

d. Have all personnel be required to wash their hands with soap and change gloves after handling each patient.

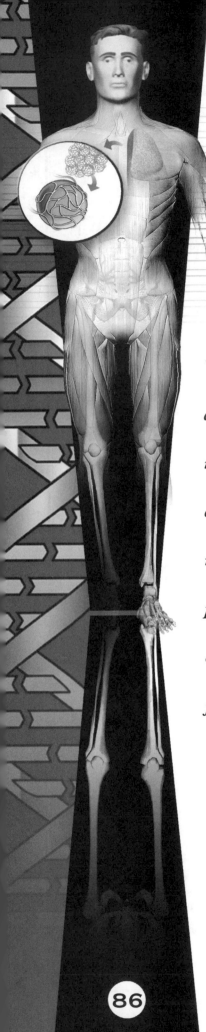

EXPLORING THE NERVOUS SYSTEM, THE BRAIN, AND PAIN

CHAPTER 11

"The brain is a swarm of cells in which everything is seemingly connected to everything else. The connections, though, follow a plan, an order, the large elements of which we are just beginning to see and understand."

(Mark Cosgrove, Ph.D.)

I n recent times children have been observed to learn motor skills after brain operations that were not thought possible. Due to various injuries, such as automobile accidents, surgeries, and other head trauma events, youngsters may have half of their brain removed. For many years, it was thought that if the right side of the brain were removed, the left side of the body would loose its normal function; likewise, if the left brain were removed, this person would lose control over the right side of the body. In adults, this loss of control is the norm. Yet, frequently, full control over the body is restored commonly in children and adolescents, even when half of the brain is removed. In these instances it appears that the brain does its own "rewiring." The right brain can take over the functions of the left brain if necessary. This remarkable characteristic of flexibility in nervous tissue is known as plasticity.

Plasticity and Complexity

P lasticity refers to the ability to do long-term adjustments or adaptive changes. New connections form and outlive an event. Each and every neuron "remembers" an event and can respond accordingly to the future. There is learning, recovery of function from an injury, and memory of past events (history). This "rewiring" in nerves is the Creator's provision for handling and adjusting to life's trauma.

Plasticity is one of two outstanding attributes of the nervous system. The other trait of the nervous system, best described with superlative terms, is its intertwined complexity. There are about 10^{11}–10^{12} neurons (nerve cells) and 10^{13}–10^{15} glial cells (support cells) in the human body. Each neuron has 10^4 connections, or synapses; this amounts to an incredible 10^{16} connections in the human body. The nervous system has the highest number of connections and degree of order, organization, and integration in the body. Only the number and organization of stars in the universe rival the complexity found in the nervous system. The colossal complexity found in the circuitry of our brains must be the fingerprint of an omniscient Creator!

The Nervous System Overview

The nervous system is responsible for sending, receiving, and processing nerve impulses. All of the body's muscles and organs rely upon these nerve impulses to function for monitoring the environment. This system is responsible for creating and maintaining communication in a central excitatory state, keeping the body ready to respond to any emergency. The nervous system is also responsible for integrating and summing signals and correlating past and present experiences. Finally, it is responsible for output, like a new action, thought, or memory.

The three systems that work together to carry out the mission of the nervous system are as follows: the central, the peripheral, and the autonomic nervous systems. The **central nervous system** is responsible for issuing nerve impulses and analyzing sensory data. It includes the brain and spinal cord. The **peripheral nervous system** is responsible for carrying nerve impulses to and from the body's many structures, and includes the many craniospinal nerves that branch off of the brain and spinal cord. The **autonomic nervous system** is composed of the **sympathetic** and **parasympathetic** systems and is responsible for regulating and coordinating the functions of vital structures in the body.

The Brain

The **brain** is the primary component of the nervous system, occupying the cranial cavity. Without its out-ermost protective membrane, the dura mater, the brain weighs an average of three pounds (1.4 kg), comprising about 97 percent of the entire central nervous system. The brain is connected to the upper end of the spinal cord (which connects through the **foramen magnum** of the skull) and is responsible for issuing nerve impulses, processing nerve impulse data, and engaging in the higher order thought processes. The brain is the human body's control center (figure 11.1). In a sense, the brain is the "head" or chief executive officer (CEO) of the body.

The brain is divided into three parts: the large **cerebrum**, the smaller **cerebellum**, and the brainstem leading to the spinal cord. The brainstem is also descriptively divided into the **medulla oblongata**, the **midbrain**, and the **pons**. Other parts include the **corpus callosum**, **hippocampus**, **hypothalamus**, **thalamus**, and **pons**. In a typical adult, the brain weighs only a little more than three pounds, yet it consumes about one-fourth of the body's total oxygen. Its large demand for oxygen, glucose, water, electrolytes, and protein makes it extremely important in terms of bioenergetics.

The human brain is a mysterious loom, weaving strands of 10 billion neurons into the fabric of thought. Perhaps this orderly loom of cellular threads blends with invisible threads of the spirit to form the essence of our personality. There is probably nothing else in the physical universe that is more complex than the human brain. The web of neurons defies description. The whole mental process consists of neurons transmitting specific chemicals between each other across synapses or gaps. As a result, each cell can communicate with every other cell at lightning speed. In one cubic millimeter (mm^3) of the brain, there are one billion connections among cells. This amounts to about 400 billion synaptic junctions in a gram of brain tissue. The brain's total number of connections rivals the stars of the universe in number, yet the connections follow an orderly plan.

Neurologists describe physiological interactions in much

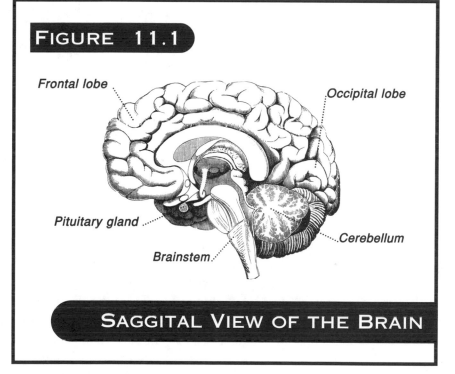

FIGURE 11.1

Frontal lobe

Occipital lobe

Pituitary gland

Cerebellum

Brainstem

SAGGITAL VIEW OF THE BRAIN

FIGURE 11.2

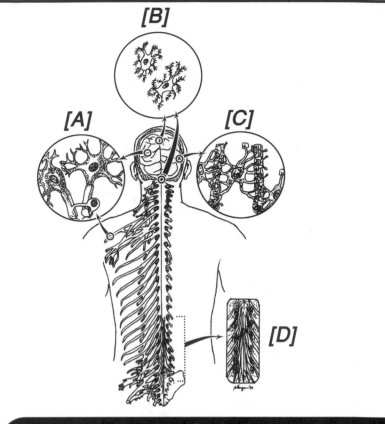

From a dorsal view, the four plexuses, neurons, and various neuroglia are illustrated.

[A] Oligodendrocytes wrap thin extensions of myelin around axons to increase the speed of neuron communication.

[B] Microglia are phagocytic cells that protect the central nervous system tissue.

[C] Astrocytes are part of the blood-brain barrier and wrap around the capillaries.

[D] Area above cauda equina, lumbar nerves, L2 and L3 depicts interlacing nature of nervous system.

INTERWOVEN COMPONENTS OF THE NERVOUS SYSTEM

detail but there are still many unknowns about the brain. In one sense, a whole person lies locked inside the cranium, protected, sealed away for managing the duties of the other 70–100 trillion cells in the body. The brain is the seat of mystery, wisdom, and unity, and it is the source of order for the rest of the body. All the body's cells ultimately report to the brain. In one sense, other body cells are defined by their loyalty to the brain. They either obey the brain's signals and thereby bring health to the body, or disobey and ultimately bring ruin to the rest of the body.

The Spinal Cord

The **spinal cord** is one of the primary portions of the central nervous system, serving as a telegraph cable which allows signals to be sent from the brain to the structures of the body and received from them in return. Extending from the medulla oblongata, through the foramen magnum in the base of the skull, to the base of the vertebral column, the spinal cord is about a 1/4 inch (0.5 cm) in diameter, and is slightly flattened. The spinal cord itself passes through the vertebral canal created by the vertebral arches, and sends out roots and branches much as does a tree. These structures contain bundles of nerve fibers that extend all the way down the body, innervating even the skin in the tips of the toes.

The spinal cord features both **efferent** and **afferent nerve pathways**, so that nerves may be transmitted to the body's structures as well as received from them. Paired sets of nerves branch out from the spinal cord along the vertebral column, with the lowest of these forming the sacral plexus of nerves. The sympathetic nerves travel alongside the spinal cord in the sympathetic nerve trunk, which features periodic clusters of nerves, called **ganglia**. The spinal cord floats in a spinal fluid that protects and nourishes it and, as with the brain, is covered by a **meningeal membrane** composed of three layers: the **pia mater,** the **arachnoid,** and the **dura mater**. Damage to the spinal cord results in inability to transmit and receive nerve impulses to and from the specific area supplied by the damaged section of the spinal cord, and all sections below it, resulting in paralysis and numbness.

The term "**plexus**" refers to a network of nerves or blood vessels. The nervous system features a number of these networks, where autonomic and voluntary nerve fibers join together. These networks include the **brachial plexus** (shoulder), the **cervical plexus** (neck), the **coccygeal plexus** (coccyx), and **sacral or lumbosacral plexus** (lower back) (see figure 11.3).

Neurons and Communication

Nerves have been discovered to communicate, or "talk with one another." This occurs through electrical and chemical signals. Electrical signals are transmitted fast and fleeting, whereas chemical signals go in and out slowly. The latter transfers information that is deliberate and with sustained action.

Interwoven Parts of the Nervous System

The interwoven components of the nervous system include the cells of the **blood-brain barrier**, the **plexuses**, and the **cauda equina**. Some of these structures are featured in Vesalius' *Fabrica*. Some cells interlaced with each other throughout the body include neurons with their glial cells. This is most notable in the blood-brain barrier where **astrocytes** are tightly bound to the neurons, just as the white and gray matter which are seamlessly interwoven (figure 11.2). The cauda equina are nerve roots on the posterior end of the spinal cord. They radiate from the spinal cord and connect to nerves in the hips and legs, and are collectively referred to as a cauda equina because they resemble a horse's tail. The nerves occur between lumbar two and three spinal nerves and are highly convoluted.

Neuron Order and Organization

Nerves are an intricate array of brain neurons and their associated brain cells (e.g., **astrocyte cells**). They transmit signals electrically or chemically to other neurons.

Neuron communication is both orderly and organized, however, there is tremendous variation in how it is done. They all have the same basic structure consisting of a cell body and two different kinds of extensions. The first extension is the **dendrite**. It receives stimuli from its immediate surroundings, from other neurons, or from sensory structures in the skin, muscle, or internal organs. Each cell has many dendrites and each dendrite has many branches (figure 11.4). This explains the origin of the word from the Greek *dendron*, meaning "a tree." Because these trees have such a large number of receiving branches, the body of any one neuron is connected to many stimuli sources. A single long extension called the **axon** (Greek for "axle") carries the impulse away from the cell body and toward other neurons and their dendrites, or directly to muscle and gland cells. Because the axon is multibranched, it, too, connects with a number of receiving structures. All of this diverse branching serves to enhance integration of the nervous system. A nerve cell may have hundreds of dendrites, but it can have only one

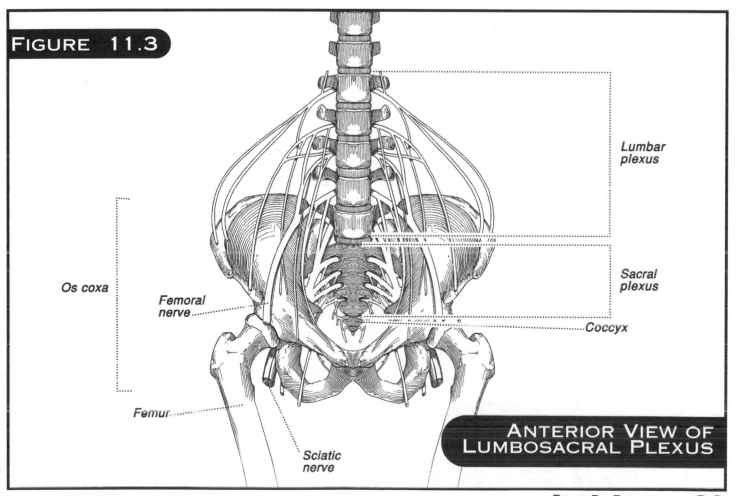

FIGURE 11.3

Os coxa

Femoral nerve

Femur

Sciatic nerve

Lumbar plexus

Sacral plexus

Coccyx

ANTERIOR VIEW OF LUMBOSACRAL PLEXUS

FIGURE 11.4

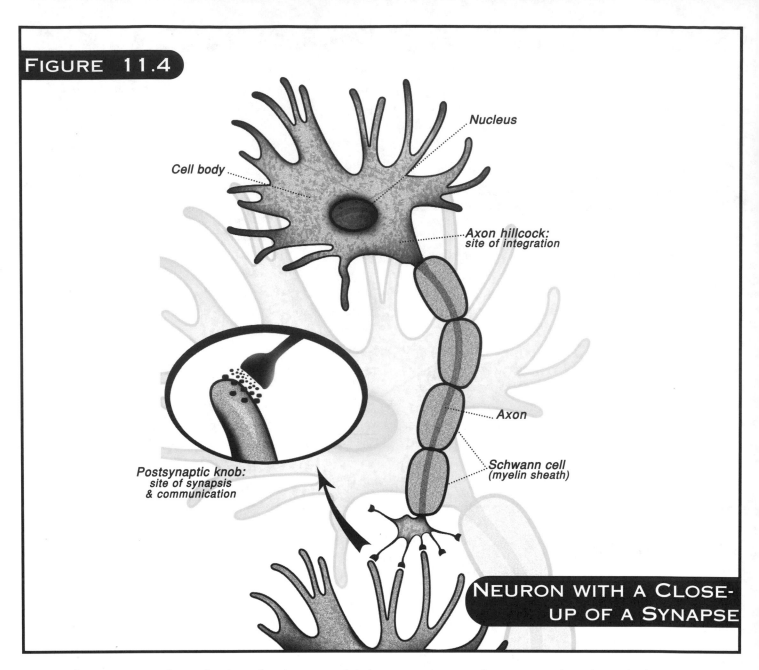

Cell body

Nucleus

Axon hillcock:
site of integration

Axon

Schwann cell
(myelin sheath)

Postsynaptic knob:
site of synapsis
& communication

NEURON WITH A CLOSE-UP OF A SYNAPSE

axon. The junction where the impulse is transmitted from one nerve cell to another is called the **synapse**, from the Greek *synapto*; "I join together." It is here that the message passes from one of the branches of an axon to one of the branches of a dendrite, or directly to the cell body.

The relationship is reminiscent of Michelangelo's magnificent *The Creation of Adam* on the ceiling of the Vatican's Sistine Chapel. In this painting, the extended right hand of God is reaching toward the outstretched left hand of Adam, but their adjacent fingers are not quite touching. There remains the smallest of spaces between them, across which an impulse must be transmitted.

Michelangelo must have believed that some divine spark of energy leaped across the gap between God and man, and much the same was at first thought about the

transmission of nerve impulses through the synapse. But as logical as it seemed, this hypothesis was not supported by later study.

When the impulse reaches the tiny intervening space, a **neurotransmitter** (a chemical substance) is released from the axon into the junction. In addition to acetylcholine, there are about 50 other messengers. The molecules of a neurotransmitter bind to receptor molecules on the dendrite or cell membrane. The binding changes the shape of the receptor; this, in turn, opens up pathways in the membrane that envelops the receiving cell. The signal stops once the neurotransmitter is used up.

Other signs of organization seen in the nervous system are the supporting cells for the neurons. These include **myelinated glial cells (or neuroglia), Schwann cells,** and **astrocytes**. Schwann cells form the myelin sheaths that cover, protect, and insulate the axon of the neuron.

The myelin sheath also speeds up the transmission of ions by allowing signals to "leap" from node to node (**nodes of Ranvier**). This is known as **saltatory jumping**.

Another supporting cell designed to regulate tight control over what enters the brain is the astrocyte. These highly integrated cells contribute to the **blood-brain barrier** and ensure that the brain will not be subjected to chemical fluctuations in the blood. Thus, they provide protection against dangerous chemicals and pathogens.

Integration at Different Levels

A single neuron may receive information from numerous neighboring neurons via thousands of synapses, some of them excitatory and some of them inhibitory. Excitatory synapses have opposite effects on the membrane potential of the postsynaptic cell. At an **excitatory synapse**, neurotransmitter receptors control a type of gated channel that allows sodium to enter the cell and potassium to leave the cell. There is a **depolarization** in the cell. Therefore, the binding of the neurotransmitter to the receptor causes the electric change. This pattern was discussed previously as the **all-or-none principle**.

At an **inhibitory synapse**, the binding of neurotransmitter molecules to the postsynaptic membrane hyperpolarizes the membrane by opening ion channels that make the membrane more permeable to potassium or to chloride, which rush out of the cell. This complex integration works much like the computer chips in your personal computer.

Pain Network as an Integrative System

Integration can be noted at the neuron level. The sensation of touch and pain is a good example of integration. Millions of touch sensors over the surface of the skin are scattered in precise accord with the body's spe-

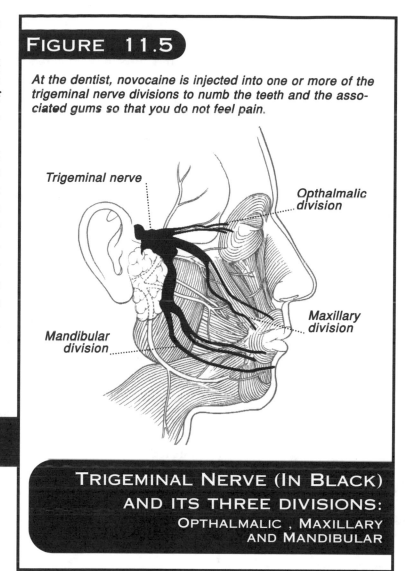

FIGURE 11.5

At the dentist, novocaine is injected into one or more of the trigeminal nerve divisions to numb the teeth and the associated gums so that you do not feel pain.

Trigeminal nerve

Opthalmalic division

Maxillary division

Mandibular division

TRIGEMINAL NERVE (IN BLACK) AND ITS THREE DIVISIONS: OPTHALMALIC , MAXILLARY AND MANDIBULAR

cific needs. The body does not seem to have any special cells dedicated to the sensation of pain because pain is tied to an elaborate network of sensors that report degrees of pressure, touch, heat, and cold.

Paul Brand and others have tried to copy this mechanism when building an artificial pain system. They achieved some success with their master engineers, electricians, and nerve physiologists in producing temporary pain receptors and signals. Let us examine a few of their studies.

These scientists blindfolded their research subjects and measured their skin sensitivity. They studied how much pressure must be applied before a blindfolded person senses an object touching his skin. Although the skin is a single organ, it displays a wide range of sensitivity to pressure. The skin must be able to sense pressure in such diverse tasks as picking food particles from our teeth, using fingers to play the guitar, or writing with a felt tip pen. The areas of skin around the fingers require a high degree of sensitivity.

Less critical areas hardly need such sensitivity. Indeed, we would tire very quickly indeed if our brains had to listen to such dainty pressure reports from the foot, which faces a daily rigor of stomping, squeezing, and supporting weight. Thus, while fingers and the tongue can detect a feather touch, other parts of the body must experience something extraordinary before they report unusual activity to the brain.

The measurements of touch threshold barely scratch the surface of the marvels of the pain network. For example, sensitivity to pressure varies depending on context. Humans can distinguish a letter that weighs 1/4 ounce from one that weighs 1/2 ounce just by holding it in their hand. But if they try to distinguish a 10-pound package from a 10.3-pound one, they cannot discern the difference. Our sensitivity to pressure is amazing, yet it does have limits.

The fingertips must be incredibly sensitive to the slightest differences in touch. But sensitivity to touch is not enough. The fingertips must also be able to withstand rigorous activity. Next time you meet a carpenter or an experienced tennis player, feel their callused hand. Life would be miserable indeed if the fingertip fired a message of pain

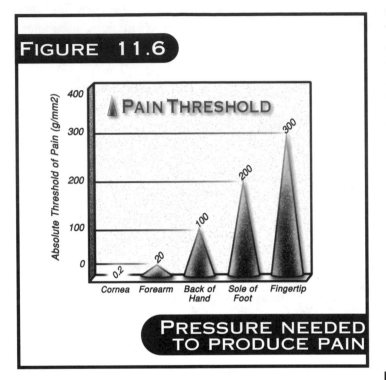

FIGURE 11.6

PAIN THRESHOLD

Absolute Threshold of Pain (g/mm2)

400
300
200
100
0

Cornea 0.2
Forearm 20
Back of Hand 100
Sole of Foot 200
Fingertip 300

PRESSURE NEEDED TO PRODUCE PAIN

to the brain each time a person gripped a tennis racket or pounded a hammer. So the design of the body includes fingers that are sensitive to pressure, but relatively insensitive to pricks. Hands and fingertips serve us well, as do the other parts of our body. All of these require sophisticated integration of the pressure network.

Another test assesses the absolute threshold of pain. In this test, the scientist measures how much pressure must be applied to a very sharp needle before the subject begins to experience pain (figure 11.6). The fingertip, for example, shows an astounding difference; it can detect a mere 3-grams/ millimeter^2 (g/mm^2) of pressure, but pain will not be felt until that pressure exceeds 300 g/mm^2. Why? The concert violinist must sense an amazing range of pressures to produce perfect sound and volume. A skilled pizza maker, swishing his hands through batches of dough, can notice as little as a 2-percent variance in its "stickiness" consistency.

After spending over a million dollars of grant money, however, Brand and his colleagues basically failed to make

a complete copy of this detailed integration of the nervous system. Their conclusion was that this integration of sensory receptors for pain could be viewed only as the fingerprint of a wise, master electrical engineer. Indeed, there is a bioengineer behind the intricate integration of the nervous system.

Design is observed in the senses of touch and pain. Touch distribution was not handed down in a random way. No accident of evolution could have produced such a marvelous matrix of touch and pain sensors found in the skin. Einstein said, "God does not play at dice." He is a wise God providing us with sensitivity in areas that could easily be damaged by high pressure. Pain is an interpretation by the brain of signals from multiple touch sensors that have been highly stimulated. The main difference between pain and touch is the number and intensity of sensors summoned. Pain is usually not thought of as a gift, but people with Hansen's disease would tell you that it is a present thoughtfully provided by a omniscient Creator (see Disease Focus 11. 1). Without physical pain, the body lacks protection against harmful agents.

The intelligent designer has also provided us with calluses to protect areas that are constantly abraded and touched (such as palms of hands, etc.) There are fewer touch and pain receptors on our back. The sensitivity of each square millimeter is programmed to the function of that body part. Our fingertips, tongues, and lips are the portions of the body used in activities that need the most sensitivity.

Intelligence

The biological basis for intelligence in man or animals is both controversial and uncertain in the world of secular science. Yet, the complex integration of information through various neurons in the cerebellum is most likely the biological basis for intelligence. Although a precise integration "circuit" is probably not known, one can confidently infer that intelligence itself is an outcome of integration. The nervous network, intelligence, and behavior are still poorly understood.

Intelligence is probably a coordinated effort by the nervous network to integrate and process signals appropriate for the particular circumstance. The completion of an intelligent activity by man may stem from a rigidly patterned neural network. The network must gather and process data from key neurons in the cerebrum. Then it must order particular sequences elsewhere in the body while blocking signals that might inhibit an effective behavior. A comparison among neurons, neural networks, and the brain indicates the parallel plans of integration. It causes us to think that there is a higher intelligence behind the design of this intricate nerve integration. Can one explain design, integration, and intelligence without a master mind?

Recall that the theory of macroevolution predicts randomness, blind chance, imperfection, expansion of the gene pool, and tinkering with nature. In contrast, a creation model predicts order, organization, boundaries to the gene pool, and integration. The nervous system has truly amazing properties. Do the properties of order, organization, and integration found in the nervous system correlate better with the characteristics of macroevolution or intelligent design?

Order and organization are two principles that are consistent with a Creator. Webster defines **order** as a condition in which everything is in its right place and functions properly. In addition, order implies there is a fixed or definite plan and system. Webster defines **organization** as a unified, coherent group or systemized whole. A divine craftsman would put things into order from the beginning, as a master carpenter would have his blueprint and materials ready for construction ahead of time. Based upon the complexity of this integration, it seems that only the greatest mind in the universe could have accomplished this.

Parallel Plans

In the human body, we see order and levels of organization. In fact, we can see parallel or congruent patterns between cellular organelles and the body organs. Although the comparison between organelles and organs is not exact, the similar functions performed by each corroborate the principle that an intelligent designer has made both. By this, we conclude that mankind has been fashioned by a wise Creator.

Parallel plans can be observed at different levels of organization. This continuity is most notable in a comparison between an organelle and an organ. The concept implied is one that suggests that a master bioengineer used a similar scheme. Engineers use the same general mechanical principles in the manufacturing of gears. This is true regardless of whether the gears are for an automobile or a watch.

There are many examples of this. The cell membrane can be compared to the human body's skin. One is the outer covering that holds the body together and the other holds the cell together. Another parallel plan can be observed between the cell nucleus and the axon hillock with the brain and the body. Each structure is involved in integrating complex signals and decision-making for the body surrounding it.

Although certain things are not identical in structure, they have similar functions. For example, the logic used in designing a computer motherboard in a computer is parallel to a neuron circuitry (figure 11.7), although their circuitry is not directly interchangeable with other systems. It took order, organization, and intelligence to make both. The evidence for design is solid and highly probable from any viewpoint. How could so many coincidences exist among living things? Was it merely a coincidence that this world was planned and thought about before time began? An all-wise inventor made the perfectly modeled parallel plans.

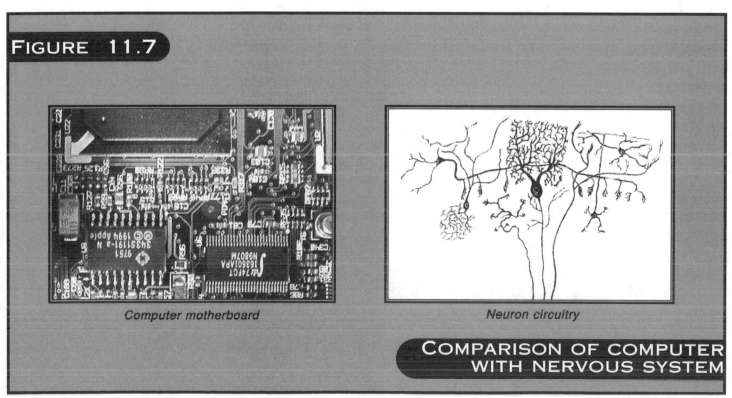

FIGURE 11.7

Computer motherboard

Neuron circuitry

COMPARISON OF COMPUTER WITH NERVOUS SYSTEM

LEPROSY AND PAIN – OUR PROTECTOR

For many centuries, **leprosy** was considered a curse of God, often associated with sin. It did not kill, but neither did it seem to end. Instead, it lingered for years, causing the tissues to degenerate and deforming the body. In biblical times, victims were required to call out "Unclean! Unclean!" and they were usually ostracized from the community. Many have thought this to be a disease of the skin. It is better classified, however, as a disease of the nervous system because the leprosy bacterium attacks nerves.

The agent of leprosy is *Mycobacterium leprae*, an acid-fast rod related to the tuberculosis bacterium. This organism, first observed in 1874 by the Norwegian physician Dr. Hansen, is referred to as Hansen's bacillus. Hence, leprosy is commonly called **Hansen's disease**. This bacterium grows in only a few places: the footpads of mice, selective tissues in armadillos, and a few other animals. Leprosy is spread by multiple skin contacts, as well as by droplets from the upper respiratory tracts.

The disease has an unusually long incubation period of three to six years, a factor that makes identification very difficult. Because the bacteria are heat sensitive, the bacillus lives in the cooler regions of the body. Its symptoms start in the skin and peripheral nervous system, then spread to various cooler parts like the hands, feet, face, and earlobes. Severe cases also involve the eyes and the respiratory tract. Patients with leprosy experience disfigurement of the skin and bones, twisting of the limbs, and curling of the fingers to form the characteristic claw hand. Facial features accompany thickening of the outer ear and collapse of the nose.

The principal drug for the treatment of leprosy is **dapsone**. Most often, leprosy patients are given two antibiotics, **rifampin** and **clofaziminem,** along with dapsone, due to increasing numbers of drug-resistant bacteria. Today, there is a great deal of hope for people with early diagnosis — triple drug therapy and they are cured for a lifetime. Even those who have had minor damage to limbs can obtain restoration therapy from Christian missions, like those Dr. Paul Brand started.

It was Dr. Brand's work with leprosy patients that illustrated, in part, why God permitted there to be pain in this world. There is a total loss of physical pain in advanced leprosy patients. When these people can't feel touch or pain, they tend to injure themselves. Tumor-like growths called **lepromas** may form on the skin and in the respiratory tract, and the optic nerve may deteriorate. The largest number of deformities develop from loss of pain sensation due to extensive nerve damage, and inattentive patients can pick up a cup of boiling water without flinching. Many accidentally let hot objects burn their fingers. In fact, some leprosy patients have had their fingers eaten by rats in their sleep and did not know it. The lack of pain receptors cannot warn them of danger.

In summary, the leprosy bacillus destroys nerve endings that carry pain signals. People who do not feel intense pressure almost inevitably damage themselves. Usually an infection sets in areas where no pain signals have alerted them to tend to the wounded area. "Thank God for pain!" says Brand. Leprosy destroys nerve endings that carry pain signals. Brand and colleagues tried to give them a substitute for pain through an artificial transducer system. However, it usually did not last for long in most patients.

He used artificial signals like warning auditory beeps to communicate pain to those who had lost their sense of touch. For a while (a few days) it worked because it was a novelty. It did not work, however, when real work was demanded, or when sports became competitive. The leprosy patients simply turned off the warning device and hurt themselves. Eventually, patients ignored all but physical pain. Brand concluded that it has to hurt to work. This is why Brand declares with the utmost sincerity, "I cannot think of a greater gift that I could give my leprosy patients than pain."

CHECK YOUR UNDERSTANDING

Nervous System

1. What are three organs of the nervous system?

2. What is the overall function of the nervous system?

3. Describe an interwoven part of the nervous system. Discuss the intricate nature for this part and how chance physiochemical processes cannot (alone) account for the level of complexity observed in the nervous system.

4. Make an illustration and discuss how a neuron illustrated the idea of irreducible complexity.

5. Describe the flexibility and plasticity of the nerves.

6. Explain one reason why pain can be thought of as a good thing.

7. Explain the concept of integration in the nervous system, both at the cellular and organ level. Give examples of each and provide sketches to illustrate your point.

CRITICAL THINKING QUESTIONS (8-11):

Going Further with Leprosy

8. Leprosy (technically called Hansen's disease) is primarily a disease of the
A) Muscular   B) Nervous   C) Skin   D) Skeletal System.

9. Hansen's disease is caused by
A) a virus   B) a spherical shaped bacterium
C) being around others with leprosy   D) *Mycobacterium leprae*.

10. A good Bible reference for what is now recognized as leprosy by medical experts is:
A) Lev. 13   B) Mark 2   C) Mark 3   D) John 3:16   E) Luke 17.

11. A good Bible reference for preventing skin diseases and leprosy by medical experts is:
A) Leviticus 13   B) Mark 2   C) Mark 3   D) John 3:16   E) Luke 17.

THOUGHTS
KNOWLEDGE
MEMORY

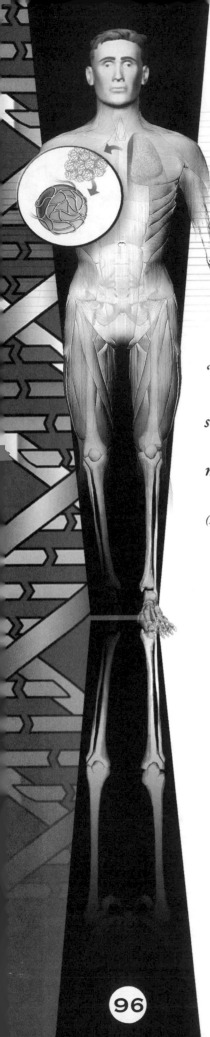

"The hearing ear and the seeing eye, the Lord hath made them both."

(Prov. 20:12)

Special Senses

All the senses work in basically the same way. Special sensory receptors collect information from the local environment and stimulate neurons to send a message to the brain. There the cerebral cortex forms a perception, a person's particular view of the stimulus. Along the way, energy is changed from one type to another through a **transducer**. All senses utilize transducers, but each sense has its own distinctive way in which it transforms energy. For example, each type of receptor is particularly sensitive to a distinct kind of environmental change and is less sensitive to other forms of stimulation. The special senses detect stimuli like light (sight), sound (hearing), odor (smell), flavor (taste), and other signals. We will concentrate on vision and hearing.

Like the multifaceted systems discussed in earlier chapters, the parts of the eye and the ear will function only as an entire unit or not at all. These interrelated parts might be called "all-or-none" systems in terms of survival. The multiple parts of the eye and the ear must work fully in place and together in precision, or the function is impaired. In order for the eye or ear to perform optimally, coordination of all the parts is required.

The way these systems operate remind us of the same principle in muscle and nerve physiology. In skeletal muscles, individual fibers contract to their fullest extent or not at all. A minimal threshold must be made in order for any action to take place. In neurons, if a stimulus is strong enough to initiate an action potential, a nerve impulse is propagated along the entire neuron at a constant strength.

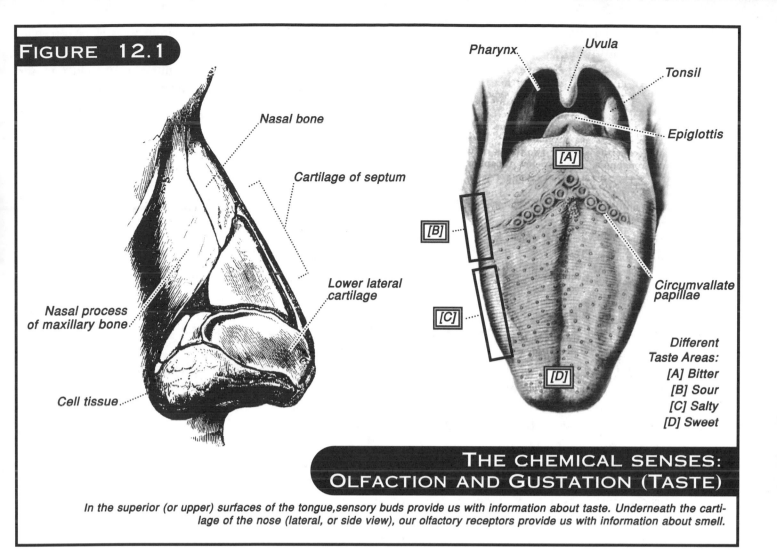

FIGURE 12.1

Nasal bone

Cartilage of septum

Lower lateral cartilage

Nasal process of maxillary bone

Cell tissue

Pharynx

Uvula

Tonsil

Epiglottis

[A]

[B]

[C]

[D]

Circumvallate papillae

Different Taste Areas:
[A] Bitter
[B] Sour
[C] Salty
[D] Sweet

THE CHEMICAL SENSES: OLFACTION AND GUSTATION (TASTE)

In the superior (or upper) surfaces of the tongue, sensory buds provide us with information about taste. Underneath the cartilage of the nose (lateral, or side view), our olfactory receptors provide us with information about smell.

Anatomy of the Eye

The eyeball lies nestled in fat within the orbital cavities (two bony sockets) of the skull, where it is situated above and lateral to the center. Of all the senses, eyesight is often considered most important. According to one estimate, four-fifths of everything we know reaches the brain through our eyes. The eyes transmit constant streams of images to the brain by electrical signals. The eyes receive information from light rays. The light rays are either absorbed or reflected. Objects that absorb all of the light rays appear black, whereas those that reflect all the light rays appear white. Colored objects absorb certain parts of the light spectrum and reflect others. When you look at something, the light rays reflected from the object enter the eye. The light is refracted by the **cornea** and passes through the watery **aqueous humor** and **pupil** to the lens. The **iris** controls the amount of light entering the eye. Then the lens focuses the light through the vitreous humor onto the **retina**, forming an image in reverse and upside-down. Light-sensitive cells in the retina transmit the image to the brain by electrical signals. The brain "sees" the image right side up.

Physiology of the Eye

The eye's anatomy and optics operate like a camera, and the eye's nervous system is comparable to a supercomputer. Yet, neither of these analogies is sufficient to fully describe the wonder of the human eye's structure and function. The eye is more than any sum of machines that humans can construct; it is a carefully crafted camera!

The eye is built like the camera except that it is infinitely more sophisticated. Some modern cameras have auto focus and automatic adjustment of the iris diaphragm. The eye has a circular iris muscle that controls the opening called the pupil. In the eye, the lens can also change its shape to focus the light rays on the retina that is comparable to the film of the camera. The lens is made of living cells that are transparent. The cornea, the window-like membrane that covers the eye, is also transparent.

The most amazing component of the camera eye is its "film," which is the **retina**. This light-sensitive layer at the back of the eyeball is thinner than a sheet of plastic wrap and is more sensitive to light than any man-made film. The best camera film can handle a ratio of 1000-to-1 photons in terms of light intensity. By comparison, human retinal cells can handle a ratio of 10 billion-to-1 photons over a dynamic range of light wavelengths of 380 to 750 nanometers. The human eye can sense as little as a single photon of light in the dark! In bright daylight, the retina can bleach out, turning its "volume control" way down so as not to overload. The light-sensitive cells of the retina are like an extremely complex high-gain amplifier that is able to magnify sounds more than one million times.

There are over 10 million rods and cones in the retina and they are packed together with a density of 200,000 per square millimeter in the highly sensitive central fovea. This is the area of highest concentration of cone cells. These photoreceptor cells have a very high rate of metabolism and must completely replace themselves about every seven days! If you look at a very bright light such as the sun, they immediately burn out, but are rapidly replaced in most cases. Because the retina is thinner than the wavelength of visible light, it is totally transparent. Each of its minute photoreceptor cells is vastly more complex than the most sophisticated man-made computer.

It has been estimated that 10 billion calculations occur every second in the retina before the image even gets to the brain! It is sobering to compare this performance with the best output of the most powerful man-made computer. Stevens reported, "*To simulate 10 milliseconds of the complete processing of even a single nerve cell from the retina would require the solution of about 500 simultaneous non-linear differential equations one hundred times and would take at least several minutes of processing time on a Cray super-computer.*"

Because there are about 10 million such cells interacting with each other in many complex ways, it would take something like one hundred years of computer time to simulate what takes place in the eye many times each second!

What makes this comparison even more striking is that nerve cells in the retina (rods, cones, bipolar neurons, and ganglion neurons) conduct their electrical signals approximately one million times slower than the conduction in circuit traces of "wires" in a man-made super-computer. If it were possible to build a single silicon chip that could simulate the retina using currently available technology, it would have to weigh about 100 pounds while the retina weighs less than one gram. The "super chip" would occupy 10,000 cubic inches of space, whereas the retina occupies 0.0003 cubic inches. The power consumption of the man-made super chip would be about 300 watts, whereas the retina consumes only 0.0001 watts. It is amazing how the efficiency of the retina far exceeds the best computer chip that man can produce!

Darwin once said that the very thought of the complexity of the eye gave him the chills. Attempts to explain the evolution of the eye, like most other evolutionary "explanations," are scientifically untestable. One must account not only for the eye, but also for an optically transparent membrane called the cornea, which bends the light rays before they enter the eye. Together with the eye, the visual cortex of the brain, which is connected to the cerebrum, it must translate optical information. The information begins as nothing more than differences in the amplitude and length of light rays and is then converted into what is perceived as three-dimensional color vision in real time. There is undoubtedly a scientific mechanism for this entire signal processing, and we now know much about it — but we are no closer to a scientific explanation of how eyes evolved in the first place than we were 150 years ago.

The human eye is an example of "compound traits," having parts that are interdependent upon each other and that do not function effectively apart from the other trait. It takes many muscles with the several eye parts (such as the cornea, the pupil, the lens, and the retina) working together, to get clear vision.

To suppose that the eye, (with so many parts all working together) . . . could have been formed by natural selection, seems, I freely confess, absurd in the highest degree.

Darwin wrote this just before he proceeded to express a rationale for how a small change may have occurred. But Darwin's argument was no explanation at all.

The human eye is among the most complex and sophisticated systems in the universe. Yet, in a critique of creation views called *Life's Grand Design*, Ken Miller describes the human eye as a "flawed design" compared to the cephalopod eye. As radically different as invertebrates are from vertebrates in their other organs, the cephalopod octopus has an eye strikingly similar to that of man.

Several evolutionary biologists claim that the vertebrate eye is functionally suboptimal, because its photoreceptors in the retina are oriented away from incoming. They make these claims because the optic wiring and support vessels of the human eye are located in front of the photoreceptor cells in the retina. These biologists claim this arrangement degrades visual quality by scattering incoming light and creating a blind spot where the wiring must poke through the retina to reach the brain. The cephalopod eye has its retina in front of the "wiring."

The critics believe that evolutionary processes produced a superior eye plan in the octopus and squid. They reason that evolutionary tinkering through natural selection must have produced both the cephalopod and human eye; eyes that are optimal and suboptimal, respectively.

On the surface, their argument seems logical. Yet the human eye is much more sophisticated than any cephalopod eye. It is both more complex and color sensitive. No human camera, artificial device, nor computer-enhanced light-sensitive device can match the contrivance of the human eye. Only a master engineer with superior intelligence could manufacture a series of interdependent light-sensitive parts and reactions.

The physiology of human vision reveals great wisdom in this unexpected design it provides for seeing objects in stereoscopic color. There are excellent functional reasons for human photoreceptors to be oriented in front. A critical tissue, the **retinal pigment epithelium** (RPE) that is located beneath the retina, maintains photoreceptor structure and function. The RPE recycles photopigments, removes spent outer segments of the photoreceptors, provides an opaque layer to absorb excess light, and performs additional functions.

The RPE is a fully functional tissue for the eye and must be located in back of the retina's photoreceptor cells in order to obtain optimal vision. If all the wiring and support vessels were behind the retina, this would leave no room for the RPE. An optimal design is one that minimizes cost and maximizes benefit. Although there is some extra energy cost to the "wiring" of the nerves in front of the retina, the benefit of the RPE next to and behind the retina provides for maximum protection of the RPE. In addition, it provides superior photoreceptor functioning and proves to be the best overall retina design for an eye.

The RPE must lie between the choroid and the bipolar cells (figure 12.2), so the human eye is not flawed as Miller contends. Rather, the conclusions of evolutionary biologists have demonstrated flawed thinking not a flawed design! In summary, the RPE must be located outside the retina to minimize blood clotting and to supply the needs for the photoreceptors. If our eye, like the cephalopod eye, had no RPE, then our vision would be greatly reduced.

Would you want to trade your eyes for those of a squid or an octopus? Cephalopod eyes are extremely nearsighted, somewhat colorblind, and unlikely to form sharp images as our eyes can. The cephalopod has eyes designed for life in the deep oceans. The human eye, like the eyes of other vertebrates, has vision that is superior to cephalopods (figure 12.3). Evolutionists have ignored these finer details of the structure and function in the human eye when they say the human eye is suboptimal to the eye of a cephalopod.

The original design of the human eye is optimal. Its coordinated details make its structure more advanced than the cephalopod eye, giving humans greater precision and visual acuity. The "imperfections," or eye impairments that some experience in vision (nearsightedness, farsightedness, and astigmatism) are the result of the degeneration (fallen nature of man) and are not part of the original plan. Upon closer inspection of the "reversed wiring" parts, we find there is "wisdom" in such a scheme.

The compound traits of the human eye make a fascinating system that requires that all its parts function together. This is another example of Paley's argument: just as a watch must have had a watchmaker, there must have existed at some time and at some place a divine artificer of the human body.

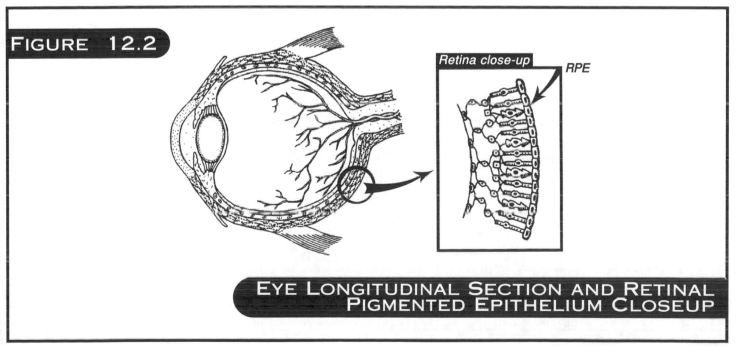

FIGURE 12.2

Retina close-up

RPE

EYE LONGITUDINAL SECTION AND RETINAL PIGMENTED EPITHELIUM CLOSEUP

The Hearing Ear

Ear Anatomy

The ear is divided into three parts: the **outer ear,** the **middle ear,** and the **inner ear**. Each section performs its own separate function in a process that converts sound waves into nerve impulses, which are then transmitted to the brain. The outer ear has two parts: the pinna and the external auditory canal. The outer ear collects and channels sound. The middle ear, or **tympanic cavity**, is a tiny cavity hollowed out of the temporal bone. It is an intermediary in the processing of sound energy. It is responsible for increasing the intensity of incoming sound waves and transforming them into mechanical vibrations that can easily travel through the inner ear. The inner ear has two parts. One is made of bone, the other of a membrane that lies inside the bone. Both have complicated shapes, and for this reason they are called **labyrinths**. Each labyrinth has three parts: **vestibule, semicircular canals,** and **cochlea**. The inner ear contains the receptor cells, which receive the mechanical vibrations and transmit them to the brain.

The human ear can detect sound frequencies of 20 to 20,000 vibrations per second. The ear also qualifies as an "all-or-none" system because it has many interdependent parts. Like vision, hearing takes place only after a cascade of mechanical, electrical, and biochemical events have occurred. There are numerous canals, fluids, and bones in the ear that transfer mechanical waves and convert them to meaningful sounds. One of the characteristics that humans share with other mammals is the presence of three small auditory ossicles (ear bones) and an outer, fleshy auricle.

The outer ear is made to receive audible signals and to transfer these vibrations to the eardrum and to the middle ear (see ear diagram, Disease Focus 12.1). The three little bones are the **malleus (hammer), incus (anvil),** and **stapes (stirrup)**. They are the smallest bones in the human body. They were named for their resemblance to tools used in the 19th century in the western United States. They transfer and amplify sound impulses through the middle ear. These ossicles are located within the cavities of the middle ear that is within the temporal bone cavity. The three bones are attached to the wall of the tympanic cavity by tiny ligaments and are covered by mucous membrane. These bones bridge the eardrum with the inner ear, transmitting vibrations between these parts.

Although some people think of the outer ear (**auricle, external auditory canal, pinna,** etc.) as the site of hearing, it is the middle and inner ears that actually do the work. The middle ear has the **tympanic membrane** on its outer side and the **cochlea** on its inner side. The **malleus** is attached to the tympanic membrane and the vibrations are transmitted from it via the malleus and incus to the stapes. The stapes, in turn, is attached to the membrane in the cochlea that is called the oval window and it moves in response to vibrations of the tympanic membrane. When the stapes presses the oval window into the cochlea, another flexible membrane in the cochlea window bulges outward to relieve the pressure.

The fact that vibrations of the tympanic membrane are transferred through three bones instead of merely one bone affords protection. If a sound were too intense, the auditory ossicles might buckle. This protection is enhanced by the action of the stapedius muscle that attaches to the neck of the stapes. When the sound becomes too loud, the **stapedius** muscle dampens the movement of the stapes against the oval window. This action helps to prevent nerve damage within the cochlea when sounds repeatedly reach high amplitudes. In the case of a gunshot, however, the stapedius muscle may not respond quickly enough to prevent nerve damage.

The inner ear contains the most critical part of the hearing mechanism, the organ of Corti. It is situated in the snail-shaped cochlea that is filled with **perilymph**. The cochlea has a twisting interior that is studded with thousands of hairlike nerve cells, each one of which is tuned to a particular vibration. When the stapes of the middle ear receives signals from the eardrum, such as a trumpet sound, the perilymph fluid inside the cochlea is set vibrating as a tidal current goes though it and transmits the signal to the auditory nerve and the brain.

Above the cochlea are three minute, fluid-filled **semicircular canals**. The **endolymph** in the semicircular canals provides us with balance but the canals do not play a role in hearing. If we start to fall, the fluid in one of the canals is displaced. Hair cells there detect a change and signal the brain that we are off-balance.

How does the complex ear anatomy correlate its functions of receiving, transferring, transmitting, and integrating mechanical waves into nerve impulses that the brain perceives as sound? Vibrating objects, such as the vocal cords of a person speaking, create percussion waves in the surrounding air. The waves from the air strike the tympanic membrane and are transferred to the middle ear through the mechanical vibrations of the eardrum. The three bones of the middle ear then amplify and transmit these movements to the inner ear. The inner ear converts the energy of pressure into more waves and these waves are sent to the oval window. Vibrations of the oval window produce pressure waves in the fluid within the cochlea and, in turn, the **auditory nerve** is stimulated.

Movement of the **perilymph** within the **organ of Corti** rotates the hairs to be displaced, thus stimulating nerve cells. These vibrations of the fluid over the hair cells are similar to the action of skilled fingers plucking the strings of a harp. The vibrations of the hair cells produce electrical signals that go to the auditory nerve. Within the organ of Corti, sensitive hair cells detect minute pressure waves and convert them to electrical signals, and this change from pressure to electrical waves is called transduction. In humans, each pitch of sound produces a maximum vibration in hair cells located at one point along the cochlea.

It is the brain that makes the interpretation and "sense" of the signal. The brain "knows" the pitch of the sound because it knows the location of the sensory neurons that are firing in response to signals from hair cells. The cochlea feeds thousands of these electrical messages from the ear to the brain, which then unscrambles the meaning of the sounds. This coordinated sequence of events is quite amazing.

The fact that all parts of the ear are necessary to produce hearing should be obvious when one considers the complex chain of mechanical and electrochemical processes involving the outer ear, the middle ear, the inner ear, the auditory nerve, and the brain. Take away any of the bones, fluids, or mechanical hairs, and hearing is impaired or deafness may result. Could such complexity arise by chance mutations and natural selection? The ear, along with the eye, carries the signature of an intelligent Designer.

In the 19th century, the famous comparative anatomist, George Cuvier, spoke of interrelated systems like these as having "a correlation of parts." Like Paley, he saw obvious signs of God's handiwork in the ear and in the human eye. Cuvier was a firm creationist and he advanced these arguments against those who believed in evolutionism. In the 20th century, many creationists have argued for design in light of the interdependence of body structures. According to Behe, as the number and quality of the related components in a system increases, we can be more and more confident that the systems arose by design. Our conviction grows that Solomon was correct in his writing (long before Paley, Cuvier, or Behe) that the eye and the ear testify to God's craftsmanship:

"The hearing ear and the seeing eye, the Lord hath made them both" (Prov. 20:12).

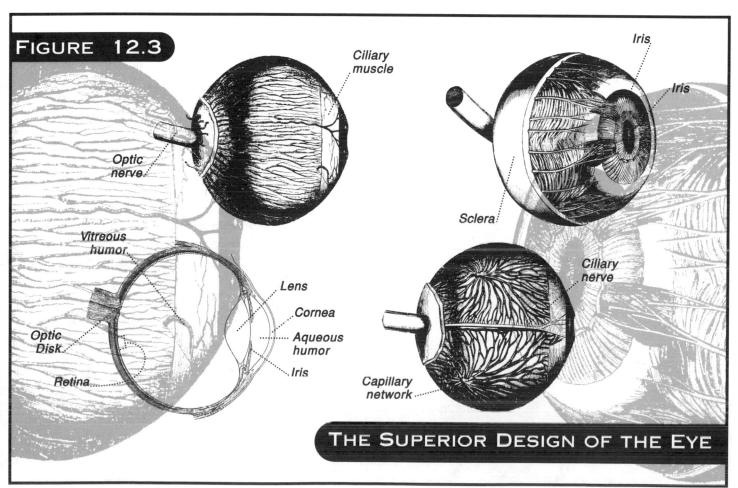

FIGURE 12.3

Ciliary muscle

Iris

Iris

Optic nerve

Sclera

Vitreous humor

Ciliary nerve

Lens

Cornea

Aqueous humor

Iris

Optic Disk

Retina

Capillary network

THE SUPERIOR DESIGN OF THE EYE

DISEASE FOCUS 12.1

OTITIS MEDIA AND MIDDLE EAR INFECTIONS

Signs of an ear infection in an infant or toddler are hard to miss: irritability and screaming incessantly, for no apparent reason other than a fever, or tugging on the affected ear. A doctor viewing the painful ear with an instrument called an otoscope sees a red and bulging eardrum. The diagnosis is otitis media, or a middle ear infection.

Ear infections occur because the mucous membranes that line the auditory tubes are continuous with the linings of the middle ears, creating a conduit for bacteria infecting the throat or nasal passages to travel to the ear. Germs of this disease usually enter through the auditory tube, most often following a cold or tonsillitis, or after swimming in a contaminated pool. Often the pathogen has migrated from the throat (a dirty place in terms of bacteria and viruses) through the **eustachian tube**. This particular route to infection is greater among young children because their auditory tubes are shorter than they are in adults. Half of all children in the United States have an ear infection by the first birthday, and 90 percent have one by age six.

Physicians treat acute middle ear infections with antibiotics. Other times children have their ears lanced with a needle in a procedure known as **myringotomy**. Because recurrent infections may cause hearing loss and interfere with learning, children with recurrent ear infections are often fitted with **tympanostomy tubes**, which are inserted into affected ears during a brief surgical procedure. The tubes form a small tunnel through the tympanic membrane so the ears can drain. By the time the tubes fall out, the child has usually outgrown the susceptibility to ear infections.

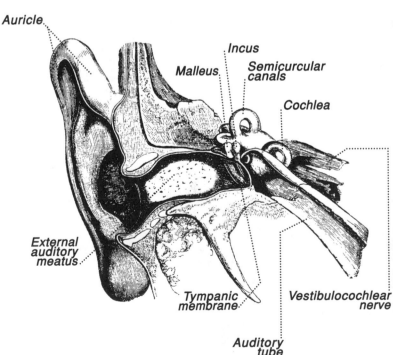

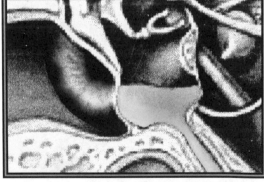

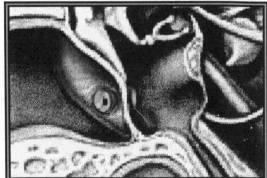

Operation on the ear drum

CHECK
YOUR
UNDERSTANDING

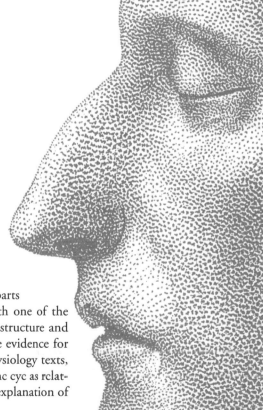

THOUGHTS
KNOWLEDGE
MEMORY

The Senses

1. Describe the basic structures and functions of the eye.

2. Describe the basic structures and functions of the ear.

3. List evidences for design of the human eye.

4. Explain the concept of transduction in relationship to the ear.

5. Why is nearsightedness and farsightedness not a flaw in the design of the eye?

6. What is otitis media? Why are young children susceptible to middle ear infections in the summertime?

CRITICAL THINKING QUESTIONS (7-8):

Going Further with the Senses

7. Many anatomy and physiology texts identify about two dozen parts that make up the composition of the eye. Describe the eye with one of the anatomy and physiology themes such as irreducible complexity, structure and function, and/or interdependence of anatomical parts. Then give evidence for intelligent design seen in the eye. Also, using physics and/or physiology texts, explain the transduction of light energy into electrical energy in the eye as related to the physiology of vision. In addition, give Dr. Paul Brand's explanation of design in the eye.

8. In many texts, about two dozen parts are identified that make up the composition of the ear. Using the idea of interdependent parts, give evidence for intelligent design seen in the ear. Also, explain how many of its parts have designed structures for the purpose of transduction of energy related to the purposeful function of hearing. In your explanation, give an explanation as to how the transduction concept is used as the basis for many artificially designed systems, such as street lights over major streets and highways.

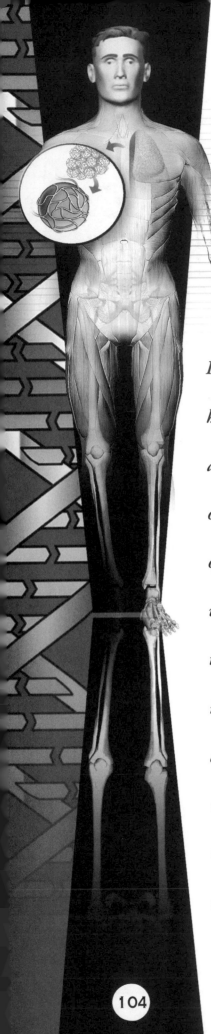

INVESTIGATING THE BODY IN BALANCE: THE ENDOCRINE SYSTEM

CHAPTER 13

It is the body that is the hero, not science, not antibiotics, not machines or new devices. The task of the physician today is what it has always been, to help the body do what it has learned so well to do on its own during its unending struggle for survival — to heal itself.

(Ronald. J. Glasser, M.D.)

The nervous system alone does not suffice for all the fine-tuning of our body's messages. Many of the chemical controls that keep us healthy and fit are instigated by extraordinarily powerful chemical messengers called **hormones**, which enter the bloodstream and exert general control over many vital bodily activities. Their mere presence in the fluids bathing certain organs can trigger remarkable action. Other glands, called **exocrine** or ducted glands, are not members of the broadly based endocrine system. Rather, they work locally, secreting substances into their cell-lined ducts, which empty either into spaces between organs or directly onto organ surfaces. Examples of exocrine glands include the sweat glands, saliva glands, mucous glands, oil glands, and mammary glands.

Endocrine System Overview

Endocrine glands are ductless: they simply release their products, which are eventually swept up by the bloodstream and taken to where their message is read. Examples of endocrine glands include the **pituitary, adrenal, thyroid, parathyroid, pineal, thymus, pancreas, testes,** and **ovaries**. Although this duct message system is much slower than the nervous system, it is very accurate and lasts much longer. Its effect lasts from minutes to months, not milliseconds. Hormones may affect many organs, not just one as do nerves, and the endocrine system frequently regulates the body differently in adults than children. Nerves tend to work the same throughout our lifetime.

When compared to neurotransmitters, hormones allow regulation of continuing processes in our bodies and concerted influence over large areas (table 13.1). Hormones circulate through the body in the blood-stream until they find the organs they are to influence. As a result, the glands that secrete hormones do not have to be near the organs they control. Overall, hormones affect the metabolism of target organs and help to regulate total body metabolism, growth, and reproduction.

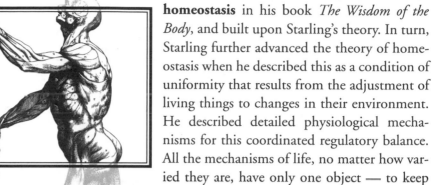

The endocrine system thus consists of glands tucked into various nooks about the body. Some are close to their spheres of influence, others far away. One of the most crucial glands of the system, the pituitary, is the size of a pea; it protrudes from a tiny stalk at the base of the brain. The efficiency of the system almost defies belief. In 1902 the British physiologist Ernest Starling discovered hormones. Historically (1923), he was also the first scientist to use the metaphor of wisdom in the inward parts to characterize the body in balance. These ideas stemmed from his observation that the body seemed to have an intuitive integration of its diverse faculties. In his delivery of the prestigious Harveian (after W. Harvey) Oration of the Royal College of Physicians in Great Britain, he spoke about the regulation of body processes, their adaptability, and the contribution of hormones that integrated signals and provided balance through feedback. For his epigraph, Starling chose a verse from the Book of Job:

"Who hath put wisdom in the inward parts?" (Job 38:36;KJV).

Starling associated the "body in balance" with the wisdom found in the inward parts designed by the Creator. He spoke about this coordinated communication among cells like the lung and kidney, and developed mechanisms describing regulatory processes, like the acid-base balance. Nine years after hearing this famous oration, Walter Cannon coined the term **homeostasis** in his book *The Wisdom of the Body*, and built upon Starling's theory. In turn, Starling further advanced the theory of homeostasis when he described this as a condition of uniformity that results from the adjustment of living things to changes in their environment. He described detailed physiological mechanisms for this coordinated regulatory balance. All the mechanisms of life, no matter how varied they are, have only one object — to keep the conditions of life constant in the internal environment.

Endocrine System: Chemical Communication

Physicians have long recognized that the body must be in chemical balance to stay healthy. If one chemical variable in the human body gets out of balance, then disorder, disease, and even death may result. Even during ancient Roman times, physicians tried to assist the self-corrective nature of the human body in overcoming disorder. *Vis medicatrix naturae* is the Latin phrase for the recuperative or self-corrective nature of the human body. Dr. Ronald Glasser emphatically says, *The body is the hero!*

Although ancient philosophers had some idea of the balanced condition in the body, it was Claude Bernard, a French physiologist of the 19th century, who developed a clear idea of chemical balance. Bernard referred to this body balance as the "**constant internal milieu.**" He recognized the power of many animals to maintain a relatively constant condition in their internal chemical environment, even when the external chemical surroundings change. A pond-dwelling *Hydra* (a tiny, simply organized animal) is powerless to affect the temperature of the fluid that soaks its cells. Yet, the body can maintain its "internal pond" temperature at 37°C, according to Bernard. His initial ideas laid the groundwork for the concept that today is called "homeostasis."

TABLE 13.1	Internal control and regulation in the human body (A comparison of endocrine & nervous systems)	
INDICATOR	**NERVOUS**	**ENDOCRINE**
Target	Muscle cells (& other neurons)	Glands (select organs)
Speed	Fast	Slow
Response duration	Short-term	Long-term
Mechanism	Electrochemical	Chemical
	Neuron changes state	(Two types: steroid & protein)
Transmission	Nerves	Blood

"Code Blue" and Emergency Hormones

In a hospital, "**Code Blue**" has special meaning. This code is given when a patient stops breathing or their heart stops. There are only 4.5 minutes, on the average, to act upon this emergency, or the patient will die if there is no intervention. The loudspeaker across the hospital says "Code Blue in Ward 25." Everyone responds differently. The physicians and nurses assigned to the "code team" bring the crash cart that contains the medications and equipment required in caring for the patient. The resident physician and an emergency specialist physician come, ready with their equipment and in their scrubs. Nursing assistants and orderlies respond to help perform CPR. The supply department brings a cylinder of oxygen and other attachments. Any visitors, custodians, and office personnel must get out of the way. Only those with critical tasks respond to the emergency. Others ignore the blue code announcement or emergency signal. Many diverse workers must act for success in an emergency. In summary, during an emergency, there must be preparedness, a plan, a purpose, a design, and forethought (intelligence) in order to save a person's life.

Specific hormones are necessary for our body to respond to emergencies. For hormones from the endocrine system, there is not a dedicated "route" to the site where the hormone will have its effect. The body does produce hormones with a specific objective in mind. Hormones are released into the circulatory system and reach every cell in the body. However, they only act upon specific cells. Hormones will only attach to specific proteins that are designed to respond and prepared to fit into the receptors on specific cells.

When **adrenaline** (also called **epinephrine**) is released into the bloodstream, it affects the cells of each gland in a different way. The entire hormone has its origin in the adrenal gland. All of the cells affected by adrenaline must have the same specific receptors. However, in some organs the target muscle or gland will dilate, and in others the target muscles or gland will constrict. All these actions take place in the body through the same hormone.

Note also that not every cell along the pathway of the circulatory system is affected. Only those cells with the specific protein receptor (cells with an "emergency action plan") are affected. Like the hospital emergency crew, only those cells with critical tasks respond to the emergency. There must be some preparedness by the body and design in the body in order for this action team of muscles and glands to work on the emergency. In summary, during an emergency, there must be preparedness, a plan, a purpose, a design, and forethought (intelligence) in order to save a person's life. This creation principle is true for the human body, even as it is for the hospital.

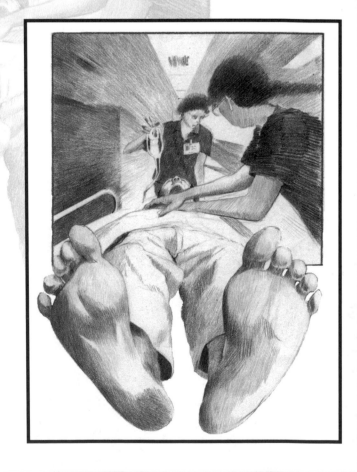

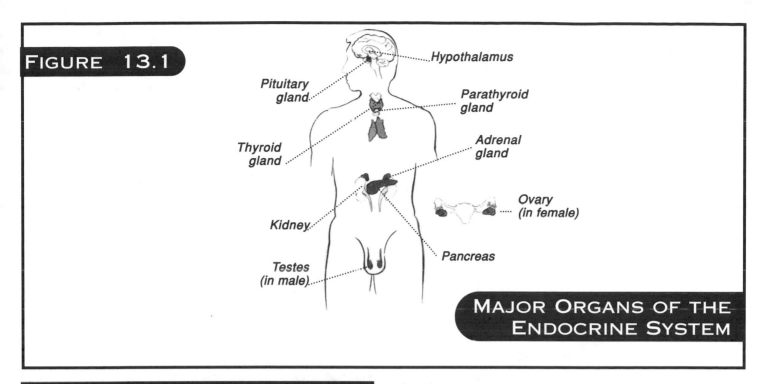

FIGURE 13.1

Hypothalamus

Pituitary gland

Parathyroid gland

Thyroid gland

Adrenal gland

Kidney

Ovary (in female)

Testes (in male)

Pancreas

MAJOR ORGANS OF THE ENDOCRINE SYSTEM

The HPA Axis

The **hypothalamus-pituitary gland-adrenal** glands (HPA Axis) are an interwoven system of glands that control many functions in the body. The **hypothalamus** consists of a tiny cluster of nerve cells located at the center of the base of the brain. This structure serves as a link between the autonomic nervous system and the endocrine system. The hypothalamus is responsible for many body functions. Its function is to integrate and ensure appropriate response to stimuli. It regulates hunger, thirst, sleep, and wakefulness. It plays an important role in the regulation of most of the involuntary body mechanisms, including body temperature, sexual drive, and the female menstrual cycle. The hypothalamus also regulates the work of the **pituitary gland**.

The pituitary (or **hypophysis**) is a small gland, no larger than a pea, located at the base of the brain in a small depression. It is controlled by the hypothalamus to which it is attached and is sometimes referred to as the master gland. The function of the pituitary gland is to coordinate the nervous and the endocrine system. Some of its hormones stimulate other glands to produce their own hormones.

This small gland is actually two glands: the anterior pituitary lobe (or **adenohypophysis**) and the posterior pituitary lobe (or **neurohypophysis**). This gland produces nine major hormones. The anterior pituitary produces seven and the posterior pituitary releases two hormones.

The adrenal glands curve over the top of each kidney in the abdomen. Although it appears to be one organ, it is actually two small glands, each weighing about 1/4 ounce (7 grams). The **adrenal medulla** is an agent of the sympathetic nervous system and is activated by nerve impulses. The

adrenal cortex is a true endocrine gland activated by **adrenocorticotrophic hormone** (ACTH) sent out from the pituitary gland. The adrenal medulla secretes adrenaline (epinephrine) and **norepinephrine** (see Design Focus 13.1) These hormones help the body reduce stress. When the **sympathetic nervous system** reacts to intense emotions, such as fright or anger, large amounts of the hormone are released. This may cause a "fight or flight" reaction, in which blood pressure rises, the pupils widen, and blood is shunted to the most vital organs and to the skeletal muscles. The heart is also stimulated.

The adrenal cortex secretes two hormones: cortisol and **aldosterone**. They help the body reduce stress and are essential for life (see Design Focus 13.2 and 13.3). **Cortisol** is an energy generator. It regulates conversion of carbohydrates into glucose and directs reserves to the liver. It also suppresses inflammation. Aldosterone regulates the mineral and water balance of the body. It prevents excessive loss of water through the kidneys and maintains the balance between sodium and potassium in the blood stream. This balance is important to the contractility of muscles.

The Pancreas and Diabetes

The **pancreas** lies just behind the lower part of the stomach. It is the second largest gland in the body and is both an endocrine and an exocrine gland. Its exocrine function is to produce digestive juices (pancreatic juices) and release them through a tube, the pancreatic duct, to the intestine. The endocrine function of the pancreas is controlling the amount of sugar in the blood. The cells that control blood sugar levels are called **islets of Langerhans**. These islands are microscopic clumps of cells scattered throughout the pancreatic tissue among the other pancreatic cells but are concentrated somewhat in the tail of the pancreas.

There are two kinds of cells in the islands: alpha and beta. The **alpha cells** secrete a hormone called **glucagon** and the **beta cells** secrete **insulin**. Insulin and glucagon work as a check and balance system regulating the body's

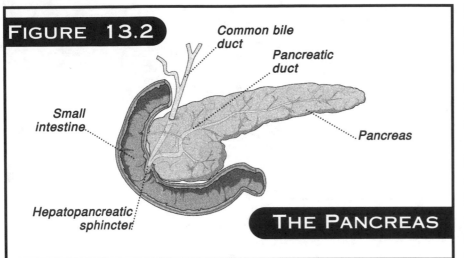

FIGURE 13.2

Common bile duct

Pancreatic duct

Small intestine

Pancreas

Hepatopancreatic sphincter

THE PANCREAS

blood sugar level. Glucagon accelerates the process of liver glycogenesis (a chemical process by which the glucose stored in the liver cells in the form of glycogen is converted to glucose). This process tends to increase the concentration of glucose in the blood. Insulin is an antigen to glucagon. As explained in chapter 1, it decreases the amount of blood glucose concentration.

Insulin decreases blood glucose by accelerating its movement out of the blood, through cell membranes, and into cells. As glucose enters the cells at a faster rate, the cells increase their metabolism of glucose. All sugary and starchy foods, such as bread, potatoes, and cakes, are broken down into glucose. In this form they can be absorbed by every cell in the body, including the cells in the liver, one of whose major roles is to store sugar. Cells absorb glucose and burn it in structures called mitochondria, using the energy it contains and producing carbon dioxide and water as byproducts. This burning-up process is the body's principal source of energy. It cannot take place without insulin.

Diabetes occurs when the pancreas fails to secrete enough insulin and so fails to regulate the glucose concentration in the blood. The normal glucose level for an average adult is about 80 to 120 mg glucose/100 mL of blood. If the islets of Langerhans secrete too little insulin an excess of glucose develops, a characteristic of diabetes mellitus, the most common disorder of the endocrine system.

High blood glucose levels stimulate the release of insulin from the beta cells of the islets. Insulin acts on just about all

body cells and increases their ability to transport glucose across their plasma membranes. Once inside the cells, glucose is oxidized for energy or converted to glycogen or fat for storage. These activities are also speeded up by insulin. Since insulin sweeps the glucose out of the blood, its effect is said to be **hypoglycemic**. As blood glucose levels fall, the stimulus for insulin release ends — another classic case of negative feedback control. Many hormones have **hyperglycemic** effects (glucagon, glucocorticoids, and epinephrine, to name a few), but insulin is the only hormone that decreases blood glucose levels. Insulin is absolutely necessary for the use of glucose by the body cells; without it, essentially no glucose can get into the cells to be used.

Without insulin, blood levels of glucose increase to dramatically high levels (for example, 600 mg/100 mL of blood). In such instances, glucose begins to spill into the urine because the kidney tubule cells cannot reabsorb it fast enough. As glucose flushes from the body, water follows, leading to dehydration. The clinical name for this condition is **diabetes mellitus**, which literally means that something sweet is passing through or siphoning (*diabetes* = Greek "siphon") from the body. Since cells cannot use glucose, fats and even proteins are broken down and used to meet the energy requirements of the body. As a result, weight loss occurs. Loss of body proteins leads to a decreased ability to fight infections, so diabetics must be careful with their hygiene and in caring for even small cuts and bruises.

When large amounts of fats (instead of sugars) are used for energy, the blood becomes very acidic as ketones (intermediate products of fat breakdown) appear in the urine. Unless corrected, coma and death result. The three cardinal signs of diabetes mellitus are: (1) excessive urination to flush out the glucose and ketones; (2) excessive thirst resulting from water loss; and (3) hunger due to inability to use sugars and the loss of fat and proteins from the body. Mild cases of diabetes mellitus (most cases of **Type II** or **adult-onset diabetes**) are treated with special diets or oral medications that prod the sluggish islets into action. For the more severe **Type I** (or **juvenile**) diabetes, injections of insulin must be given periodically through the day to regulate blood glucose levels.

Glucagon acts as an antagonist of insulin. Low blood levels of glucose stimulate its release by the alpha cells of the islets. Its action is basically hyperglycemic. Its primary target organ is the liver, which it stimulates to break down stored glycogen to glucose and to release the glucose into

CORTISOL AND STRESS:
NEGATIVE FEEDBACK FROM THE ADRENAL CORTEX

"Cease from anger, and forsake wrath:
fret not thyself in any wise to do evil" (Ps. 37:8).

IT ONLY CAUSES HARM TO THE BODY.

Humans have a pair of adrenal glands, one above each kidney. Some cells of the **adrenal cortex**, the outer portion of an adrenal gland, secrete hormones such as glucocorticoids. **Glucocorticoids** help maintain the concentration of glucose in blood and help suppress inflammatory responses. Cortisol, for instance, blocks the uptake and use of glucose by muscle cells. It also stimulates liver cells to form glucose from amino acids.

A negative feedback mechanism operates when the glucose level in blood declines below a set point. This chemical condition is known as hypoglycemia. When the hypothalamus detects the decrease, it secretes CRH in response. This releasing hormone stimulates the anterior pituitary to secrete **corticotropin** (ACTH). In turn,

ACTH stimulates cells of the adrenal cortex to secrete cortisol, which helps regulate the glucose level in blood. How? Cortisol stops muscle cells from taking up glucose that blood is delivering through the body. These cells are major glucose users.

Emotions like anger, worry, and fret have been shown to harm our body due to high levels of cortisol released during these times of negative thinking. During severe stress, painful injury, or prolonged illness, the nervous system overrides feedback control of cortisol secretion. It initiates a stress response in which cortisol helps to suppress inflammation. If unchecked, prolonged inflammation damages tissues. That is why doctors often prescribe cortisol-like drugs for asthma and other chronic inflammatory disorders.

---

the blood. No important disorders resulting from hypo- or hypersecretion of glucagon are known. Glucose levels are very important in homeostatic control. For example, the adrenal glands and the alpha and beta cells in the pancreas control the amount of glucose in the blood, which in turn affects the balance between hunger and satiety. There are many other complex relationships between glands and body regulation.

Homeostasis: Interdependent Processes That Regulate the Body

The word homeostasis comes from two Greek terms, *homeo* (alike or the same) and *stasis* (standing or remaining). Thus, the word means remaining the same. It is applied to the internal chemical conditions of living things. An American physiologist, Walter B. Cannon (1871–1945), coined the term homeostasis to describe Bernard's original idea of balance and constancy of chemical conditions in living organisms. Cannon's idea was first published in a book, *The Wisdom of the Body*, in 1932.

The "wisdom of the body" points to a wise Creator who lovingly provides and sustains life through these essential homeostatic mechanisms. Cannon viewed the body as a community that consciously seeks out the most favorable conditions for itself. It corrects imbalances in fluids and salts, mobilizes to heal itself, and deploys resources on demand. Homeostasis includes not only the constancy of chemical conditions inside an organism, but also the feedback mechanisms that maintain that constancy.

Homeostasis applies to all organisms, but this discussion will be limited to some phases of homeostasis in the human body. The mechanism of homeostasis can be observed in most of the 11 body systems. The movement of a pendulum is an analogy for homeostasis. The moving pendulum represents the fluctuation of a physiological variable, such as body temperature or blood pressure, around an ideal value.

Disturbance in either direction could move the variable into the abnormal range, or into a harmful state. If the disturbance is so extreme that it goes "off the scale" or outside the range of what is tolerable, disease and consequently death can result. Body regulation of these systems is controlled by the nervous and endocrine systems. The divine Designer has obviously set limits or boundaries on changes in the human body.

Thermostat Wars and Control of Body Temperature

Did you ever wonder why your body temperature remains about 98.6°F whether you are exposed to freezing temperatures in the winter or to temperatures above 100°F in the summer? Man is said to be homeother-

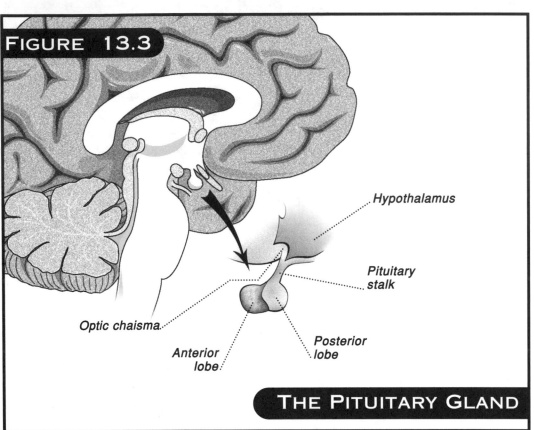

FIGURE 13.3

Hypothalamus

Pituitary stalk

Optic chaisma

Posterior lobe

Anterior lobe

THE PITUITARY GLAND

mic which means that he maintains a constant temperature regardless of the temperature of his environment. In homeothermy, the hypothalamus is responsible for our fairly stable temperature.

There are two main ways man's body temperature is regulated to remain constant. First, the amount of heat lost or removed from the body is controlled. More heat is produced by metabolism than is needed (unless the environment is quite cold), so excess heat must be removed. Sweating is one method of removing the heat. When you exercise vigorously or the air around you is warm, sweating increases. When you are still or the surrounding air is cool, sweating decreases. Evaporation of sweat removes excess heat.

The body also removes excess heat from the blood in the skin. When you get hot, your skin gets red. This is because blood vessels in the skin enlarge, permitting more blood to

flow near the surface of the skin. The heat in the blood warms the skin and this heat is transferred from the skin into the air. When you are cold, your skin turns pale because the blood vessels contract, keeping the blood deeper in the body so that less heat is lost to the air. If there is much pigment in the skin, the red color or the paleness will not be as evident as it will be in lightly pigmented people.

The second way body temperature is regulated is by controlling the amount of heat produced. When muscles contract because of chilling, this causes shivering and chattering of the teeth. You might walk about and rub your hands in order to generate heat. These processes generate heat. When the air is warm, as on a summer day, your muscles relax so that less heat is generated. This is one reason you may sometimes feel physically lazy during hot weather.

The heat-regulating center in the brain is in the **diencephalon**. Nerve endings in the skin are sensitive to temperature changes. When stimulated, these nerve endings send messages to the heat center. Neural messages are also sent to the sweat glands, blood vessels, and muscles, directing them as necessary to keep the temperature of the body constant. In summary, these are balanced interactions necessary to maintain homeostasis in the body. These interdependent biochemical connections are additional examples of what Behe calls irreducibly complex systems in the body. If you take away any one of these vital internal control mechanisms, the body will be unable to maintain or regulate its steady state. These evidences support the belief that an all-wise Creator produced the body fully formed.

Balance in the Body's Urinary System

Further evidence of design comes from one of the most unlikely systems — the urinary system. The kidneys appear to have the kind of organization that resulted from a divine Planner. I am convinced that the kidney is one of the unsung heroes of the body. These bean-shaped structures function primarily to regulate the body's extracellular fluid. This function is accomplished through the formation of urine.

Urine is plasma that has been filtered and modified. In the process of urine formation, the kidneys regulate (1) the blood plasma volume and, in turn, blood pressure; (2) the concentration of waste products in the blood; (3) the concentration of electrolytes in the plasma; and (4) the plasma pH. Because the design inference is most evident in complex and interdependent feedback systems, we will focus on the last two functions of the kidney. Most people think of the kidney as a janitoring system; however, the kidney (along with the lung) is responsible for keeping the body in balance. In this next section, this homeostatic role of the kidney is emphasized.

Water Balance

The term "balance" suggests a state of **equilibrium**, and in the case of water and electrolytes it means that the quantities entering the body are equal to the quantities leaving it. Maintaining such a balance requires mechanisms to ensure that lost water and electrolytes will be replaced and that any excesses will be expelled. In fact, an in-depth study would show it is an optimal balance, one that minimizes metabolic cost to the organ and system, and at the same time maximizes benefit (fluids, electrolytes, and energy) to the entire body. This **optimal balance** is a result of nearly perfect efficiency of the body systems. As a result, the quantities of water, electrolytes, and hydrogen ions within the body are relatively stable at all times.

It is important to remember that water balance and electrolyte balance is interdependent, because the electrolytes are dissolved in the water of the body fluids. Consequently, anything that alters the concentrations of the electrolytes will necessarily alter the volume of the water by adding solutes to it or by removing solutes from it. Likewise, anything that changes the concentration of the water will change the concentration of the electrolytes by making them either more concentrated or more diluted.

Water and electrolytes are not uniformly distributed throughout the tissues. Instead, they occur in regions, or compartments, that contain fluids of varying compositions. The movement of water and electrolytes between these compartments is regulated, so that their distribution remains stable. Water balance exists when the total intake of water is equal to the total loss of water.

The primary regulator of water output is urine production. The volume of water excreted in the urine is regulated mainly by activity in the distal convoluted tubules and collecting ducts of the nephron. The epithelial linings of these segments of the renal tubule remain relatively impermeable to water unless vasopressin, or **antidiuretic hormone** (ADH), is present. The action of ADH causes water to be reabsorbed in these segments and, thus, to be conserved. In the absence of ADH, less water is reabsorbed and the urine volume increases.

Electrolyte Balance

An electrolyte balance exists when the quantities of the various electrolytes gained by the body are equal to those lost. The **electrolytes** (substances that release ions in water) of greatest importance to cellular functions are those that release the ions of sodium, potassium, calcium, magnesium, chloride, sulfate, phosphate, and bicarbonate. These substances are obtained primarily from foods, but they may also occur in drinking water and other beverages. In addition, some electrolytes occur as byproducts of various metabolic reactions.

Ordinarily, a person obtains sufficient electrolytes by responding to hunger and thirst. When there is a severe electrolyte deficiency, however, a person may experience a strong desire to eat salty foods. The concentrations of positively charged ions, such as sodium ($Na+$), potassium ($K+$), calcium ($Ca +2$), and hydrogen ($H+$), are particularly important. Certain concentrations of these ions, for example, are necessary for the conduction of nerve impulses, contraction of muscle fibers, and maintenance of cell membrane permeability. Sodium ions account for nearly 90 percent of the positively charged ions in extracellular fluids. The primary mechanism regulating these ions involves the kidneys and the hormone **aldosterone**. This hormone is secreted by the adrenal cortex. Its presence causes an increase in sodium reabsorption in the distal convoluted tubules and the collecting ducts of the renal tubules. Thus, it is not surprising that conditions that alter sodium ion balance also affect potassium ion balance. When God formed man from the "dust of the earth" (Gen. 2:7), He did it with great precision.

The sodium/potassium ion balance is regulated by aldosterone from the adrenal cortex. Aldosterone also functions in regulating potassium. In fact, the most important stimulus for aldosterone secretion is a rising potassium ion concentration, which seems to stimulate the cells of the adrenal cortex directly. This hormone enhances the reabsorption of sodium ions and at the same time causes the secretion of potassium ions into the renal filtrate.

The concentration of calcium ions in extracellular fluids is regulated mainly by the **parathyroid glands**. Whenever the calcium ion concentration drops below normal, these glands are stimulated directly, and they secrete parathyroid hormone in response. Parathyroid hormone causes the concentrations of calcium and phosphate ions in the extracellular fluids to increase.

pH Balance

One of the most important functions of the kidneys is to maintain the balance of the acids, bases, and salts in the blood. Body fluids must remain at the optimal pH (relative measure of acidity or alkalinity in solution) level in order to resist extreme acidosis or alkalosis. During exercise, more acids are produced. There are two ways of correcting the excess of acid or hydrogen ions. One is by buffers, which are chemicals that neutralize strong acids or strong bases in the bloodstream.

The second means of controlling acidity is the respiratory system that helps maintain constant conditions in your body. One of the byproducts of aerobic metabolism is carbon dioxide. It forms carbonic acid in the blood that is broken down into bicarbonate that gives off CO_2 to the exposed air. The kidneys remove excess acids resulting from metabolism, chiefly lactic acid, a byproduct of anaerobic metabolism and the same acid that is found in sour milk. The liver has a wondrously intricate mechanism for changing excess lactic acid back into glucose that can be used for energy.

The respiratory center in the brain stem working with the endocrine system helps regulate hydrogen ion (H+) concentration in the body fluids. By controlling the rate and depth of breathing, a drop in the hydrogen ion concentration in the body fluids accompanies this loss of carbon dioxide, because the released carbon dioxide comes from carbonic acid.

$$H_2CO_3 \longrightarrow CO_2 + H_2O$$

Conversely, if the body cells are less active, the concentrations of carbon dioxide and hydrogen ions in the plasma remain relatively low. As a consequence, the breathing rate and depth are decreased.

The Kidneys

Another means of controlling **acid-base balance** is the removal of excess acids from the body. This removal takes place in the nephron by the excretion of hydrogen ions from the kidneys. These ions are secreted into the urine by the epithelial cells that line certain segments of the renal tubules. By controlling the amount of electrolytes, acids, and water removed from the blood, the kidneys regulate the quantity and composition of the blood at an optimal functional level.

The various regulators of hydrogen ion concentration operate at different rates. Acid-base buffers, for example, function rapidly and can convert strong acids or bases into weak acids or bases almost immediately. For this reason, chemical buffer systems sometimes are called the body's first line of defense against shifts in the pH.

Physiological buffer systems, such as the respiratory and renal mechanisms, function more slowly, and constitute secondary defenses. The respiratory mechanism may require several minutes to begin resisting a change in the pH, and the renal mechanisms may require one to three days to regulate a changing hydrogen ion concentration.

Acid-Base Imbalance

One reason to believe the scientific support for the design inference is that the delicate and complex balance would have had to have been planned from the beginning, or nature has to overcome tremendous obstacles that are nearly impossible, to evolve the level of complexity necessary to achieve homeostasis through gradual physiochemical mechanisms (i.e., mutations and natural selection). Creeping towards balance is highly improbable.

The kidneys regulate acid-base balance by the secretion of H+ ions into the tubules and the reabsorption of bicarbonate (HCO_3-). The slightest imbalance of body fluids with H+ ions leads to acidosis. In **acidosis**, the ratio of CO_2 to HCO_3- increases in the extracellular fluid because of the production of CO_2 or increased H+ formation from metabolites. As you will soon see, the slightest imbalance may be deleterious, if not disastrous, in consequences if imbalance were sustained. On the other hand, the slightest imbalance of body fluids with OH- ions leads to alkalosis. In **alkalosis**, the number of basic ions increases in the extracellular fluid, thus elevating the pH. Some changes in body fluid pH cause marked alterations in the rates of chemical reaction in cells and in overall body function. Acidosis may lead to death as a result of coma, and alkalosis may lead to death as a result of tetany or convulsions.

Homeostatic examples illustrate the wisdom, skill, and care of the Creator for the body's chemical needs by providing such a precise balance in the "dust of the earth" (Gen. 2:7). Ordinarily, the body fluid hydrogen ion concentration is maintained within a very narrow pH range by the actions of chemical and physiological buffer systems. However, disease conditions may disturb the normal acid-base balance and produce serious consequences. For example, the pH of arterial blood is normally about 7.4, and if this value drops below 7.35, the person is said to have acidosis. If the pH rises above 7.45, the condition is called alkalosis. Such shifts in the pH of body fluids may be life-threatening and, in fact, a person usually does not survive if the pH drops to 6.8 (or rises to 8.0) for more than a few hours.

Acidosis is caused by an accumulation of acid or a loss of

base, resulting in an increase of the hydrogen ion concentration of body fluids. Conversely, alkalosis is caused by a loss of acid or an accumulation of base, accompanied by a decrease in hydrogen ion concentration.

In summary, the consequences for our bodies when water, electrolytes, and/or pH get out of balance are disease, permanent disorder, and sometimes even death. The consequences may be severe when the pendulum of balance is off one way or the other. Natural selection, mutation, and chance physiochemical processes hardly could explain the body in balance.

Homeostasis in Household Appliances

Cybernetics is a term applied to the science of controls in both living and non-living systems. Technically, homeostasis applies to living systems only, but there are systems like homeostasis designed by human engineers. The cybernetics of non-living systems deal with feedback mechanisms as in the case of home heating and cooling systems. Examples of homeostatic-like controls in household appliances and temperature control systems include thermostats in refrigerators, air conditioners, and furnaces. Each of these thermostats controls the temperature of an appliance or the entire home. When the temperature drops below the desired level, the thermostat turns the furnace or heating element on. The furnace is turned off when the temperature rises above a certain level. If the temperature continues to rise, the air conditioner will be turned on. It is shut off when the temperature drops to the level set on the thermostat. With these systems, the temperature of a house can be kept within a narrow optimal range year around. Both heat production and its removal are regulated by a kind of "electromechanical homeostasis."

Parallels can be drawn between the

control of the temperature of a house and temperature control in homeothermal animals. In both cases there is a stimulus, a receptor, a control center, and an effector. The receptor detects fluctuations in some variable of the animal's internal environment such as a change in temperature (stimulus). The control center processes information it receives from the receptor and directs an appropriate response by the effector.

When the temperature falls below a set point, the thermostat switches on the heater (the effector). When the thermometer detects a temperature near the set point, the thermostat switches off the heater. This type of control circuit is called a negative feedback system because a change in the variable being monitored (heat) triggers a response that counteracts the excess of that same variable — heat. Negative feedback mechanisms prevent small changes from becoming too large. Most homeostatic mechanisms involving diverse body systems in humans operate on the principle of negative feedback.

This similarity may leave the impression that the systems are alike and animals are entirely mechanistic. Closer inspection, however, reveals a vast difference, because homeostasis is far more complex than temperature controls in household appliances. The thermostat in the refrigerator or house is stimulated only by air temperature. In living systems, the rate of metabolism, which is controlled by hormones,

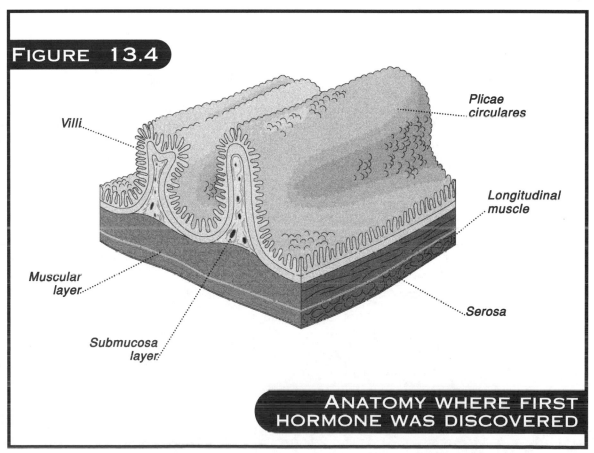

FIGURE 13.4

Villi

Plicae circulares

Longitudinal muscle

Muscular layer

Serosa

Submucosa layer

ANATOMY WHERE FIRST HORMONE WAS DISCOVERED

affects temperature independently of the environment. Also, fever results when the temperature setting is raised as a result of infection of **pathogens** (germs).

Homeostasis is a phenomenon in living systems and is vastly more involved than control systems in appliances invented by man. The complex system of checks and balances has been invented by a superior cause, the Creator. The inventor is superior to the invented. The advanced thinking that went into His systems far exceeds anything man has been able to develop. How marvelous and wise is the Bioengineer of the human body!

Wisdom in the Inward Parts

Homeostasis is the Creator's common blueprint for constancy in the human body. We have explored how design principles operate in the excretory system and how homeostasis, order, and the boundaries of the urinary system serve to protect the human body. Homeostasis is an organized and irreducible property of order that maintains the body's delicate balance through feedback (usually negative). This delicate balance is the mark of a creative genius — an intelligent designer if you will.

It is the constancy of homeostasis that is the condition of free and independent life. All the mechanisms of life, no matter how varied, have the purpose to keep the conditions of life constant in the internal environment (paraphrasing Bernard). God, who is discerned in nature, must be doing much of His work in the "milieu interieur." It is homeostasis, the dependability and steadiness of the internal environment, that keeps us alive. The structure of the kidneys is based on their critical role in maintaining homeostasis.

It was a Bible-believing physiologist, Ernest Starling, who discovered hormones. In 1902 two British physiologists, Starling and Sir William Bayliss, discovered **secretin**, a hormone enhancing digestion of foods in the **duodenum** (small intestine). These men were the first scientists to use the term "hormone" for chemical messengers that regulated body reactions. They named it for the Greek word, ορμαω; "I excite." It was discovered from the early days of research that hormones were very specific in their target. Starling was also the first scientist to use the metaphor of "wisdom in the inward parts" to characterize homeostasis. His ideas stemmed from his observation that the body seemed to have an intuitive integration of its diverse faculties. In his delivery of that prestigious lecture to physicians in Great Britain, he expanded on the concept of hormones as chemical messengers and regulators to chemicals that maintained precise balance through highly specific instructions to cell receptors that governed normal growth, development, and wellness. Starling saw a correlation between the Bible verse and biology in Job 38:36;KJV:

"Who hath put wisdom in the inward parts or who hath given understanding to the heart?"

In the Hebrew original, *sechvi* is the word translated "heart," a term so distinctive that this is the only place in the Bible where it occurs. Starling saw the mind and heart as equivalent. Therefore, the wonder of the human body is not only in the wisdom of its endocrine physiology but also in the breadth of its mind or intelligence. Starling associated the "body in balance" and man's intelligence with the wisdom found in the inward parts designed by the Creator.

Nine years after hearing this famous oration, Walter Cannon coined the term homeostasis in his book *The Wisdom of the Body*, and built upon Starling's theory. In turn, Starling further advanced the theory of homeostasis when he described this as a condition of uniformity that results from the adjustment of living things to changes in their environment. He described detailed physiological mechanisms for this coordinated regulatory balance. All the mechanisms of life, no matter how varied they are, have only one object – to keep the conditions of life constant in the internal environment.

Indeed, the Creator put wisdom in the inward parts (Job 38:36). This wisdom is evident in the process of homeostasis: balance, order, regulation, and chemical feedback. It is the Creator who has given understanding to the mind of man as he has discovered the laws that the Creator set in motion in the human body. In the endocrine system, its glands and hormones, we find a plan, purpose, and design to maintain our health and wellness.

Homeostasis is a universal characteristic of all living things. We have studied homeostatic control in humans, but these systems are also found throughout the animal kingdom. There are many variations in the way this is done, but the basic principle is the same. Most human homeostatic control systems involve three or more components: the endocrine, nervous, and one other system, coupled with many biochemical reactions. Homeostatic controls are irreducibly complex in nature. This irreducible complexity in humans involves the intricate living controls, whereas non-living control mechanisms are quite simplistic by comparison. It is most unlikely that such an intricate and delicate balance would have developed by chance from genetic mutations that are largely nuetral or harmful!

DESIGN FOCUS 13.3

A MERRY HEART DOETH GOOD LIKE A MEDICINE

"A merry heart doeth good like a medicine: but a broken spirit drieth the bones"
(Prov. 17:22).

Modern medical science now confirms what ancient Greek physicians and biblical writers both believed. In experiments with laboratory animals, injury to certain areas of the brain can lead to immune system changes. These changes affect specific resistance to disease, which refers to the immune system's ability to recognize, attack, and remember particular foreign molecules, such as viruses and bacteria. Specific resistance to disease is carried out by **lymphocytes**, called **B-cells** and **T-cells**.

The "thinking on good things" phenomenon has been known for years — positive attitude can assist the immune system's activities while stress can place a burden on the system. In 1991, *The New England Journal of Medicine* published a watershed report showing a direct link between mental state and disease. That study demonstrated a correlation between level of psychological stress and susceptibility to infection by a common cold virus. Due to the appearance of this article in a prestigious journal, this publication marked a turning point in medical acceptance of the mind/body connection — in particular, of the notion that stress and psychological factors could affect the function of the immune system. In this study, Sheldon Cohen at Carnegie Mellon University inoculated volunteers with measured doses of a cold virus — five different viruses were tested — or a placebo, a non-infectious "dummy" shot. As expected, some of the volunteers came down with colds and some did not. But among the volunteers injected with any of the five different respiratory viruses, the chance of getting a cold (or respiratory infection) was directly proportional to the amount of stress the volunteers said they had experienced during the past year. The study was the first well-controlled demonstration that stresses can increase the risk of infection.

The physiological discoveries, along with several clinical studies of illness ranging from the common cold to AIDS, have given rise to the rapidly growing field of **psychoneurimmunology** (PNI). PNI is an outgrowth of more than half a century of research on the physiology of stress. Later, medical scientists at Ohio State University identified physiological mechanisms responsible for these findings. Providing proof of this phenomenon has been difficult, but the Glassers are among those determined to show that a correlation exists between stress and reduced immune activities. Already, they have demonstrated reduced activity in natural killer cells in blood taken from students during exam week. Also, they have shown that in herpes-infected students, the virus is more active when exams are occurring (a reflection of reduced body defense).

The Glassers gave Ohio State students hepatitis B vaccinations and then tested for antibody response. Not surprisingly, the more stressed-out and anxious students were, the more they consistently responded with lower antibody levels. Lower antibody levels lower the specific defenses against hepatitis and would leave them prone to infection. Perhaps, these students might have contracted hepatitis B more readily if the virus were present. In summary, this line of medical research has demonstrated that both general and specific defenses against disease are lowered when we allow stressful situations to get the best of us.

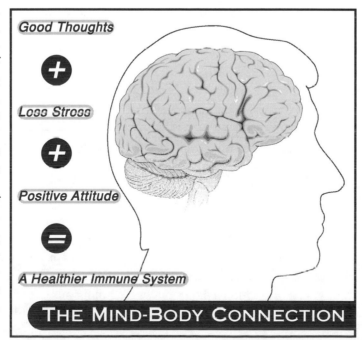

Good Thoughts
+
Less Stress
+
Positive Attitude
=
A Healthier Immune System

THE MIND-BODY CONNECTION

DISEASE FOCUS 13.4

DIABETES AND DISABILITY

Diabetes is growing in the United States in tidal wave proportions. There are nearly 16 million people in the USA (5.9% of the U.S. population) with diabetes, and in some groups of Native Americans as many as 50% of all adults are at risk for diabetes. It is the sixth leading cause of death by disease. There is a growing medical concern in western nations due to changes in lifestyle. As Americans become more "couch-potato-like" they increase the likelihood of becoming diabetic. Many people are diabetic and do not know it. The risk is high that over time, circulation in their limbs will decrease and permanent damage will occur in their appendages, particularly their lower legs and feet. They risk amputation unless restorative work is intervened by a podiatrist or physical therapist.

Like those suffering from Hansen's disease (leprosy), diabetics may lose their sense of pain in their extremities. Diabetes is unlike leprosy in that bacteria do not cause it, but rather it is the unwanted lipids (fats) and high glucose that cause the damage. Often, diabetics have painful, tingling sensations in their upper legs, but lose some sensation in their feet. If they lose a sense of pain and touch in their feet, they may damage their toes, heel, and arches. The sense of touch and pain are critical in maintaining healthy feet.

How Diabetes Cripples

When sugar levels remain elevated in the bloodstream, lipids accumulate in the limb blood vessels and restrict circulation in places like the feet. The low oxygen in their feet lead to low sensation and pain in the limbs and consequently patients injure themselves. Diabetics with restricted blood flow in their hands and feet frequently lose fingers and feet. Amputation occurs more often in feet because their feet are more likely to develop ulcers, sores, and tingling sensations.

The cellular metabolism of an untreated type I diabetic is similar to that of a starving person. Since insulin is not present to aid the entry of glucose into body cells, most cells use fatty acids to produce ATP. Organic acids called ketones (ketone bodies are products of fatty acid metabolism) accumulate. They cause a form of acidosis called ketoacidosis that lowers the blood pH and this may result in death. The burning of stored triglycerides and proteins also cause weight loss. As the lipids are transported by the blood from storage depots to cells, lipid particles are deposited in the blood vessel walls. This deposition leads to antherosclerosis and causes a multitude of cardiovascular problems, including heart disease, peripheral vascular disease, and gangrene. A major complication of diabetes is the loss of vision due to cataracts. Excessive glucose attaches to the lens proteins, causing cloudiness or damage to blood vessels to the retina. Several kidney problems also may result from damage to renal blood vessels. The major cause of disability among patients with insensitivity, is that of plantar ulcerations of the feet. Plantar (foot) ulcerations will persist or reoccur to gradually destroy the foot without intervention. If a diabetic develops grossly deformed feet, it is recommended that they have surgical correction for their feet and wear protective footwear until healing takes place.

Seldom are foot ulcers seen in the presence of an intact nervous system. It is generally felt that there are three causes for tissue damage and ulceration: 1. poor blood circulation, 2. high pressure on the sole (e.g. results from a blow, wound, or accident), and 3. repetitive stress in specific areas of the feet. Any of these may lead to severe injury that will require restorative surgery and orthopedic shoes. Patients must be trained to not apply too much pressure to their feet, or they may lose their feet.

Once again we see how Paul Brand's research on our created pain network protects us from destroying ourselves. Yet, chronic pain itself can destroy, as a visit to a pain center will illustrate. Unchecked pain saps physical strength and mental energy and can come to dominate a person's entire life. Somewhere between the two extremes, painlessness and incessant chronic pain, most of us live our days. There is a tremendous danger to those who lose the sense of pain. For without pain telling us that something is wrong, we go on to injure ourselves further. So the pain network is something we can thank God for. It is our protector and is another evidence of design in our awesome anatomy. This is an unexpected wisdom in the inward parts.

CHECK YOUR UNDERSTANDING

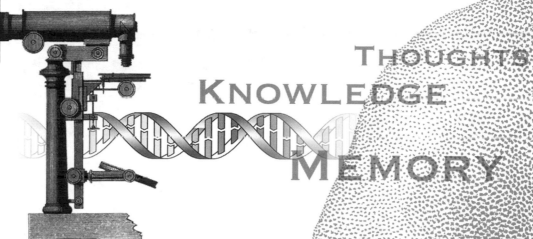

THOUGHTS

KNOWLEDGE

MEMORY

Endocrine System

1. What are three organs or components of the endocrine system?

2. What is the overall function of the endocrine system?

3. Describe an interwoven part or nature of the endocrine system. Relate this to Starling's idea of "wisdom in the inward parts."

4. Describe and illustrate the interwoven components and structure of the pituitary gland.

5. What is one of the hormones produced by the adrenal gland? What is the function of that hormone?

6. What gland controls temperature regulation? And what can result if it malfunctions?

7. Define homeostasis as it relates to the endocrine system.

8. Homeostasis is a physiological term that was coined by the American physiologist Walter Cannon in 1932. It refers to the ability of an organism to maintain the stability of its internal environment by adjusting physiological processes. Discuss the similarities of the humoral theory of body organization in the interior millieu in an attempt to explain homeostasis. Explain the role of antagonistic negative feedback process in the maintenance of homeostasis.

9. Who discovered hormones? List and define different classes of hormones.

10. Name two other contributors to the theory of homeostasis and give the contribution for each.

11. How is a "merry heart" like a medicine? Explain how laughing can help relieve stress and thus reduce disease.

12. Use creation theory to explain one homeostatic mechanism in the endocrine system.

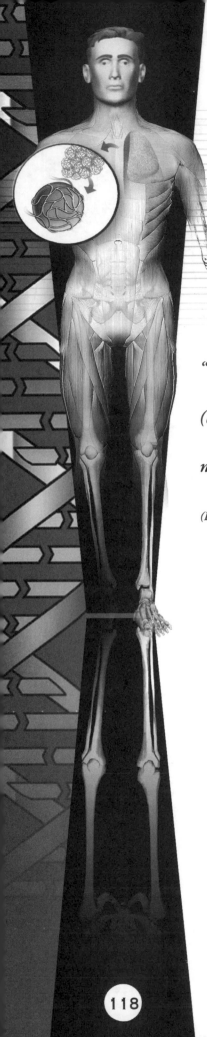

"Thou hast set a bound

(boundary) that they may

not pass over"

(David, Ps. 104:9).

We find in the Bible that the Creator has placed boundaries in creation and in the human body (Job 38:10–11; Jer. 5:22). He has placed genetic limits on variation within the various kinds of organisms (Gen. 1) and has also placed protective barriers surrounding cells, tissues, and organs in the human body. The boundary concept may be seen in limiting the entry and exit of chemicals and pathogens. Every organism must be able to maintain its boundaries so that its insides remain distinct from everything outside. In this chapter, the patterns involved in maintaining boundaries will be illustrated with examples from the human body. First, we explore the broader concept of boundaries and then we describe specific boundaries that serve to keep pathogens out of the body.

An external living membrane that encloses its contents, selectively allowing helpful inflow and preventing harmful flow of chemicals, surrounds every human body cell. Boundaries protect the body's insides from outside pathogens. Each cell has a protective covering, a membrane that limits it. Of the 75 trillion body cells, most are surrounded by friendly human cells that share the same adaptive functions and live in harmony. All cells have these living barriers provided by the Creator to control what goes in and what comes out.

Our Body Defense Systems

In this chapter, we examine three body systems that form "boundaries" protecting our body from invading pathogens and harmful chemicals. These three systems include the lymphatic, immune, and integumentary systems. These systems overlap in both their structure and function.

FIGURE 14.1

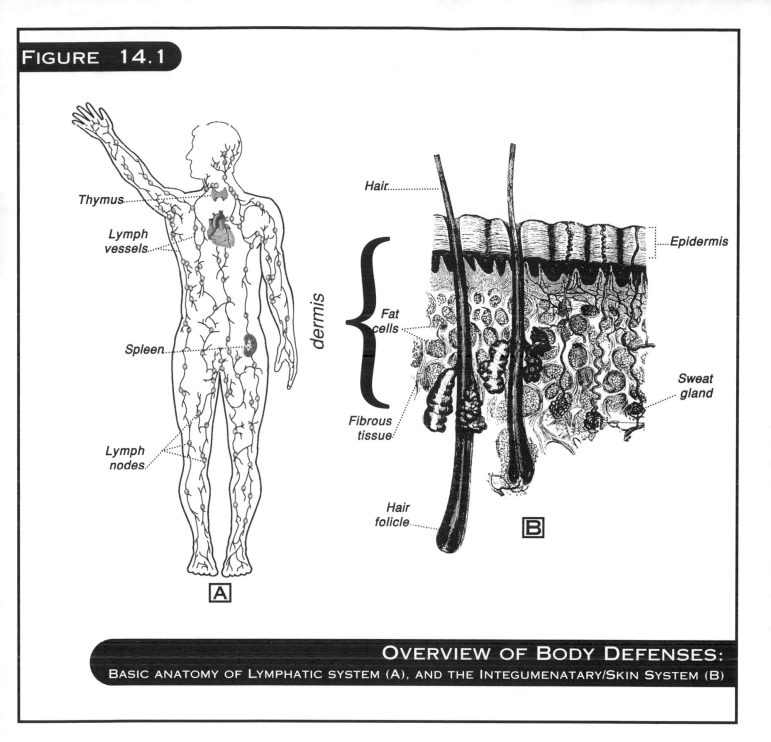

Thymus

Lymph
vessels

Spleen

Lymph
nodes

dermis

Hair

Fat
cells

Fibrous
tissue

Hair
follicle

Epidermis

Sweat
gland

A

B

OVERVIEW OF BODY DEFENSES:
BASIC ANATOMY OF LYMPHATIC SYSTEM (A), AND THE INTEGUMENATARY/SKIN SYSTEM (B)

Biologists generally refer to the system of anatomical parts, organs, and physical structures that assist in our body's defense system against pathogens and toxins as the lymphatic system. On the other hand, the functional system of body defenses is generally referred to as the immune system. This generally refers to specific cells, antibodies, and other proteins that provide us with defense against disease. The lymphatic and immune systems are just flip sides of the same coin. Generally, microbiologists and physiologists will refer to the body defenses as the immune system, whereas, anatomists and developmental biologists will refer to the lymphatic system.

The lymphatic system consists of both the lymph vessels and the lymphatic organs. The lymphatic vascular system consists of many tubes that collect water and solutes from interstitial fluid and transport them to the circulatory system ducts. Its main components are lymph capillaries and lymph vessels. The lymphoid organs include the lymph nodes, the spleen, bone marrow, the thymus, tonsils, small patches in the small intestine (Peyer's patch), and the appendix. The lymph nodes are strategically located by design at intervals along lymph vessels. Before entering the blood, lymph is filtered as it trickles through at least one node. A mass of lymphocytes takes up residence in the nodes after forming in the bone marrow.

The Lymphatics: Awesome, Distinct, and Interwoven

The lymphatic organs are awesome in structure and distinct in function. The anatomy of the diverse lymph nodes are marvelously interwoven and provide further evidence of intelligent design by the Skilled Craftsman. Each lymph node contains leukocytes that win victories over highly specific pathogens and toxins. The lymphatic system and the cardiovascular system share closely intertwined structures that are joined by capillaries. The lymphatic system was once thought to be part of the circulatory system since it consists of lymph, a moving fluid that comes from the blood and returns to the blood by way of the vessels. Lymph nodes with their capillaries are the most obvious interlacing fabric in the body's primary defense base. The nodes are small oval structures that interweave with lymph capillaries, blood capillaries, and reticular connective fibers and tissues. A capsule of dense connective tissue that extends strands and covers each lymph node is called a **trabercula.** These extensions divide the node into compartments, provide support, and interlace with blood vessels into the node interior. The superficial region of a lymph node, the **cortex**, contains many follicles. The deeper region of a lymph node is the **medulla**. Lymph nodes are a "military base" that deploy soldier cells, B- and T-lymphocytes, to a location where "cell wars" occur. Once a bacterium, virus, or toxin invades the body, T-cells and B-cells quickly go into "battle" from the interwoven, reticular fibers and travel with the flow of lymph to the "war" zone. Other leukocytes warn the body of danger and assist in filtering and cleansing the lymph to keep it pure.

There are more than 100 tiny lymph nodes. These are mainly in the neck, groin, and armpits, but are scattered all along the lymph vessels. The most clinically important nodes are illustrated in Figure 14.1. They act as barriers to infection by filtering out and destroying toxins and germs. The largest lymph gland in the human body is the **spleen**. The **cervical lymph nodes** are located in the neck. They are divided into two sets: superficial and deep. The **deep cervical glands** are large glands that are situated near the pharynx, esophagus, and trachea. When you have a sore throat, white blood cells mass together in these nodes to fight the infection, which is why your throat will often feel swollen and tender.

The **axillary lymph glands** are located in the arm, in the armpit, and near the elbow (Figure 14.1). They are divided into two sets: superficial and deep. These lymph nodes receive lymph from the vessels of the arm and the upper nodes receive lymph from vessels in the upper chest area near the breast and the mammary glands. There are about 35 lymph nodes in this area. Most of the lymph nodes are located in or near the armpit to limit the spread of cancerous cells in the chest. If cancer forms in the breast area it often spreads to the nodes because the lymph can carry cancerous cells. The lymphatics of the leg are divided into two sets, superficial and deep. The superficial are called the **inguinal lymphatic glands**, illustrated in Figure 14.1. These nodes vary from eight to ten in number and surround the large **Great Saphenous Vein**. These glands frequently become enlarged during disease. Infectious diseases of the upper leg and groin area will usually cause these glands to become inflamed. The swollen glands are signs that the body is launching a "war" against the germs that have invaded. In addition to containing lymphocytes, the lymphatic system also produces other white blood cells and generates antibodies. The body is able to eliminate the products of cellular breakdown and bacterial invasion through the flow of blood and lymph through the lymph nodes.

Two very large areas are of significance in this system. They are the **right lymphatic duct** that drains lymph fluid from the upper right body quarter above the diaphragm and down the midline, and the **thoracic duct structure** roughly 16 inches long located in the mediastinum of the **pleural cavity** which drains the rest of the body. It is through the actions of this system including the spleen, the thymus, lymph nodes, and lymph ducts that our body is able to fight infection and to ward off invasion from foreign invaders. Lymph plays an important role in the immune system and in absorbing fats from the intestines. The lymphatic vessels are present wherever there are blood vessels and transport excess fluid to the end vessels without the assistance of any "pumping" action.

In addition to the functions of defense, the lymphatic system serves to provide fluid in homeostatic balance and fat absorption. Lymph helps with the distribution of fluids and nutrients in the body, because it drains excess fluids and protein so that tissues do not swell up. *Lympha* (lymph) means *"clear spring water,"* in Latin. Therefore the lymph keeps other body fluids pure and in balance with the rest of our body cells. The lymphatic system absorbs fats from the digestive tract from the **lacteals** of the small intestine. These fats have entered the lacteals from the intestinal villi. This lymph transports the fatty content, called **chyle**, to the venous circulation and eventually is distributed or metabolized elsewhere in the body. Attached to parts of the villi, we observe another provision by the Creator to defend the body against minor poison, toxins, and germs. Whenever we eat food that might be "poisoned," the gastrointestinal tract has some protection. Located within the walls of the small intestines is a cluster of small nodes referred to as **Peyer's patches**. They are specialized aggregates of lymphatic follicles to combat minor food poisoning. Once again we observe the protective care of the Creator of the human digestive tract.

The **thoracic duct** is the channel for the collection of lymph from the portion of the body below the diaphragm and from the left side of the body above the diaphragm. It is a long duct, approximately 16 inches in the average adult. It extends from the lower spine to the **left subclavian vein** where it drains. The **lymphatic duct** is much shorter than the thoracic duct, only about 1/2 of an inch long. It receives lymph from the right side of body above the liver and empties into the **right subclavian vein** and **internal jugular vein**. Together with the thoracic, these ducts empty between 4 and 10 mL of lymph into the blood every minute. The subclavian vein is a continuation of the **axillary vein** (armpit vein) from the upper arm.

Tonsils by Design Defend the Body

Tonsils have long been overlooked as an important body defense. If you view the tonsils through a creation lens, you will quickly see that the tonsils are not a "useless" organ as some have claimed, but have been made with the function and purpose of defending the mouth and throat against infectious disease. Anatomists recognize three types of tonsils: **palatine, lingual,** and **pharyngeal (adenoids)**. There is a pair of palatine and lingual tonsils, as well as a cluster of adenoids (making up one pharyngeal tonsil). For hundreds of years, the five tonsils were thought be vestigial organs (optional organs to be disposed). Tonsils are unusually large groups of lymph nodules and diffuse lymphatic tissue located deep within the oral cavity and the nasopharnyx. They form a protective ring of lymphatic tissue around the openings between the nasal and oral cavities and the pharnyx. This ringed boundary helps to provide a protection against bacteria, viruses, and other potential pathogens in the nose and mouth (Figure 14.3).

The palatine tonsils were once thought to be organs that gave more trouble than service to the body. Today, creation scientists believe they help to contain respiratory infections by maintaining boundaries. Tonsils keep an infection local and limit the possibility of it becoming systemic. They contain germ-killing cells that help protect against upper respiratory tract infections, such as strep throat. Adenoids (also called pharyngeal tonsils) are a mass of lymphatic tissue, similar to the (palatine) tonsils, that is attached to the back

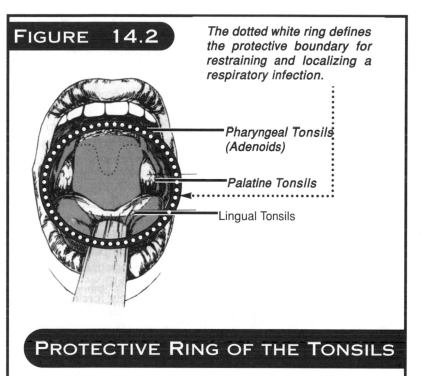

FIGURE 14.2

The dotted white ring defines the protective boundary for restraining and localizing a respiratory infection.

Pharyngeal Tonsils (Adenoids)

Palatine Tonsils

Lingual Tonsils

PROTECTIVE RING OF THE TONSILS

wall of the nasal pharynx. An individual fold of such nasopharyngeal lymphatic tissue is called an **adenoid**.

The surface layer of the adenoids consists of ciliated epithelial cells covered by a thin film of mucus. The cilia, which are microscopic hair-like projections from the surface cells, move constantly in a wavelike manner and propel the blanket of mucus down to the pharynx proper. From that point the mucus is caught by the swallowing action of the throat and is sent down to the stomach. The adenoids also contain glands that secrete mucus to replenish the surface film. The function of the adenoids is protective. The moving film of mucus tends to carry infectious agents and dust particles inhaled through the nose down to the pharynx, where the epithelium is more resistant. Immune substances, or antibodies, are thought to be formed within the lymphatic tissue, which, combined with phagocytic action, tends to arrest and absorb infectious agents.

The lingual tonsils are a pair of oval-shaped organs located at the back of the tongue behind the taste buds in the mucous membrane covering the tongue. They enlarge gradually from birth to seven years of age and then shrink. Each oval tonsil consists of a large number of lymphoid follicles. The lingual tonsils are part of the lymphatic system and are important to the body's defense against dangerous bacteria.

The circle of tonsils corral germs and limit the number of bacteria entering bloodstream. The tonsils appear to restrain the spread of bacteria and viruses thereby limiting the number of systemic infections. Occasionally, tonsils enlarge with an associated respiratory infection. This is because their location in the mouth and throat is near several respiratory organs. In rare instances, there may be repeated infections by respiratory pathogens that cause strep throat (*Streptococcus pyogenes*) and colds (adenoviruses). These germs may cause swelling and inflammation of the adenoids and may permanently enlarge them. This may be dangerous because large adenoids obstruct breathing through the nose and interfere with sinus drainage. Today, surgical removal of the tonsils (tonsillectomy) is occasionally recommended for children with permanently enlarged adenoids. In most cases, however, tonsils provide protection against respiratory infections spreading and are another example of intelligent design. The once classified "vestigial" organs are now considered fully functional!

A branch of biology called immunology involves the study of how the body protects itself from agents of disease called pathogens, or germs. The word immune comes from a Latin root word that means "freedom or protection from taxes or burdens." Taken together, the immune system usually protects us from getting sick and enables us to battle infectious disease successfully. The primary role of the immune system is to recognize pathogens and destroy them. In addition, the immune system prevents the proliferation of mutant cells, such as cancer cells. When the immune system is working properly, it protects the human body from infection. When it is not working or when a boundary is breached, the failure of the immune system can result in localized or systemic infections.

Our immune system acts against specific foreign chemicals and particles based upon prior memory. These foreign particles are called antigens. Antigens include protein-polysaccharide complexes that are part of bacteria, viruses, and protozoans. Once an antigen enters our body, the defense system starts to protect us through an immune response. First, the body must recognize the antigen as a harmful invader and then it must neutralize or destroy it. Both of these steps involve certain types of white blood cells called lymphocytes and neutrophils. Lymphocytes are produced by bone marrow, the red tissue in the hollow part of bones.

Lymphocytes enter the blood and lymph vessels. Cells that mature in the thymus gland are called T-lymphocytes. Others are called B-lymphocytes because they are processed and mature in the bone marrow, or liver. T-lymphocytes are further subclassified into helper T-lymphocytes and cytotoxic T-lymphocytes.

Helper T-cells (also called CD4 cells) act as the directors of the immune system. They identify the enemy and rush to the spleen and lymph nodes, where they stimulate the production of other cells and activate important cells such as cytotoxic T-cells. Once recruited and activated by helper T-cells, cytotoxic T-lymphocytes specialize in destroying cells of the body that have been invaded by foreign organisms. They also destroy cells that have turned cancerous.

B-lymphocytes act as the "biologic arms factory" because they produce millions of potent chemical weapons called antibodies. They reside in the spleen or lymph nodes, where the helper T-cells induce them to replicate. B-lymphocytes produce specific antibodies in response to particular pathological agents.

The process continues with macrophages which are large monocytes that are able to "eat" pathogens and also consume other members of the immune system that have been overcome in the struggle. Macrophages clean up the debris after helper-T, killer-T, and B-lymphocyte cells have stopped the invaders. Phagocytosis, or "cell eating" occurs when the pseudopods of a macrophage engulf harmful parasites or microorganisms. This is one way that blood serves to cleanse the body of waste and foreign material.

A third type of T-cell, the suppressor T-lymphocyte (also called CD8 cell), is able to slow down or stop the activities of B-cells and other T-cells. Suppressor T-cells play a major role in calling off the attack after an infection has been con-

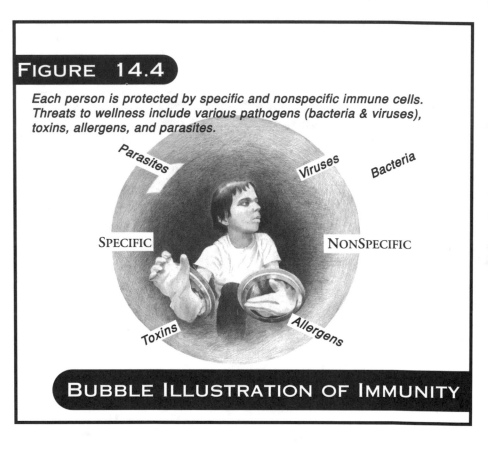

FIGURE 14.4

Each person is protected by specific and nonspecific immune cells. Threats to wellness include various pathogens (bacteria & viruses), toxins, allergens, and parasites.

Parasites Viruses Bacteria

SPECIFIC NONSPECIFIC

Toxins Allergens

BUBBLE ILLUSTRATION OF IMMUNITY

quered. This is a simplified version of how our body defenses work at the cellular level. In short, this cell team, working in conjunction with natural defense chemicals like interferons, keeps our bodies protected against those outside harmful invaders.

The immune system is somewhat like a protective bubble around the human body, shielding us against pathogens and forming an invisible boundary (figure 14.3). These vital functions are best illustrated through the case study of a young man who lacked an immune system from birth. David Vetter was the first long-term survivor of severe combined immunodeficiency (SCID) and became known as the "boy in the bubble" or the "bubble boy" through the popular press and television.

David the "Bubble Boy"

In 1971, David Vetter was born without a functioning immune system. Faced with what was, back then, a fatal situation, doctors placed the boy in a completely sterile environment. First, David was placed in a small "bubble" crib. They were "buying time" until they could figure out what to do.

After receiving generous donations, they built him a one-room bubble, and after 12 years David had a two-room bubble and a "space suit" to walk in. The experiment ended in February 1984, when David the "bubble boy" died. His death provided a clear link between the Epstein-Barr virus and cancer. With no "compatible" relatives to provide him with immune cell-producing bone marrow, David had to wait for the technology to rid donated marrow of the cells that would attack his own. After David spent 12 years in the bubble, doctors hoped the technology was ready, and the boy received treated bone marrow from his sister. Eighty days after the transplant and still in a germ-free environment, David developed some of the clinical signs of mononucleosis, a condition caused by the Epstein-Barr virus. Doctors brought him out of isolation for easier treatment, hoping his sister's marrow cells had taken hold and would protect him from the microbes the rest of us encounter every day. Her cells had not established themselves, and David died about four months after the transplant. What killed him was not the immediate failure of the transplant but cancer. David's B-cells became disrupted because of the proliferation of the Epstein-Barr virus that caused a rare form of cancer.

The autopsy revealed small, whitish-pink cancer nodules throughout his body, and closer study showed that these cells all contained Epstein-Barr virus — a pathogen that he could have gotten only through his sister's bone marrow. The cancer came from the transplant itself, according to William T. Shearer who was the lead physician on David's case. David had a B-cell cancer of a type similar to Burkitt's lymphoma, and while Shearer cannot say with certainty, the two types of cancer kicked off in the same way.

David is the most famous case of SCID, the gene for which is carried on the X-chromosome. His life was most significant because he was the first long-term survivor, and in his death a great deal was learned about the immune system. Ten years after his death the gene causing SCID was isolated from a cell line that originated with David. SCID usually involves a deficiency of the enzyme adenosine deaminase (ADA). This genetic deficiency leads to a failure of the lymphocytes to develop properly, which in turn causes the failure of the immune system to function (similar to AIDS).

A conclusion that we can draw from David's life is that the immune system acts like a protective bubble around the human body, protecting against pathogens. It provides an invisible barrier to localized and systemic infections.

FIGURE 14.4

This diagram shows a progressive break in the basement membrane of epithelial tissue due to bacteria, like Salmonella, that contain powerful endotoxins. In step A, Salmonella attaches to the cell. In step B, the cell is induced to rearrange actin fibers and ingest pathogen by endocytosis. In step C, the pathogen leaves the cell by exocytosis. In step D, the bacterium multiplies. In step E, Salmonella invades surrounding tissue by destroying epithelium. This toxin may disrupt Peyer's patch (lymphatic tissue in the GI tract) and the intestinal wall barrier. The disruption makes room for more bacteria to colonize the tissue. Dysentery, fever, and bloody diarrhea are possible symptoms from bacterial food poisoning.

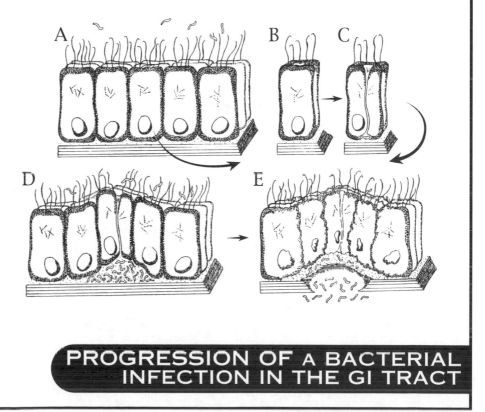

PROGRESSION OF A BACTERIAL INFECTION IN THE GI TRACT

DISEASE FOCUS 14.1 Broken Boundaries

Most of the time, enteric bacteria inhabit the gastrointestinal (GI) tract (A) mutualistically. They are most abundant in the colon (B), but are also found in the small intestine. As long as boundaries are maintained in the intestines, the body remains healthy. In fact, most bacteria in the GI tract are beneficial, providing useful vitamins and inhibiting the growth of pathogens. However, when boundaries are broken, bacteria invade (figure 14.4). The establishment of infection frequently involves an invasion of host tissues when the boundaries are broken. In the lettered sequence, A through E, there is a progressive break in the basement membrane of epithelial tissue because of pathogenic bacteria strains that release enterotoxins. This poison may disrupt Peyer's patch and/or the intestinal wall barrier. This disruption makes room for more bacteria to colonize the tissue. Dysentery, typhoid fever, and bloody diarrhea are possible. In addition, fatal diseases like hemolytic uremic syndrome are possible if toxins from *E. coli 0157:H7* spread in the bloodstream from the GI tract to the kidney. Injury, disease, and death are possible when boundaries like these are broken.

Another way of visualizing the immune system is an umbrella protecting our body from the raindrops falling from the sky. When the umbrella is intact, we stay dry; when it breaks, we get wet. In the case study of David, his "umbrella" was the bubble and it protected him from the "rain" of viruses, bacteria, parasites, allergens, and toxins (see figure 14.3). The immune system is both impressive and invisible.

The invisible boundary that protects us against pathogens is made up of numerous and diverse interdependent cell types, such as macrophages, neutrophils, natural killer cells, T-lymphocytes, and B-lymphocytes, that are interdependent upon each other. Once again, we observe that many diverse parts in the immune system must all be present for an effective body defense. It is difficult to conceive how a gradual, Darwinian mechanism of mutation and natural selection over billions of years could produce the awesome interaction between the parts of the immune "cell team."

Anatomical Boundaries in the Body

The intact skin and the mucous membranes that extend into the body cavities are among the most important resistant factors. Unless penetration of these barriers occurs, disease is rare. Penetration of the skin is a fact of everyday life. For example, a cut or abrasion allows staphylococci to enter the blood, and a mosquito bite acts as a hypodermic needle permitting various pathogens to enter the inner body. Yellow fever viruses, malaria parasites (*Plasmodium* sp.), certain rickettsiae, and plague bacilli are but a few examples. Other means of penetrating the skin include splinters, tooth extractions, burns, shaving nicks, and injections.

Certain features of the mucous membranes provide resistance to parasites. Cells of the mucous membranes along the lining of the respiratory passageways secrete mucus that traps heavy particles and microbes. The cilia of mucous membrane cells move particles along the membranes and up the throat, where they are swallowed. This mechanism is referred to as the mucociliary escalator. Stomach acid then destroys any swallowed microorganisms. A natural protection to the gastrointestinal tract is provided by stomach acid, which has a pH of approximately 2.0. Most organisms are destroyed in this environment. Notable exceptions include typhoid and tubercle bacilli, *Helicobacter pylori* (the ulcer bacterium), protozoan cysts, immature helminth stages, polio, and hepatitis A viruses. Bile from the gall bladder enters the system at the duodenum and serves as a chemical barrier. Duodenal enzymes digest proteins, carbohydrates, fats, and other molecules in microbes.

All parts of the body surface exposed to the outside world are covered with epithelial cells. These cells are packed tightly together and rest on a thin layer of noncellular material, the basement membrane. The parts of the body that are exposed to the outside world include the skin and mucous membranes of the genitourinary tract, the respiratory tract, and the alimentary tract. Although they are inside the body, they are nevertheless exposed to the external environment through the intake of food and air.

Each region of the body has, in addition to the tight packing of the epithelial cells (with tight junctions), other mechanisms to keep microbes from gaining entry and colonizing. Skin cells are shed regularly. Ciliated cells of the respiratory tract transfer mucus-entrapped microbes out of the lungs and into the throat where they are first swallowed and then destroyed by stomach acid. The peristaltic movement in the intestine moves potential pathogens out of the body, and the flushing actions of the urinary tract are its main defense against potential pathogens.

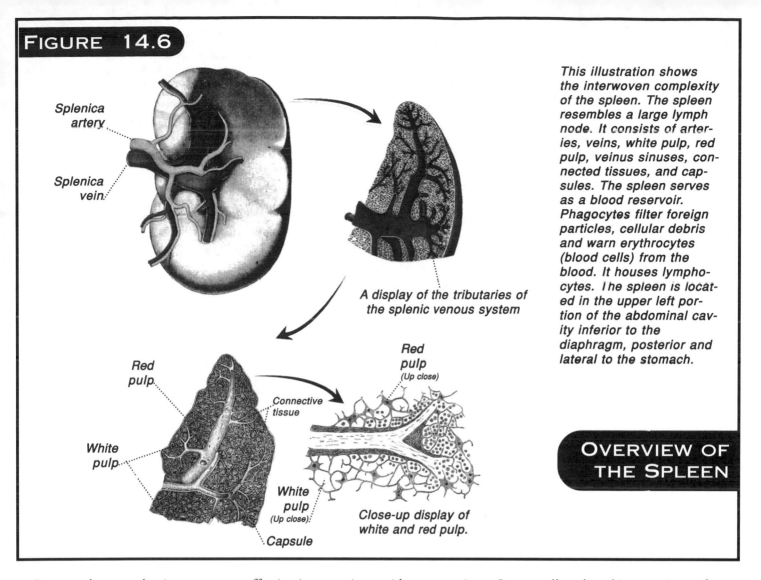

FIGURE 14.6

Splenica artery

Splenica vein

A display of the tributaries of the splenic venous system

This illustration shows the interwoven complexity of the spleen. The spleen resembles a large lymph node. It consists of arteries, veins, white pulp, red pulp, veinus sinuses, connected tissues, and capsules. The spleen serves as a blood reservoir. Phagocytes filter foreign particles, cellular debris and warn erythrocytes (blood cells) from the blood. It houses lymphocytes. The spleen is located in the upper left portion of the abdominal cavity inferior to the diaphragm, posterior and lateral to the stomach.

Red pulp

White pulp

Connective tissue

Red pulp (Up close)

White pulp (Up close)

Capsule

Close-up display of white and red pulp.

OVERVIEW OF THE SPLEEN

Because these mechanisms are very effective in removing organisms, a germ must adhere to or attach to host cells as a necessary first step in the establishment of infection. As a general rule, both germs and host cells are negatively charged and therefore tend to repel each other. For attachment to occur, the repulsive force must be overcome.

Some pathogens, such as streptococci that are responsible for tooth decay, possess polysaccharides that form a sticky network of fibrils (called the glycocalyx) that allows bacteria to attach to surfaces nonspecifically. Other bacteria use pili, hair-like structures (resembling cilia) found on their surface, that allow them to adhere to the urinary tract. The numerous pili help them to anchor to surfaces while they exploit their environment.

The Skin and Integumentary System

The skin is an organ because it consists of different tissues that are joined to perform specific activities. It is the largest organ in surface area and weight. In adults, the skin covers an area of about 22-feet^2 (2 m^2). The skin is not just a simple, thin covering that keeps the body together and pro-

vides protection. Structurally, the skin consists of two principal parts. The outer, thinner portion, which is composed of epithelium is called the **epidermis**. The inner, thicker, connective tissue part is called the **dermis**.

The skin has at least six functions:

1. **Regulation of body temperature.** In response to high environmental temperature or strenuous exercise, the evaporation of sweat from the skin surface helps lower an elevated body temperature to normal. Changes in blood flow in the skin also help regulate body temperature.
2. **Protection.** The skin covers the body and provides a physical barrier that protects underlying tissues from physical abrasion, bacterial invasion, dehydration, and ultraviolet radiation. Hair and nails also have protective functions, as described shortly.
3. **Sensation.** The skin contains abundant nerve endings and receptors that detect stimuli related to temperature, touch, pressure, and pain.
4. **Excretion.** Small amounts of water, salts, and several organic compounds (components of perspiration) are excreted by sweat glands.

5. **Immunity.** Certain cells of the epidermis (Langerhans cells) are important components of the immune system that protects against pathogens.

6. **Synthesis of Vitamin D.** Exposure of the skin to ultraviolet radiation helps with the production of vitamin D, a substance that aids in the absorption of calcium and phosphorus from the digestive system into the blood.

The skin's various nerves, glands and structures intertwine to produce the integumentary network; below the outer epidermis. **Apocrine** and **eccrine** glands secrete the waste products from the body. Sebaceous glands secrete the oil needed in lubricating and waterproofing the skin. In both the epidermis and dermis, special sensory structures like the **Mesiner's corpuscles** allow for the feeling of pressure and pain. However, even beyond all of these intricate structures, the individual skin cells also demonstrate the fabric-like design. Within each cell there are complex stitchings which bind together the individual cells. These tiny fibers in the cell membranes are called **desomones.** These intricately woven fibers help "stitch" the skin together. Desmosomes are also called **anchoring junctions.** These junctions function like rivets, fastening cells together into strong epithelial sheets. Intermediate filaments made of **keratin** reinforce desmosomes.

If we view the skin through a creation lens, we see a beautiful fabric or tapestry. In contrast, evolutionists view the skin as a random, haphazard histology in its origin. The evidence, however, reveals that the skin's mechanism for repair is intricate, a histology that favors wound healing. Our skin is merely a small segment of the woven masterpiece from the skilled Craftsman. Since God is the Creator of the integumentary system, He can restore those incisions that the skin experiences. He knows just what to include in the restoration of body parts; after all, He is the original fabric designer! He has masterfully designed and set in place the necessary components of the skin, so that the body lacks nothing.

The skin has the largest surface area of any organ in the body and is the heaviest. On the surface are the sensitive papillae, and within are certain organs with special functions, such as the sweat glands, hair follicles, and sebaceous glands. The skin protects the internal organs of the body against infection, injury, and harmful sun rays. It also plays an important role in the regulation of body temperature. The skin consists of three layers: the epidermis, the dermis, and the hypodermis.

Bacteria and viruses cannot penetrate the tightly knotted cells of the skin. As long as the skin is unbroken, it is one of our most effective defenses. Normal flora, harmless bacteria that live on the skin, protect the body by attacking harmful bacteria that try to take up residence. The acidity of the skin also helps to ward off harmful bacteria. When bacteria break down the oil on the skin, more acid is produced and the bacteria are prevented from reproducing by their own waste products.

Mucous Membranes

The nose and mouth have a sticky coating of mucus that is secreted from the mucous membranes. These mucous membranes consist of an epithelial layer and underlying connective tissue layer. Mucous membranes line the entire gastrointestinal, respiratory, urinary, and reproductive tracts. They form a common internal boundary within the body. Mucus prevents the tracts from drying out. Some pathogens that can survive on the moist secretions of the mucous membrane are able to penetrate the membrane if they are present in sufficient numbers. Although mucous membranes do inhibit entrance by bacteria, they offer less protection than skin and nails.

Streptococcus pneumonia, a normal resident of the nose and throat, is frequently an opportunist. When its numbers are low, it does not cause infection. During times of stress, however, the immune system's defenses are lowered. As these bacteria grow in numbers, an infection can result. When defense barriers are broken, a case of pneumonia may result.

The first sign of disease is an inflammation of the pulmonary tracts. The bacteria may be identified by their cell formation in pairs. Advanced symptoms include fever, difficult breathing, and chest pain. The lungs have a reddish appearance because blood vessels are dilated. Bacteria can invade the blood stream and the pleural cavity around the lung, and occasionally inflammation, fever, and tonsillitis characterize strep throat where lymph nodes in the neck become enlarged.

In summary, there are boundaries inside our bodies at the cellular and tissue level. They provide protection against dangerous pathogens and chemicals that might harm us upon entry. We can be good stewards of our bodies by keeping our skin clean and being careful not to touch our nose and mouth with our fingers that may have been contaminated by pathogens. Fortunately, if boundaries of the human body are broken, the Creator has made provision for defenses against infectious disease. These functional body defenses are collectively placed in the immune system.

Recall, enteric microbes like *E. coli* make up the normal flora in the intestines. These symbiotic bacteria are usually friendly, but should not be considered altogether harmless. Even placid bacteria cannot and must not get inside the body or they may become pathogens. Infection from microbes, if left unchecked, can lead to disease and eventually death. Our defensive cells recognize them as foreign and proceed to attack and destroy them. Fortunately, there are epithelial membranes lining the entire gastrointestinal tract and other inside organs that maintain the body's

Outer Layers for Protection

In the Hebrew mind, fine clothing was something highly regarded. Job describes his skin and flesh with the word *lâbesh**. The KJV translators used the word "clothed" in Job 10:11 to describe the skin and outer flesh. These are protective layers or boundaries for the rest of the body. This word is similar to the Greek and Latin word *tunica* (literally, wrap around), or tunics. Anatomists use this word to describe the various layers of skin, other epithelial tissues in the body, blood vessels, and epithelial tissues throughout the body.

Inward Parts for Intricate Function

The Bible also describes other body parts in God's creation. These include the words *râgam* (translated "curiously wrought, embroidered, variegated, or interwoven"), and *sûwk* (translated "fenced, knit, shut in, or entwined"). These words have been used to describe the human embryo, fetus, the bones, tendons, muscles, kidneys, heart, lungs, and ureter throughout the Bible. Note also its connection of *râgam* to *râphah*; these come from a similar root word in Hebrew. *Râgam* is used to describe the cross-stitched, or interwoven, design in the body and *râphah* is used in the context of healing, where the great physician stitches together our broken and wounded body (see Design Focus 14.2). Both words come from a similar root. The healing method used by Jesus to heal the blind man is similar to the procedure used by the intelligent designer to make the human eye. After all, Jesus is both the Great Physician and the Creator (Col. 1:16). Jesus has the power

and skill to heal any illness because He is our Maker and is well acquainted with our blueprint.

In conclusion, clothing and various types of cloth seem to be God's word picture to help us better understand His design of the human body. In addition, we see the care He has taken to provide both outer protective barriers, as well as our intricate and highly developed inward parts that have cross-stitching in them. No wonder Job said there is wisdom in the inward parts, and David said he was fearfully and wonderfully made!

*Hebrew phonetic spelling of words.

Four Stages of Healing Observed in the Skin

1. Normal skin (an interwoven fabric)
2. Inflamed skin (the fabric torn)
3. Phagocytosis of dead neurotrophils (fabric cleaner)
4. Fibrosis (mending the stitches)

boundaries. These boundaries can also be seen as a marvelous and adaptive mechanism that makes the human body unique. These membranes allow needed substances to enter while they exclude potentially damaging chemicals and pathogens. Hence, boundaries are needed for our health and well being. These facts fit quite well with the idea that an all-wise Creator prepared these various barriers to protect the body from harm.

Inside the cranium, there is a distinct membrane, the blood-brain barrier, that limits the entry and outflow of chemicals, such as around the brain. Cells surrounding the brain are designed to regulate tight control over what enters the brain. The astrocyte cells primarily regulate substances that pass in or out of the brain (see figure 11.2). Astrocytes and other neuroglial cells ensure that the brain will not be subject to chemical fluctuations in the blood. Thus, they provide protection against dangerous chemicals. They work like a sieve, screening larger molecules from smaller ones at the brain's edge.

Interwoven Designs

Dermis of the Skin

Most of the skin, nails, and hair are made up of tightly knit cells and cell products. The interwoven design is easily seen in the skin's dermis. The dermis is the thick, relatively soft middle tissue of the skin. It shields and repairs injured tissues and is about four times thicker than the epidermis (outer layer of the skin). The dermis consists mainly of protein collagen, which builds scar tissue to mend cuts and abrasions. Hair roots, muscles, nerve endings, sensory receptors, sweat glands, blood and lymph vessels all form the interlacing tapestry. The dermis nourishes the epidermis and is the most intricate layer, or tunic, of the integumentary skin. Underneath the dermis is the hypodermis, which is a fatty subcutaneous layer.

The Spleen and Reticular Fibers

The spleen is closely associated with the circulatory and the lymphatic systems. It is an abdominal organ that lies between the bottom of the stomach and the diaphragm. It plays a role in the maintenance of blood volume, production of some types of blood cells, and recovery of material from worn out red blood cells. It is involved in the removal of blood cells and bacteria from the blood.

In the cross-section of the spleen may be seen the various coats and layers of splenetic tissue. The spleen is covered by an external, serous coat that lubricates the outside of the spleen with serous fluid to protect it against friction against the other viscera. Immediately within the serous coat is the internal, fibrous coat of the spleen. It forms the framework of the organ and follows the vessels within the spleen, forming sheaths around them. From these sheaths extend the fibrous bands that bind the sections of the spleen together, much as the fibers of a sponge. The sacs enclosed are called areolae, and within the areolae is the pulpy tissue of the spleen. This pulpy tissue is a reddish-brown, and is where the blood is filtered to remove bad cells, convert their hemoglobin to bilirubin, and return the iron from the destroyed cells back to the blood.

Lymphatic Nodes

The lymphatic system consists of lymph, a moving fluid that comes from the blood and returns to the blood by way of the lymphatic vessels. Lymph carries some nutrients around the body, especially fat. It also distributes germ-fighting white cells. Lymph resembles plasma, but is more diluted and contains only about five percent proteins, one percent salts, and extractives. It is formed from bits of blood and other body liquids, called interstitial fluid or tissue fluid, that collect in the spaces between cells. Some of the interstitial fluid goes back into the body through the capillary membrane, but most enters the lymphatic capillaries to become lymph. Along with this interstitial fluid, the lymph also picks up any particles that are too big to be absorbed through the capillary membrane. These include cell debris, fat globules, and tiny protein particles. The lymph then moves into the larger lymphatic vessels and through the lymph nodes, and eventually enters the blood through the veins in the neck region. Lymph has no pump of its own. Its flow depends upon blood pressure and the massaging effect of the muscles.

Lymph nodes, the most obvious interwoven fabric in the defense system, are small oval structures. Lymph nodes are the size of kidney beans and generally are located in clusters near veins at strategic points along medium-sized lymph vessels at the knee, elbow, armpit, groin, neck, abdomen and chest. Blood is cleaned and filtered in the lymph nodes, and germ-fighting cells gather there during illness. This filtration process prevents bacteria, cancer cells, and other infectious agents from entering the blood and circulating through the system. The lymph nodes are the centers for production and storage of some of the white blood cells, namely the lymphocytes and monocytes, which are important elements of the body's immune mechanism. During any kind of infection, the nodes enlarge in their area of drainage due to the multiplication of lymphocytes in the node.

DESIGN FOCUS 14.2

JEHOVAH RAPHA AND LISTENING TO THE GREAT PHYSICIAN

God revealed himself as *Jehovah Rapha* in the context of great sickness occurring around His people. *Rapha* means "to cure, to repair, to heal, to mend back together," or restore one to health or usefulness. Usually the word "heal," or "healing," is used in conjunction with Jehovah Rapha. In addition, "healing" implies sewn together, mending, stitching up, binds to, or adheres on. God is involved in the restoration of lives by pulling things together that are out of joint. He stitches our life into a beautiful tapestry, including dark threads (black and gray) mixed with silver and gold threads on the underside and a beautiful cloth picture on the top side. He is the Master Surgeon in our life. He can mend broken strands because

He is the Creator who has woven life together from the beginning. This is the nature of Jehovah Rapha. While many Egyptians were suffering from plagues, God protected His people when they obeyed Him. I think the Israelites were receptive to God's voice and His instruction of health principles in the Levitical law. Most likely, God's people listened due to the dramatic contrast of Egyptians experiencing plague and sickness, while they experienced good health and blessing. God often gets our attention during times when we and/or our neighbors are sick. It appears that we are more ready to hear God's prescriptions for life, death, health, and sickness when He has our attention. Let us all listen to the Great Physician.

CHECK YOUR UNDERSTANDING

THOUGHTS

KNOWLEDGE

MEMORY

Immune and Lymphatic Systems

1. List at least three organs of the immune system.

2. What is the overall function of this system?

3. Distinguish between the immune system and the lymphatic system. Why are body defenses so critical to living a long life?

4. Describe and give an example of an interwoven part of the immune and lymphatic system.

5. Draw a picture of and discuss how a lymph node illustrates irreducible complexity or is evidence for an intelligent designer.

6. What are the affects of an immunodeficiency (e.g., SCID or AIDS) in the body? What boundaries are broken in the body?

Integumentary System

1. List at least three organs or components of the integumentary system.

2. What is the overall function of the integumentary system?

3. Describe an interwoven part of the integumentary system.

4. Discuss how the skin is an interwoven element that illustrates irreducible complexity and include a drawing.

5. What causes acne?

6. Describe one infectious disease that affects the digestive system. Explain its cause and how it occurs in figure 14.3. Illustrate (with a diagram) this disease and its infection of body structures.

7. *BONUS:* In past years, the news media have shared dozens of stories of how *E. coli 0157H7* in tainted hamburger meat and apple juice has led to the death of numerous young children. Explain how the bacterium *E. coli* (normally harmless in the intestine) breaks one of the body's natural boundaries in the excretory system and causes health care professionals to apply kidney dialysis in order to save the child's life. Explain how IV fluids are pumped into the body to maintain homeostasis.

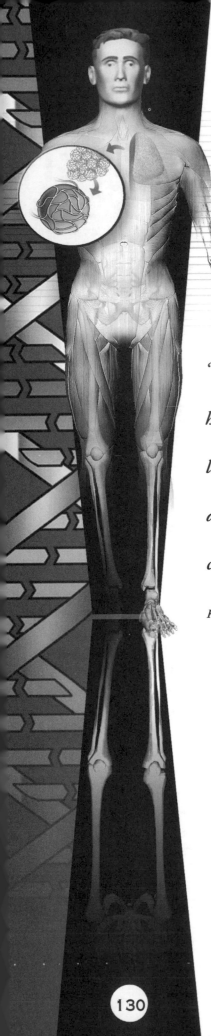

CLASSIC AND CONTEMPORARY EXPLORATIONS IN THE HUMAN BODY

CHAPTER 15

"The history of anatomy has an interesting parallel with the history of the dissection of human cadavers."

Kent Van De Graaff, 1998

The origin of the patterns observable in creation is a topic that has fascinated biologists since the time of the ancient Greeks. It was not until the time of William Harvey, however, that man's physiological and anatomical exploratory endeavors utilized the scientific method and demanded proofs from repeatable experiments. Beginning with the time period of Vesalius and Harvey, man began to really understand the *"wisdom of the inward parts"* and sought to understand the products of the Creator's design and His plan for the human body. In those days, many explorers of the human body began *"thinking God's thoughts after Him."* In this chapter, we present an exposé of classic and contemporary explorers of the human body which includes pioneering creation scientists, proponents of design, and current investigators whose beliefs are unknown.

The Reformation Era

The **Reformation** era was one in which man returned to the Scriptures. The Reformation in Europe loosed the grip of superstition and allowed a renewal of the study of nature and the use of exact descriptions for living and preserved things. This was especially helpful in the advancement of knowledge of human anatomy and physiology as biologists began to experiment with living animals and observe human cadavers. The return to the authority of the Scriptures, the hallmark of the Protestant movement, made people very interested in the natural world which the God of Genesis had made. These scientists wanted to discover the secrets that God concealed in nature (Prov. 25:2) and, wherever possible, to use their discoveries for the benefit of others. As science turned to biblical principles, a great new era began, the era of modern science. This is particularly true in human anatomy and physiology. A few hundred years later, Pasteur and Lister built upon similar principles in microbiology, just as George Cuvier did in pathology. As biology turned to biblical principles, science grew. Today, if man rejects this divine revelation and accepts Darwinism and evolutionism, science goes backward. Modern science does not conflict with biblical principles. Only by holding to the truth of Scripture and a biblical world view can man hope to learn more of God's creation.

Andreas Vesalius (1514–64) was a Belgian anatomist and physician whose dissections of the human body and descriptions of his findings helped to correct misconceptions that had prevailed since ancient times. Vesalius was born in Brussels, Belgium. At Paris, he studied medicine and developed an interest in anatomy. In 1537, Vesalius obtained his medical degree and a job as a lecturer on surgery. During his research, Vesalius showed that the anatomical teachings of Galen, revered as infallible standards in medical schools, were primarily based upon the dissections of animals rather than cadavers. Galen's books were used as a guide to explaining the inward structures and functions of the human body, in spite of many errors.

Vesalius wrote the revolutionary text *De Humani Corporis Fabrica* to counter Galen's false teachings. The volumes were completely illustrated with characteristically delineated engravings based on his own drawings of what he observed firsthand during his cadaver dissections. The theme of design, or divine craftsmanship, can be seen throughout his drawings and may reflect his Roman Catholic beliefs in a Creator. These seven volumes were the most accurate and comprehensive anatomical texts to date and they led to his appointment as physician to Holy Roman Emperor Charles V.

Vesalius' Classic Masterpiece

De Humani Corporis Fabrica (*On the Fabric of the Human Body*), printed in Basel in 1543, endures as the Renaissance classic that describes the design of the human body while it updated and amended the misconceptions in the publications of past scientific writings. Following the organizational style of Galen, considered the first anatomist, Vesalius was able to correct many of his predecessors' errors by studying human cadavers instead of animal remains. Condemned criminals, considered worthless and unworthy of proper burial, served as the models. At times, graves were robbed to provide the bodies needed for dissection and illustration. Leonardo da Vinci also recorded dissections of the human body that are considered classic works of art and are scientifically correct. Unfortunately, however, he never published his drawings and they remained unknown for many years.

For its time, this text (*De Humani Corporis Fabrica*) contained revelations on the makeup of the human body. Also, it was noteworthy for its extensive series of illustrations coupled with Vesalius' comprehensive text describing the human anatomical structures exposed by his dissections. The visual representations were drawn and transferred to woodcuts by artists of the Titian school. Unfortunately, Vesalius never credited the artists. Some names are offered as possible candidates, and Titian himself is named in the speculations. The series of engravings that illustrates these volumes are captivating, not only for the studied detail they elaborate but for the poses. The settings that frame these visions are mesmerizing, and some may be regarded as enchanting and/or macabre. Its production led to Vesalius' recognition and an appointment as physician to the imperial court – an honor analogous to the modern-day Nobel Prize.

The volume is approximately 16 by 11 inches and consists of more than 700 pages divided into seven sections or books. The first book deals with the bones of the body, the second with muscles. Books three and four describe the veins and arteries. Section five delves into the abdominal organs, while book six explores the thoracic contents. The crowning seventh section details the contents of the head. The engravings are integrated within the text, which are enriched with captions, cross references, and marginal annotations.

Leonardo Da Vinci

Leonardo Da Vinci (1452–1519), the original Renaissance man (one who displays talents in all fields), is generally recognized as the famous painter whose portrait of an unknown woman, the *Mona Lisa*, is the greatest artistic work from the Renaissance era. He was, however, far more than that. He was also an architect, sculptor, musician, and engineer.

Evidence of Leonardo's interest in knowledge of technical matters is clearly recognized in the many drawings and sketches that he left behind. His famous drawing of the human figure in perfect proportion with the square and the circle shows the harmony between Renaissance artistry and mathematics(15.2). The meticulous notes that accompanied

FATHER OF MODERN SURGERY
REJECTS DARWINISM

Joseph Lister (1827–1912) was acquainted with the principle of maintaining boundaries better than anyone alive in his generation. Lord Lister, a devout Quaker physician, is best known for pioneering aseptic surgical methods. Lister is also known as a co-founder of germ theory, as the physician for Queen Victoria, for the first successful use of permanent artificial limbs, and for working with wound infections. Lister identified himself on numerous occasions as a Bible-believing Christian who believed in special creation and rejected Darwinism.

Lister was a British physician who revolutionized surgery by preventing infection in surgical wounds. Lister, impressed with Pasteur's work on fermentation, completed his bacteriological studies. In particular, he investigated lactic acid fermentation and milk spoilage. Lister thought of milk spoilage as a type of infectious disease. Lister made the connection between how a specific bacterium causes "lactic ferment" in milk and how bacteria in surgical wounds often causes gangrene and pyemia in humans. Lister's laboratory studies of "milk diseases," in conjunction with Pasteur, led him to study "surgical diseases." Based on his observations of bacteria in air contaminating milk in flasks, Lister was able to apply the germ theory during his operations. He was also the first to be successful with the implantation of artificial limbs because he was able to keep them germ-free.

Lister wondered if minute organisms might also be responsible for the pus that forms in surgical wounds. He then experimented with a phenolic compound (**carbolic acid**), applying it at full strength to wounds by means of

Louis Pasteur and the
"Germ Theory of Disease"

Joseph Lister
"The Father of Modern Surgery"

FIGURE 15.1

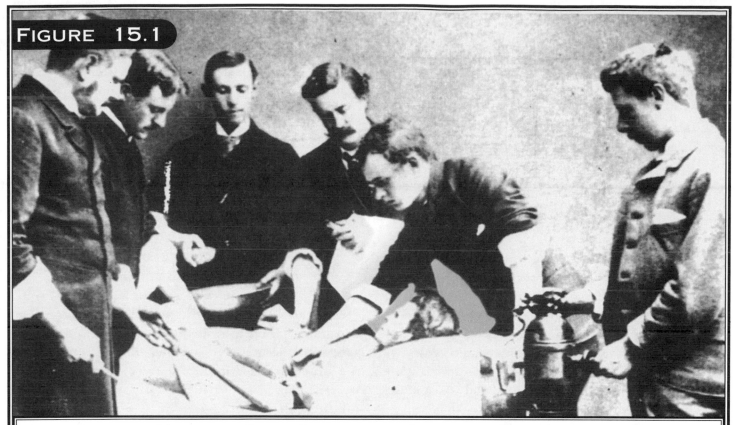

VICTORY OVER INFECTION. LISTER AND SPRAY.
Lister's discovery of antiseptics being used by these doctors who are performing an 1871 surgery in Edinburgh (Scotland). A carbolic acid (phenol) aerosol is sprayed with this instrument. It showers an antiseptic mist over the patient to kill the pathogens that cause infection providing a Victory Over Infection.

a saturated rag. Lister was particularly proud of the fact that after carbolic acid wound dressings became routine for his patients, the patients no longer developed gangrene. Later, Lister improved his antiseptic surgery to exclude bacteria from wounds by maintaining a clean environment in the operating room and by sterilizing instruments (figure 15.1). These procedures were preferable to killing the bacteria after they entered wounds because they avoided the toxic effects of the disinfectant on the wound. His technique of asepsis, along with hand washing, meant that most patients no longer suffered from new germs introduced during surgery. *The British Medical Journal* stated that "he [Lister] had saved more lives by the introduction of this system than all the wars of the 19th century together had sacrificed" (Nester et al., 1998, p. 202).

Early in his life, Lister suffered persecution because of his rejection of Darwinism. In one case, he may have been discriminated against in a competitive medical school exam because his ideas did not align with a medical school examiner on Darwin's views of comparative anatomy. Later, he contended with Darwinists over abiogenesis. Many Darwinists in the 1880s still believed in spontaneous generation and felt that germs in wounds could magically appear from nowhere. Like Pasteur, Lister dismissed this ancient, disproved idea. Lister had to defend his idea of biogenesis, that any bacteria found in wounds were a result of contamination in the surgery room. His answer was asepsis, clean hands, and a clean hospital. Perhaps he had read Bible passages like: "*This is the law…make a difference between the unclean and the clean*"(Lev. 11:46–47) and "Depart ye, go ye out from thence, touch no unclean thing; go ye out of the midst of her; be ye clean, that bear the vessels" (Isa. 52:11).

In conclusion, Lister revolutionized medicine because he practiced good science. This practice of good science was preceded by a Christian heritage and was grounded in the Bible. In the tradition of Louis Pasteur and Robert Koch, Lister applied the germ theory through his public promotion of cleanliness and sanitation to various governments and institutions all around the world, encouraging them to reduce tuberculosis and other major infections. The germ theory of disease is one of the most important concepts that needs to be understood in the age of AIDS and other deadly infectious diseases. Remember these historical events the next time you are in surgery or use Listerine mouthwash or toothpaste (Lister's namesake).

the sketches gave invaluable information that helped guide humanity to where it is today.

As a young man, Leonardo regularly participated in cadaver dissections and intended to publish a textbook on anatomy with an anatomy professor. When Leonardo died, his notes and sketches were lost and not discovered for more than 200 years. Leonardo's illustrations helped to create a new climate of visual attentiveness to the structure of the human body. He was intent on accuracy and his sketches are incredibly detailed. He experimentally determined the structure of complex body organs such as the brain. He made wax casts of the brain to study its structure. He also constructed models of the heart valves to demonstrate their action. Only a master could achieve the detail and accuracy of the sketches of Leonardo da Vinci. "The painter who has acquired a knowledge of the nature of the sinews, muscles and tendon," Leonardo wrote, "will know exactly in the movement of any limb how many and which of the sinews are the cause of it, and which muscle by its swelling is the cause of sinew's contracting."

A classic word picture that Leonardo used to describe the human body is one that envisions it as a machine. The body and a machine both perform work. Other Renaissance scholars also used this same analogy. At the close of the 15th century, Leonardo da Vinci made the most comprehensive study of the human body, yet he saw neither superfluous nor defective structure in man. In fact, he described the human anatomy as one of beauty and complexity. In addition, he made sketches of the body, in a study of proportions, and compared them with the most sophisticated machines in his time. Because the body was so masterfully engineered like a "machine," it has been the subject of many artists' work through the centuries.

Michelangelo

Michelangel Buonarotti

(1475–1564), perhaps the greatest artist of all time, exerted an enormous influence in the fields of art and science. He, too, was universally acknowledged as a supreme artist in his own lifetime because of the dramatic realism and sense of movement that were characteristic of his work. Unfortunately, his followers all too often present us with only the master's outward manner, like his muscularity and gigantic grandeur, but they miss the inspiration. There has never been a more literally awesome artist than Michelangelo: awesome in the scope of his

FIGURE 15.2

VITRUVIAN, BY LEONARDO DA VINCI, SHOWS THE PROPORTIONS OF THE HUMAN BODY.

imagination, awesome in his awareness of the significance – the spiritual significance – of beauty. Beauty was to him divine. It was one of the ways God communicated himself to humanity.

Isaac Newton

Isaac Newton, the "Father of Modern Science," contributed more to the scientific progress of mankind than any other individual before or since. Building upon the foundations and groundwork set by others, Newton strived with his brilliant mind to understand God's most basic laws of the physical universe.

In 1687, Newton published his discovery of the universal law of gravitation. He called the work *Mathematical Principles of Natural Philosophy*, also known as *Principia*. His universal law says that every particle of matter in the universe attracts every other particle of matter with a force that is directly proportional to its quantity of matter, and this force decreases proportionally as the distance between particles increases. Newton also explained the three laws of motion. These laws dealt with the concepts of inertia, the relationship of acceleration to physical force, and the action and reaction to force. He then related the three laws into the concept of momentum or the "quantity of motion."

Newton, who spent much of his life studying the Bible, searched for truth about God's creation and came to realize that there are profound facts about God's creation and governance of it that will forever elude the efforts of scientists that try to explain. He believed that studying creation would reveal the "fingerprints of God." It has been said that Newton's works are "the foundation stone of modern thought." Along with many other famous scientists

---

DISEASE FOCUS 15.2

THE BIBLE AND THE GERM THEORY

Since his fall, man has struggled to conquer disease, one of the curses brought upon him by sin. Only in the past two centuries, however, has man made great strides toward curing and preventing disease. Knowledge of anatomy and physiology grew during the 17th century, but progress in microbiology did not grow very much until the 1850s. In the 1870s, biologists began to link microorganisms with the presence of disease. Pathogens include forms, such as viruses, bacteria, molds, protozoans, rickettsiae, and multicellular parasites.

Louis Pasteur and **Robert Koch** were able to associate specific bacteria with certain diseases. Pasteur first developed his ideas of the germ theory from his work on fermentation of milk, butter, beets, beer, and wine. Then, Pasteur solved anthrax and rabies disease plagues by treating sheep and dogs using the germ theory concept. Pasteur applied his germ theory to vaccinating people against deadly diseases. Prior to Pasteur, the connection between microorganisms and disease was not apparent since many microbes were known to be beneficial for humans and did not cause disease.

During the 1800s, physicians such as Ignaz Semmelweis and Joseph Lister began to understand the role of microbes in causing disease and they applied aseptic principles in their medical practice. Semmelweis washed his hands in solutions of chlorinated lime (a strong disinfectant) prior to delivering babies, and the dreaded puerperal fever declined. Lister experimented with a carbolic acid (a phenol), introducing it into wounds during surgery by means of a saturated rag. This technique, along with hand washing, meant that most patients no longer suffered from gas gangrene, poisoning of the blood, or amputation because of surgery. By the end of the 19th century, patients were less likely to die in the operating room because of disinfected surgical instruments and washing hands. Both Louis Pasteur and Joseph Lister expressed faith in God, and were to some extent "listening" to the Creator to solve medical plagues of their day. The practices of cleansing one's hands, instruments, and other objects date back to ancient Israel when Moses instructed the Israelites about purification. This was not just spiritual cleansing; it also had a useful medical purpose. Long before Semmelweis, Pasteur, Koch, and Lister, the Creator instructed His people in ancient times to distinguish between the unclean and the clean, the antiseptic principle (Lev. 11: 47). In addition, He instructed man, in the Levitical law, about other disease principles such as quarantine, sanitation of body wastes, and disinfection, long before the Golden Age of Microbiology.

of his day, Newton believed in creation and sought to understand the laws, set in motion by God, that govern it. Newton is frequently quoted, in regards to his study of science, as "thinking God's thoughts after Him." His studies were an extension of His faith in God.

Harvey and the Heart

It was not until the early 1600s that William Harvey gave the explanation of blood circulation that we recognize and know as fact today. Harvey, as mentioned in chapter 9, laid to rest many misconceptions that Galen had brought about through his work. In contrast to Galen, William Harvey's view of the heart and circulation rested not on books or on the opinions of his predecessors. They were based on direct ocular observations, dissections, and experimentation. In 1628, Harvey published a small book written in Latin called *Exercito Anatomica de Motu Cordis et Sanguninis* in *Animalibus*, which is translated as *An Anatomical Dissertation on the Movement of the Heart and Blood in Animals* (Harvey, 1628 reprint). It was that book that led to the understanding of the circulation of blood that we have today.

Harvey's ideas had been by far the most widely accepted of several competing theories of blood flow, but *De Motu Cordis* (as it is usually called) would, in time, bring about the ultimate demise for them all. Harvey used a combination of quantitative and qualitative methods to make a series of easily confirmable observations and measurements that led him to his conclusion. He proclaimed in one striking sentence the entire contents of chapter 14 in his monumental book:

> It must be of necessity concluded that the blood is driven in a round by circular motion in creatures and that is moves perpetually; and hence does arise the action and function of the heart, which by pulsation it performs; and lastly that motion and pulsation of the heart is the only cause (Harvey, 1628, p. 91).

With his work, Harvey no doubt meant to lay to rest the misguided confidence of his readers in those mystical attributes of the heart so dearly cherished by church people, kings, and commoners alike. Perhaps his message was not lost on Charles, though the royal patient must have taken consolation in knowing that his doctor believed so strongly in cardiac supremacy that he compared the heart's indispensability to that of the king himself.

Although the implications of Harvey's contribution were not at first universally appreciated, the publication of *De Motu Cordis* opened the way to a profusion of studies. These studies were aimed at elucidating aspects of cardiac function and the details of the various functions of its elements, such as blood pressure, the pulse, and the activity of cardiac muscle. Finally, in the late 18th century, physicians began to use the fruits of findings based on Harvey's principles to help them understand the diseased hearts of their patients. By the first decade of the 19th century the technique of percussion had been developed, by which it was possible to estimate the size of the heart by tapping on the chest. In 1817 the stethoscope was invented and cardiology advanced further.

Harvey had built upon the anatomical approach of **Paracelsus** (1490–1541). Paracelsus believed that if the structure of the body was to be learned, direct observation was essential rather than textbook anatomy. The combined work of these two men, Paracelsus and Vesalius, revolutionized the study of anatomy and brought about advances in the way science and medicine were done.

The importance of Paracelsus' work was that it clearly demonstrated that the flow of blood through the body is really a circulatory movement. This movement flows one way through the arteries, capillaries, and veins, all forming conducting channels. Harvey referred to the intricate and orderly circulatory patterns in the heart as the "fabric of life."

During this time period, it is remarkable that Harvey used the scientific method of exact experimentation and mathematical calculation to support his theory. He had no microscope capable of revealing the capillaries, but he reasoned that there must be such a connection between arteries and veins. Like the Darwinists of today, many people in Harvey's day refused to accept his explanation, especially those who favored the established ideas of Galen. **Marcello Malpighi** later demonstrated capillaries by means of a light microscope, in 1632. This discovery once and for all vindicated Harvey.

As Harvey discovered, the heart is actually two pumps, right and left, with a septum between the two sides so that the blood does not go from one side to the other. The left pump is somewhat larger and stronger than the right pump. Its function is to receive blood from the lungs in its upper chamber, or atrium, and send it out all over the body from its lower chamber, the ventricle. If you look at the heart of a preserved specimen you will note that the atrium has very thin walls. When it is contracted, it is very small. Notice the correlation of structure and function; the ventricles are designed to pump blood over far distances to the lungs and entire body, as indicated by their more muscular chambers. Atria are designed for receiving venous blood and pumping it downward only a short distance, to the larger, stronger ventricles. Hence, atria have thinner walls.

Harvey found the vessels involved in blood circulation also show a planned form-and-function relationship. When examining a cross-section of a vein, capillary, and artery, one can see a single layer of tissue called the endothelium. In veins and arteries, a muscular layer and a protective layer of connective tissue surround the endothelium. The arteries have a thick muscle layer to aid in pushing blood out to the body tissues farthest from the heart. The layers of the veins are thinner and more flexible than those of similarly sized arteries. This attribute fits their function of returning blood to the heart. Like Isaac Newton, Harvey believed the study of the human body would reveal the "fingerprints of God." Harvey's belief in God as the wise creator of the universe was accepted and considered the standard. It was not until the time of Darwin that the tide changed.

New Horizons

Several new projects have recently developed to advance the study of anatomy. These projects are being used more in educational settings to provide a phenomenal view of the human body, unavailable to previous generations of students. Two endeavors are the **Human Visible Project** and the **Vesalius Project**. Through these projects, scientists, once again, are beginning to rediscover and explore the evidences of the fabrica design.

Human Visible Project

Joseph Paul Jernigan spent much of his adult life involved in violent crimes. The convicted murderer was executed by the state of Texas in 1990. Since then, however, Jernigan has become a model for many students across the country – not a role model, but a scientific model. Jernigan's dead body was sliced, photographed, and digitized 1,800 ways to become the world's first computerized human cadaver. Teachers, doctors, and scientists now use Jernigan's "virtual cadaver" as a research and educational tool (figure 15.2).

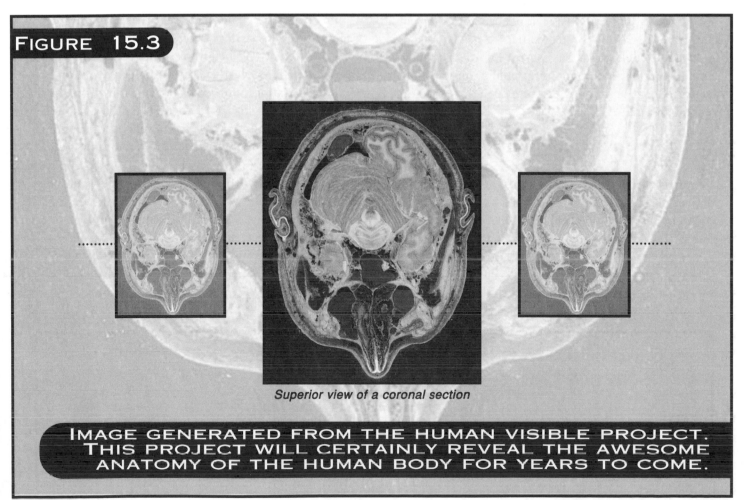

FIGURE 15.3

Superior view of a coronal section

IMAGE GENERATED FROM THE HUMAN VISIBLE PROJECT. THIS PROJECT WILL CERTAINLY REVEAL THE AWESOME ANATOMY OF THE HUMAN BODY FOR YEARS TO COME.

THE HUMAN GENOME PROJECT

The **Human Genome Project** (HGP) is an international research program designed to construct detailed genetic and physical maps of the human genome, to determine the complete nucleotide sequence of human DNA (over 3.5 billion base pairs), to localize the estimated 100,000 genes within the human genome. The U.S. government has invested over $3 billion to elucidate the entire DNA sequence that makes us human. The scientific products of the HGP will comprise a resource of detailed information about the structure, organization, and function of human DNA, information that constitutes the basic set of inherited "instructions" for the development and functioning of a human being. Because of new sequencing technologies, the project was bascially completed in the Summer of 2000. Improved technology for biomedical research will thus be another important product of the HGP. The acquisition and use of such genetic knowledge will have momentous implications for both individuals and society. It will pose a number of policy choices for public and professional discussion. Analysis of the ethical, legal, and social implications of genetic knowledge, and the development of policy options for public consideration are therefore yet another major component of the human genome research effort.

Joy in the Journey

Francis S. Collins, M.D., Ph.D., is the director of the Human Genome Project based at the National Institute of Health in Bethesda, Maryland. Dr. Collins showed great passion for his project — the mapping and sequencing of the human genome. As an enthusiastic Christian, Collins is concerned about how the public, especially physicians, view genetic research. He strongly believes that genetic research can provide seeds of hope for healing and alleviating human suffering. Dr. Collins feels that he is following the example of the Great Physician, Jesus Christ, who healed hundreds of people during His three-year ministry. Dr. Collins is a committed Christian who believes in an intelligent designer and believes in the sanctity of life.

When Dr. Collins was asked why he chose medical genetics as a specialty, his answer was simple: "The simplicity and elegance of the DNA molecule immediately appealed to me." He also finds great joy in discovery and for him the journey into discovering the genes that cause disease has brought great happiness because he knows that such knowledge may lead to cures for specific genetic disorders. He is motivated by this verse: "*And Jesus went about all the cities and villages, teaching in their synagogues, and preaching the gospel of the kingdom, and healing every sickness and every disease among the people*" (Matt. 9: 35*)*.

For Dr. Collins, genetics has been a natural extension of the medical research that he made for decades. Dr. Collins believes that locating specific genes for specific genetic disorders, such as cystic fibrosis, will lead the way for gene therapy and help those afflicted. Although such information can clearly lead to effective treatments, Collins is cautious and is aware that knowledge in the wrong hands can also lead to destruction. Cautiously optimistic, Collins believes sequencing the human genome will help people better appreciate the Creator's design for life and ultimately help those who suffer from birth to have extended life with dignity. He would agree with Dr. Marshall W. Nirenberg (winner of the Nobel Prize in medicine, 1968):

When man becomes capable of instructing his own cells, he must refrain from doing so until he has sufficient wisdom to use the knowledge for the benefit of mankind.

Human Genome Project. Karotype for each type of the 23 human chromosomes (haploid set of chromosomes shown in diagram).

CHECK YOUR UNDERSTANDING

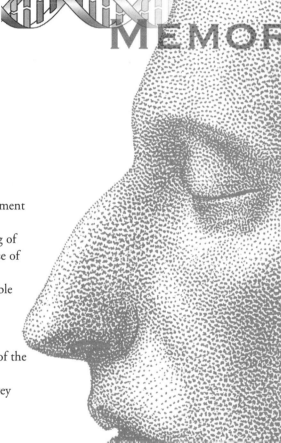

Classic and Contemporary Explorations in Human Biology

1. List three details about the contributions that Harvey made in the study of circulation.

2. What qualities made Andreas Vesalius' work, *De Humani Corporis*, a masterpiece of human anatomical studies and what made the text so revolutionary?

3. What misconceptions, stemming from Galen's works, pertained to blood and blood flow? Also, what permitted the farcical philosophies of Galen to pervade science for so long? What parallels exist between the philosophies of Galen and modern evolutionary thinking?

4. List details on how the work of Joseph Lister (and others) revolutionized surgery, and discuss how their work led to the germ theory of infection.

5. Discuss the germ theory and its importance in the advancement in the study of the causative agents of disease. Explain.

6. Essay: Discuss the role of cadaver dissection in the teaching of gross anatomy. Also, give reasons why you think that the use of cadavers may never completely come to an end.

7. Give reasons why the Vesalius Project and the Human Visible Project are beneficial in the study of the gross anatomy of the human body.

8. Consider the moral and ethical issues involved with the use of cadavers. The Bible says that the body is the temple of the Holy Ghost — does this apply after death?

9. One of the most important contributions of William Harvey was his research on the topic of:
   a) circulation of blood. b) the microscopic structure of spermatozoa. c) the detailed structure of the kidney. d) striped appearance of skeletal muscle.

10. The anatomical masterpiece *Fabrica* was the work of:
    a) da Vinci b) Harvey c) Vesalius d) Leeuwenhoek

11. You learned that Galen relied on dissections of animals other than humans in an attempt to understand human anatomy. Discuss the value and the limitations for using real specimens in a human anatomy laboratory. What advantages (and disadvantages) are gained by studying human cadavers vs. dissecting virtual images of human cadavers.

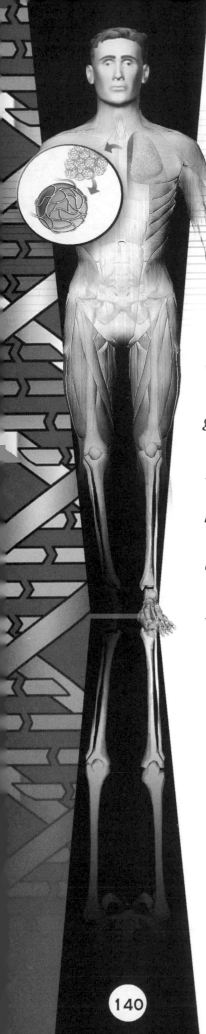

THE WISDOM OF THE BODY

CHAPTER 16

"The invisible hand that governs the universe with 'perfect intentionality' — has worked for the good of those who love him."

R. C. Sproul (1996, cover jacket)

So far, designs in the human body have been examined system by system, particularly in anatomy. These patterns have been systematically shown to be logical and at times wondrous. For the most part, a Creator of the universe, of living organisms, and particularly of mankindhas been shown in this book. Although confidently asserted these as truths, this is a minority opinion among professional biologists today. Most "professionals" (earned doctorates) assume an evolutionary origin of mankind has been shown. As we have already examined, this idea clashes with the position taken by the founders of many fields in biology, such as Vesalius, Harvey, Pasteur, Lister, Virchow, and Cuvier. In this chapter, we examine both the "doctrine" of evolutionary dogma and modern movement to recognize creation and design.

Evolutionary Dogma:

"Nothing in Biology Makes Sense Except in the Light of Evolution"

This is the title, thesis, and brazen pronouncement of the geneticist and committed evolutionist Theodosius Dobzhansky. Almost 30 years later, Steven Jay Gould (1999) maintains, "Evolution is not a false peripheral subject but the central start and organizing principle of all repeated biological science." It is Darwinian evolution, they maintain, that is the glue that holds all areas of biology together. This theme has become a watershed for the secular scientist. This idea has been cited hundreds of times in magazines, journals, and conference presentations that invoke evolution as fact. The article also proposes that evolution be integrated with everything in biology. Dobzhansky, Gould, Dawkins, and Huxley are the most influential evolutionists of the 20th century. What would cause these biologists to make such bold claims that nothing makes sense in science except in the light of evolution?

Molecular Evidence

In his article, Dobzhansky cites unreliable evidence. The same logic would be used for the famous molecule of heredity, DNA. Does this mean that all these vastly different organisms have genetic roots from one common ancestor as Dobzhansky maintained? It is more logical to argue that these biomolecules owe their existence to a common designer, not a common ancestor. Since all cells utilize DNA to reproduce, it is logical that the Creator would use the same molecule and efficient plan in creating cells. Secular biologists think that the universality of this information sequence in nearly all cells is evidence for a common ancestor of all life. But it is just as logical to view the same plan being used to code proteins in all living organisms. This is why the Mustang and Taurus have more in common with each other than do Ford cars and sailboats. It is the creation according to a common plan. Certainly as one looks at the code that is DNA, one would think of a code-giver.

Microevolution in Fruit Flies

Dobzhansky also spoke of subtle changes within varieties of fruit flies in Hawaii as evidence of "evolution" occurring today. There is no question that throughout the years various selective pressures have given advantage to some populations of flies and not others. Creationists certainly would agree to these minor changes called microevolution and to natural selection. **Natural selection** was even suggested 24 years before Darwin by a creation scientist named Edward Blyth. The question a student should ask is whether these minor variations in fly types lead to big changes (mega- or macroevolution). The answer may be given as a clear "No," using a variety of science methods. There is neither clear experimental evidence nor fossil from which one can extrapolate from micro to macroevolution. From beginning to end, we start with and end up with fruit flies — nothing more, nothing less. Science relies upon observation skills, and all that is observed are fruit flies.

Is Evolution a Fact?

Macroevolution is unfortunately taught as a scientific (empirical) fact. Nearly 30 years after Dobzhansky's pronouncement, this argument continues with evidence of change in **antibiotic-resistant bacteria**.

Many newspaper and popular accounts of evolution frequently cite the growing medical threat of multidrug resistance in bacteria as proof for evolution.

Antibiotic-resistant bacteria are hardly evidence for macroevolution. Although creation scientists acknowledge changes of antibiotic sensitivity in bacteria where genes are traded and transferred among them, these bacteria are still the same kind. Recently, an expedition to the Arctic uncovered the bodies of three men who perished in an 1845 expedition. Samples of bacteria were taken from their intestines and it was found that some of the bacteria were indeed resistant to modern-day antibiotics. This is just as the creation scientist would predict. There have always been some populations of bacteria that have had genes conferring a resistance to antibiotics.

Plasmid transfer, conjugation, and **transduction** are most likely the mechanisms for changing antibiotic resistance among bacteria. These mechanisms, however, allow for horizontal change, but not vertical evolution, in bacteria that are necessary for macroevolution to take place. Medical microbiologists, physicians, and hospital technologists are all interested in tracking the patterns of change in bacteria for practical reasons — being able to provide an effective antibiotic that will eliminate disease. Fortunately, they do not have to worry that the bacteria will evolve into a fungus or some other microbe. The bacteria are still bacteria and remain so. Therefore, the practitioner can resolve the resistance factor with new and better antibiotics.

We can say, therefore, that science done in the present (empirical science) would not support an extrapolation from very minor changes to macroevolution. Put another way, the only changes we see are horizontal (minor), certainly not large changes that would yield new kinds. No macroevolution has occurred in the past, and none is occurring in the present. There's no reason to believe it except that the alternative is unthinkable to the secular mind. We would do well to investigate some of the alleged evolutionary evidences that biologists claim to possess. Several of their evidences actually support the creation model.

Human Evolution

Java Man, Peking Man, Piltdown Man, Nutcracker Man, and *Ramapithecus* are all false starts on the trail from ape-like creatures to man. Evolutionary thinking has caused people to spend millions of dollars and thousands of man-hours looking in vain for links that will never be found. But the search continues for man's ancestor, because many still believe that "*Nothing in biology makes sense except in light of evolution.*"

Imperfections

Richard Dawkins continues the theme of evolution as a fact when he states, "*No serious biologist doubts the fact that evolution has happened, nor that all living creatures are cousins of one another*" (1996, p. 287). He discusses the imperfections in nature, such as the aberrations of eyesight in humans. He turns to Darwinian evolution to explain the gradual tinkering of natural selection and chance mutation and to explain the evolution of the eye. He discusses how a neutral evolutionary force over time makes images to the eye sharper and sharpest. He uses these examples of poor eyesight in man as proof of nature's tinkering with traits to produce superior eyesight. Yet there are no examples for this type of evolution seen today, nor is there a history of eye transitions observed in the fossil record.

Defects and Disease

Even though there is no fossil record to support things like eye evolution, the question lingers, "If your God is so intelligent and loving, why are there so many defects in the human body — disease, and painful things in this world." The answer in short is that we do not claim to have "perfect design," but rather intelligent design due to the fallen condition of mankind. In this section we deal with consequences "after the Garden of Eden."

Imperfections of the eye (nearsightedness, farsightedness, and astigmatism) are merely a consequence of the fall of man. In the biblical account of creation, man was not merely made a complex animal, but a creature made in the image of God. Shortly after his creation, man stained this image by disobedience to his Creator. Man's image became tarnished and any of his "imperfections," defects, and diseases are consequences of his fall from perfection. Yet, in spite of being marred by sin, we still observe many wonders in the human body. The intelligent design and many adaptations found in the human body are perfect testimonies to the Creator's wisdom and greatness. Man continues to be sustained by the one in whose hand is the soul of every living thing, and the breath of all mankind (Job 12:10). We might summarize

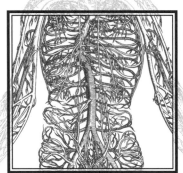

man's divine image as flawed, but not eliminated.

Recall that Leonardo da Vinci saw man as the pinnacle of creation and a spectacular object of study in spite of his fall. Da Vinci, during the Renaissance period, made the most anatomically comprehensive study of the human body. Although he did not view man as perfect, he saw humans as possessing the most wonderful and magnificent design in nature. He saw neither superfluous nor defective structures in man. Leonardo da Vinci looked for ways to describe this masterpiece of engineering, beauty, complexity, and symmetry. In his study of body proportions, he frequently made the analogy between man and machine.

Dealing with Imperfections

The human body has been willed into existence by a loving Creator and placed on a planet that, despite all its pain and fear, contains much beauty and goodness. We can still develop a consistent outlook of gratitude, undergirded by trust in the One who made us. Dr. Paul Brand still concludes the human body and all nature has been made wondrously even after searching many of the dark spots and blemishes on the world. How could a truly good God allow such blemishes to exist? Dr. Brand took them on one by one. Disease? Did you know that 90 to 95 percent of all bacteria do not cause disease? Rather, many are healthful, not harmful. In fact, some are essential for our living as discussed in chapter 7. Plants could not produce oxygen and animals could not digest food without the assistance of bacteria. Most agents of disease diverge from these necessary organisms as only slight mutations.

What about birth defects? Although there are environmental events that cause DNA to mutate and lead to imperfections at birth, there are many complex details in biochemistry that are needed and must work right just to produce one healthy child. The great wonder is not that birth defects exist but that millions more do not occur. Could a mistake-proof world have been created so that DNA spirals would never err in transmission? No scientist could envision such a system without the possibility of error in our world of physical laws.

Even at its worst, our natural world shows evidence of careful design. Imagine a world without tornadoes or hurricanes — calamities that carry the damaging label "acts of God." When hurricanes and monsoons do not come, the delicate balance of weather conditions gets upset, and killer droughts inevitably follow. How would you improve upon the world?

Dr. Brand's professional life has centered on perhaps the most problematic aspect of creation – the existence of pain. He emphatically insists on pain's great value, holding up as proof the terrible results of leprosy – damaged faces, blindness, and loss of fingers, toes and limbs – that nearly all occur as side-effects of painlessness.

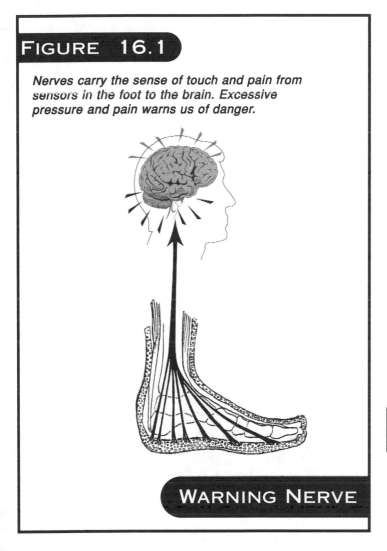

FIGURE 16.1

Nerves carry the sense of touch and pain from sensors in the foot to the brain. Excessive pressure and pain warns us of danger.

WARNING NERVE

Leprosy destroys nerve endings that carry pain signals. People who do not feel pain almost inevitably damage themselves; infection sets in, and no pain signals alert them to tend to the wounded area. Even the best artificial pain systems do not produce the sensation these people need to have protection against injury. "Thank God for pain!" and "Pain is the gift nobody wants," are Brand's conclusions after observing people who lack it.

Like Dr. Brand, we can develop gratitude, trust, and appreciation regarding those things that may contradict our intuition. Some designs at first glance seem flawed, but a deeper investigation reveals wisdom beyond man's imagination. As thinking creation scientists, we may struggle

with perplexing patterns in nature. Until Adam and Eve sinned, human bodies were without flaw. After the fall of man, however, humans have been subject to disease, decay, and death. God promises to give the Christian a new body someday that will be free from death and the necessity of pain. Some questions may never be answered in this lifetime. Ultimately, another world is coming where perfection will be restored.

In this present world, we must understand that nerve cells wear out and die, never to be replaced. Eventually eyesight, muscle coordination, and mental awareness will fail us all. Because of an accumulation of years of deposits, the blood vessels eventually narrow, diminishing the life-giving flow of blood. Heart disease, heart attacks, and strokes lay people in the grave on a daily basis. These are the resulting symptoms of old age. Eventually this well-designed machine, the human body, wears out. Three thousand years ago, King Solomon described this inevitable plight in Ecclesiastes 12: 1, 6, 7:

> *Remember now thy Creator in the days of thy youth, while the evil days come not, nor the years draw nigh, when... the silver cord be loosed, or the golden bowl be broken, or the pitcher be broken at the fountain, or the wheel broken at the cistern. Then shall the dust return to the earth as it was: and the spirit shall return unto God who gave it.*

Yet, in spite of aging, decay, and disease, the design of the human body is still a marvel of engineering. Man has yet to improve on a single design with an artificial substitute.

More Living Designs

The greatest biochemical discovery of the 20th century was the unraveling of the chemical structure of chromosomes. Recall, the language of genetics is founded in the pairs of nucleotide bases (A, T, C, G, and U). The sequence of bases in DNA and RNA is actually a code for amino acids, the building blocks for proteins, such as albumin, immunoglobulin, fibrinogen, and other proteins found in blood.

A remarkable analogy exists between human language and genetic language. By common agreement, numbers are the elements of computer language that are used by intelligent humans to code for letters. Similarly, the elements of the biochemical code (the four nucleotide bases) were organized by an intelligent cause to code for amino acids. Ultimately, the letters that humans use, as delineated by computer code, are assembled to form words for the purpose of communicating concepts. In the same way, amino acids, as delineated by the genetic code, are assembled to form proteins for the purpose of producing living components, like erythrocytes, leukocytes, and platelets. The similarity between the two codes is great enough to support a general conclusion by our "principle of uniform experience." There must be an intelligent cause for both.

Intelligent humans devised the computer code in a fashion similar to the way an intelligent cause devised the genetic code. We note that human intelligence is external to the computer code, and we stipulate that an intelligent cause is external to the genetic code. Thus, the intelligence is not latent within the genetic language itself, as the pantheist might assume. The similarity in the DNA code exists because the Creator used a similar plan to fashion the diversity of life on earth. Likewise, the numbers in the computer code have no meaning, unless words and language exist external to the order. Similarly, the sequence of bases in DNA has no meaning without the amino acids. The machinery external to the code builds proteins in red blood cells.

Not only is the intelligence external to the genetic code, but the intelligence must have incredible sophistication. It can be concluded that, because man is just beginning to understand DNA structure, the origin of life was caused by a source with greater intelligence and manipulative ability than man. Yet even this is still an insufficient picture of the structure of this cause. DNA is only a small part of the simplest cell's complexity. Without the ability to reproduce itself, the DNA would eventually succumb to destruction. The process of replication, therefore, is essential to life. Without transcription and translation of DNA into cellular materials, the information is useless.

Thus, transcription and translation are necessary for life, as well. Upon consideration of these and the tremendous complexities of even the simplest cell, it becomes clear that the origin of the red blood cell must be assigned to a cause with incredible intelligence and manipulative ability.

Compared to the functional complexity of cells like erythrocytes, leukocytes, and platelets, man's most noteworthy technological achievements seem primitive. The discovery of the unique design and functional complexity of living organisms has caused many to doubt the naturalistic origin of life

components in man. Logic demands that the languages of life (DNA, RNA, and amino acids) be interpreted as indicators of God's work.

Explanatory Filter

For many years, recognizing design has been informal and intuitive. More recently several design proponents have more formally taken steps to identify in nature what constitutes intelligent design. According to Behe (1996), the argument for design is "when a number of separate, very unlikely events combine to produce something as complex as life, we suspect that the conditions were intentionally arranged for the purpose."

Intelligent design makes our thinking more precise and

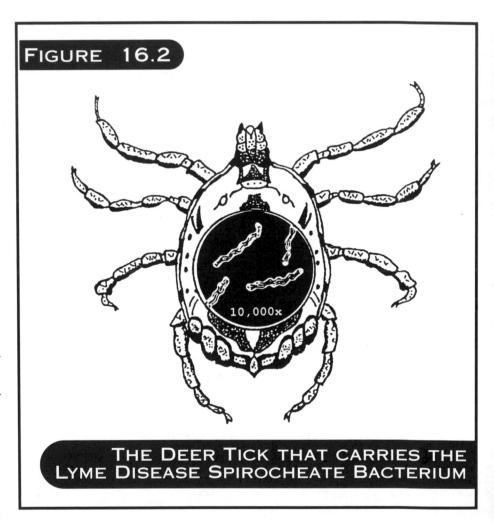

FIGURE 16.2

10,000x

THE DEER TICK THAT CARRIES THE LYME DISEASE SPIROCHEATE BACTERIUM

our logic more scientific. Most of us are engaged in a form of rational activity that, without being tendentious, can be described as inferring design. Inferring design is a perfectly common and well-accepted human activity. People find it important to identify events that are caused through the purposeful, premeditated action of an intelligent agent, and to distinguish such events from events due to either

DETECTIVE WORK AND THE NATURE OF SCIENCE

Detection of Design is Like Detecting Disease

Let us focus on how the cause of **Lyme disease** was discovered and how it compares to detecting created design in living things. In both cases, scientists look for clues that might correlate a cause with an effect. An **epidemiologist** looks for a specific microbe with an infectious disease, studies the pattern of disease distribution, and applies statistics to find the probable cause of a given disease. Those looking for clues of design in living things must find things that cannot be explained by chance physiochemical processes. Detectives need keen observation, problem-solving ability, and critical thinking skills.

Discovery of Lyme Disease's Cause

In 1975, the Connecticut Health Department received hundreds of calls about cases of what appeared to be arthritis in children in Lyme, Connecticut. Despite being assured by their physicians that arthritis was not infectious, the callers were not satisfied. A state epidemic investigation was put into action. Public health officials began trying to locate all those who had a sudden onset of swelling and pain in the knee or other joints. This odd disease seemed to occur from late spring throughout summer and lasted from a week to a few months.

Most patients had symptoms in three stages. The first stage was characterized by a skin rash that began as a red spot or bump and slowly enlarged. Second-stage symptoms included influenza-like fatigue, chills, fever, headache, stiff neck, and backache. In the third stage, swelling and tenderness accompanied by pain would afflict certain joints of the body. These symptoms developed in most untreated cases, beginning about six months after the rash, and slowly disappearing over years. It was later discovered that bacteria multiplying and spreading across the skin disseminated into the body tissues through the bloodstream. Immune reactions to this process produced tissue damage. Health officials began calling this affliction "Lyme arthritis."

The clustering of cases was most reported in wooded areas along lakes and streams. This suggested that the disease was transmitted by an arthropod. As officials investigated further, they found that people who had a household pet were more likely to be affected than those who weren't pet owners. The importance of this finding was emphasized when most patients reported that their arthritic symptoms were preceded with an unusual bull's-eye skin rash that spread to a six-inch ring. The officials began to suspect ticks as the carriers of the bacteria. Pet owners would be more likely to come into contact with ticks that their dogs and cats had picked up in the woods.

As scientists outside of Connecticut studied the problem, they found **spirochete** bacteria in the guts of many of the ticks. The spirochete was named **Borrelia burgdorferi**. Later, it was determined that this microbe was the cause of Lyme disease. Thereafter, physicians began to treat Lyme disease effectively with antibiotics. Presently, scientists have recommended prevention techniques like wearing protective clothing, tick repellents, and using a vaccine named Lymerix. In short, the detection of ticks has helped to alleviate suffering from Lyme disease. The process of detecting causes of disease is often tedious and time consuming, but the outcome of saving lives makes this effort worthwhile. Likewise, learning to detect design in nature and telling others about their finding may ultimately help people discover their Creator and in turn find life more abundantly.

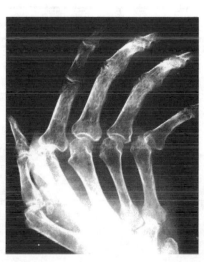

Lyme arthritis (right) as revealed by an x-ray of the right hand. Notice the swollen joints.

law or chance. Design theory unpacks the logic of this everyday activity, and applies it to questions in science. There's no magic, no vitalism, and no appeal to the occult supernatural. Inferring design is rational, objective, and nearly universal.

According to Dembski, the key step in formulating intelligent design as a scientific theory is to delineate a method for detecting design. Such a method exists, and in fact, we use it implicitly all the time. The method takes the form of a three-stage **explanatory filter**. Given something we think might be designed, we refer it to the filter. If it successfully passes all three stages of the filter, then we are warranted asserting it is designed. In general, the filter asks three questions, and in the following order: (1) Does a law explain it? (2) Does chance explain it? (3) Does design explain it? To see how the filter works in practice, consider the case of the interwoven pattern.

Is It Designed?

Any scientific idea must go through a filter to determine its truthfulness or validity. In order to say something is designed, from a scientist's perspective, we must first demonstrate that neither law nor chance can explain it alone. Let's examine the claim in this book that human body parts that have an interwoven pattern (and its synonyms) are a result of intelligent causation. At the first stage, the filter determines whether a law can explain the thing in question. Clearly, if a law can explain something, it cannot be proven as designed. Things explainable by a law are therefore eliminated at the first stage of the explanatory filter.

Suppose, however, no law is able to explain the pattern we think is designed. We then proceed to the second stage of the filter that determines whether the thing in question might be reasonably expected to occur by chance. Clearly, if something can be explained by reference to chance, it cannot be attributed to design. Things explainable by chance are therefore eliminated at the second stage of the explanatory filter.

In terms of the interwoven pattern, there is no law that is able to account for its occurrence, nor is there any plausible probability that might account for its occurring by chance. In this case, we bypass the first two stages of the explanatory filter and arrive at the third and final stage. Vast improbability predicts design if we notice that the interwoven pattern is specified.

We find that the interwoven pattern of DNA is specified in its base pairing and that its message is ordered beyond any random probability. Chance or law cannot explain – therefore, it must be designed. It is this category of specified things and having a very low chance of random occurrence that tells us the pattern is not an accident. The third stage of the explanatory filter therefore presents us with a choice. We must accept the logic of common experience that tells us that human body parts that have multiple, interdependent parts are designed and, in turn, created by a Designer. If we reject this intuitive conclusion, we deny the truth. This has been the habit of skeptics and atheists. They reject this marvelous interweaving and say that it is all a product of time and chance.

For some of them, they see this "apparent" design, not "real" design. In this next section, we will examine similar patterns in the human body that have made it through the filter.

TABLE 16.1	Interdependence in the Human Body

TERM	EXAMPLE
Cell team	B- and T-lymphocytes of the immune system
Compound traits	The eye and its external muscles
Interwoven molecules (interlacing, intertwined)	DNA with its coiled histones
Interdependent parts	Nephron, capillaries, and renal tubules of the excretory system
Irreducible complexity	Blood clotting cascades

DESIGN FOCUS 16.1

THE STAR-SPANGLED BANNER AND THE SECOND LAW

Decay of the American Flag Over 200 Years

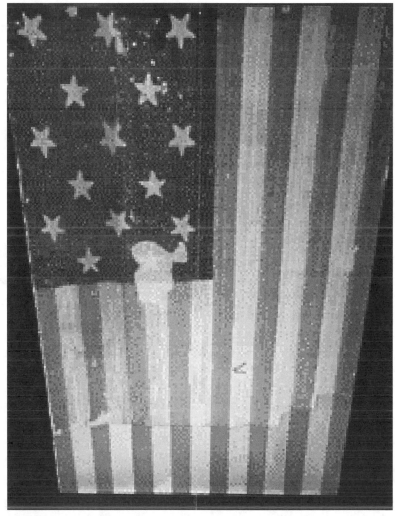

The famed **Star-Spangled Banner**, the flag that flew in 1814 during the War of 1812 in the United State represents a great historical moment. Since its manufacture in 1812 it has continued to decay. Tens of thousands of dollars have gone into restoration of this great flag. So, over time, fabric does not become more complex and highly integrated, it deteriorates. The evolutionist claims that if you have enough time, then, the blind watchmaker working with mutation, selection and the right environment will produce complex tapestries.

Despite the evidence, the second law of thermodynamics (**entropy**) doesn't seem to apply to living things according to the evolutionist. Entropy is a fundamental law in nature that predicts that disorder will always increase in all structured systems. They would rather imagine that human evolution is an exception to the law of decay. So which model – evolution or creation – makes more sense and is consistent with entropy? Things do not go uphill without energy, some directed force, and/or intelligence.

How then could random chance and natural selection forces produce something as highly integrated as a kidney nephron and a capillary network in an intestinal villus? It is highly improbable. A tornado going through a junkyard is more likely to produce a 747 jet than for the formation of even one interwoven body part from macroevolution. Therefore, they must have been fashioned by the Creator!

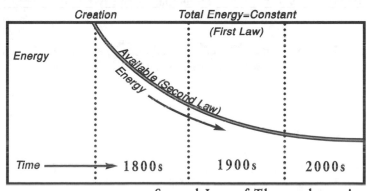

Second Law of Thermodynamics

Interdependence

In many respects, the theme of interdependence is the strongest evidence for creation. The concept of interdependence of body parts is one of the most recognizable themes in the disciplines of biochemistry, cell biology, and human anatomy and physiology. It is repeated in many diverse sets of cells, organs, and organ systems. The famous comparative anatomist George Cuvier, in the 18th Century developed a similar notion of irreducible complexity, calling it the correlation of parts. Cuvier, a firm creationist, advanced this argument in debates against evolution. In the 20th century, other scientists, such as Dean Kenyon, Michael Denton, and Michael Behe have also argued for design in light of the evidence of the interdependence and complexity of body structures.

Related terms used by various authors to describe this phenomenon of interdependence include adaptation package, cell team, compound traits, emergent properties, irreducible complexity, molecular team, and synergism. This resulting condition of interdependent body parts working together is that the sum of the actions is greater than the separate, individual actions. A summary of terms with examples is given in table 16.1.

Living cells, as well as specific organs in the human body, will not work unless every part is there at the same time. There is a tremendous advantage to cooperation in the body at all levels from the molecular to the systematic level.

Detective Work

In analyzing the human body systems and their origin, you need to become a sleuth. Sleuths are detectives, trackers, or bloodhounds who search for a criminal, or an elusive clue. The way to check the plausibility of an origin's model is to consider circumstantial evidence. In a murder case with no eyewitnesses, detectives must rely on the strength of such evidence.

Epidemiologists, or medical detectives, discover an epidemic in progress and define circumstances under which a disease spreads. They look for clues that might correlate a specific microbe with an infectious disease, studying the pattern of disease distribution, and applying statistics to find the probable cause of a given disease (See Disease Focus 16.1). Sleuths need keen observation, problem-solving, and critical thinking skills. Sleuths possess traits like those of "Sherlock Holmes": patience, persistence, discipline, and creativity. They must be open to new methods while maintaining their traditional traits of being a good "bloodhound."

FIGURE 16.3

DETECTING DESIGN

NOTHING IN BIOLOGY MAKES SENSE EXCEPT IN LIGHT OF THE EVIDENCE

As you examine new data in the organization of the human body, we encourage you to think critically, like a detective would. Be aware of the assumptions that go into each way of thinking, from a design versus a blind watchmaker (chance) perspective. You will want to utilize a variety of methods and skills to understand the nature of human body origins. Should the disciplines of human anatomy and physiology be explained by special creation or by macroevolution? You must make an intelligent choice.

Conclusions

In conclusion, intelligent design in the human body may be observed in the purposeful arrangement of individual parts in the 11 body systems. The idea of design flows naturally from the data and from arguments from the Bible. The products of the human body appear not to be by chance and necessity, but rather they appear to be planned. New data from medical research verifies the time-tested analogy that the human body and its functions are like a finely tuned computer. The Creator knew what completed and functional systems look like, then took steps to bring the systems into being. The human body, in its most critical components, appears to be the product of intelligent activity.

Design is most evident when a number of separate, interacting components are ordered in such a way as to accomplish a function beyond the individual components. In general, the greater the specificity of the required, interacting components to produce a specific function, the greater the probability and confidence that its origin was by intelligent design.

As examined, the processes in the human body are very complex in the 11 body systems and are evidences that some designer is responsible for this marvelous body plan. Isaac Newton said, "In the absence of any other proof, the thumb alone would convince me of God's existence." Today, more and more scientists are once again agreeing with Newton. For over a century, very few scientists had a satisfactory, scientific answer to Darwin's theory, but an increasing number of professional biological scientists see intelligent design as a reasonable alternative to evolution.

The wonder of the human body is not new. In fact it was revered long ago. As we study the intricacies of the human body, we must conclude that its design was not only intelligent, but was wonderful because it is a product of a personal and skilled Creator. In fact, King David got it right when he penned these words over 3,000 years ago:

For Thou hast possessed my reins: Thou hast covered me in my mother's womb. I will praise thee, for I am fearfully and wonderfully made: marvelous are thy works, and that my soul knoweth right well. My substance was not hidden from thee, when I was made in secret, and curiously wrought in the lowest parts of the earth. Thine eyes saw my substance yet being unperfect.

DESIGN FOCUS 16.2

THE HUMAN BODY, CROWN OF CREATION

Design, purpose, and amazing patterns are revealed in the human body as the handiwork of our wonderful Lord. Each vertebrae of the body has an even number of segments. Each hand has an even number of muscles and tendons in its forearm. The Master Craftsman fashions a masterpiece that human hands have never, and will never, be able to duplicate. He is a skilled engineer, stringing a network of nerves – a system of communication that makes the telephone systems in our largest cities seem simple in comparison. He adds muscles and ligaments, each in the exact size, not too long nor too short, planned skillfully to suspend, support, and act as the guy wires of a suspension bridge. Then a framework, architecturally perfect, of lime and other minerals for reinforcement, molding and shaping each bone for the stress and strain its location calls for without any precision instruments, without any trial fitting or experimental tests. He built each bone perfectly. All the wonders of construction and yet more! Is it by chance? Meditate upon this saying of a famous mathematician of the 18th century. Abram de Moivre, in 1718, said, "The same Arguments which explode the Notion of Luck, may, on the other side, be useful in some Cases to establish a due comparison between chance and Design: We may imagine Chance and Design to be as it were, in competition with each other, for the production of some sorts of Events, and may calculate what Probability there is, that those events should be rather owing to one than to the other" (Dembski, 1998, p. v.).

Who Is This Architect?

You may wonder who is this great **Architect of the human body**. He made us, bought us, heals us, and gives purpose to our lives. In Genesis, He is the one who declared us to have been made "very good." In Exodus, He is *Jehovah Rapha*, "the One who heals." In Job, He is the **Intelligent Designer** who fashioned our inward parts with wisdom. In Psalms, the He is the **Maker of Mankind** that is fearfully and wonderfully made. In Isaiah, He is the **Colossal Creator** who cares for us. In Luke He is the **Great Physician**. In Colossians, He is **Christ the Creator** who holds us together with invisible forces (molecular bonds, like DNA). In Ephesians, He is the **Skilled Craftsman** who compacted and knit us together. In John and Revelation, He is none other than **Jesus Christ**!

And in thy book all my members were written, which in continuance were fashioned when as yet there was none of them (Ps. 139: 13-16).

Contemporary interpretation of blood clotting mechanisms by scientists is analogous to the interpretation of historical events made by various "wise men" during the day of Daniel and the reign of Belshazzar. The ancient Babylonian prophet Daniel was a man who understood science (Dan. 1:4), gifted by God to interpret difficult enigmas. At a critical point in history, the Creator's hand became visible (Dan. 5) and wrote a message on the wall of Belshazzar's palace for all to see. Although many of the king's choice scholars read the inscription, only Daniel, a man who understood that God was omniscient (all knowing) could tell the meaning of the cryptic words. He was able to interpret the "handwriting on the wall," (Dan. 5:5). Daniel understood this writing because he trusted God to reveal the solution to this unsolved mystery.

Today the message is not one of written revelation, but one that is more subtle: the revelation of God's glory in His handiwork (Ps. 19:1), the human body. Sometimes molecular biologists encounter cryptic messages and unsolved mysteries in determining the mechanisms behind physiological patterns and pathological conditions. Sometimes dental researchers encounter anatomical anomalies, like the facial, sphenomandibularis muscle, and find its function puzzling. Biochemists study "biological messages" in the language of life, DNA, and in the intricacies of blood clotting and the immune response. In a sense, these microscopic observations are modern examples of "handwriting on the wall." As creation scientists, we must follow Daniel's example by asking God to illumine the mysteries, the themes, and the enigmas encountered in today's biological world. It is the Creator who gives understanding to these patterns. Although the secular scientist works by his own "light" and ignores God in this thinking about the natural world, the creation scientist, in contrast, looks to the Creator's Word to illumine his mind for understanding. It is there that he finds truth.

In Daniel's day, the message from the hand was one of impending judgment. Today, with an understanding of Scripture and a prudent study of biological "fingerprints," one can see a message in the physiological patterns. Today, the message is that the designs in the human body were crafted by an all-wise Maker and He cares for you, His creation. This same Creator is also judge, and His word says that we will all be accountable to Him someday (Rom. 1:29). One can still see clear writing on the wall: that someday we will meet our Maker who has been sending subtle messages to us all along. He is present in our world.

The watchmaker is not blind as some contend, nor is evolution the "glue" that holds all biology together. But, rather, it is the hand of the Creator that holds all things together by His power (Col. 1:16–17). Therefore, the best scheme that links (or "glues") all biology together is intelligent design. Nothing makes sense in biology, except in the light of evidence! There are dozens of examples of interwoven complexities, or fabric-like designs, in the body for the open-minded biologist. The invisible attributes observed in human anatomy challenge the Darwinian dogma for an evolutionary origin of humans. The Psalmist said that he was fearfully and wonderfully made. A modern paraphrase is that our body displays an awesome and distinctive blueprint. If we were to explore further the histology of wound healing, bone restoration, and tissue regeneration, we would discover more fingerprints of the Great Physician. *Jehovah Rapha* has the power to heal the body because He is the One who made it. The same "cell-stitching" that He designed in His original blueprint can be restored when the body is injured. He is able to mend it back together because He is the Master Craftsman.

Although God may be invisible to our physical eyes, He provides us with sufficient "light" to "see" Him with spiritual eyes. The Bible is our divine revelation and the Father's world is our natural revelation. Both illumine our minds with evidence to understand the patterns of the human body. The wisdom of God is revealed in the living Word, Jesus Christ; in the written Word, the Bible; and in nature. The natural "fingerprints" from His invisible hand are a testimony to the Creator's glory and His care for all life (Ps. 8:4; 19:1). The fact that this Creator also gives us a plan and purpose for life is our fortress, our shield, and our very great reward. This book only scratches the surface of human anatomy, but we have presented adequate evidence to testify that the human body themes are in fact "fingerprints" from His invisible hand. There is in fact, "wisdom in the inward parts"!

CHECK YOUR UNDERSTANDING

THOUGHTS
KNOWLEDGE
MEMORY

Wisdom of the Body

1. Explain why intelligent design is the theme that links all biology themes. Why is evolution (molecules to man) not the "glue" that holds all biology together?

2. List several examples of microevolution.

3. Explain the principle of uniform experience and how it relates to the intelligent design.

4. Illustrate how you might recognize design in DNA (and other living systems).

5. Discuss how disease, decay, and death fit into a creation model of life.

6. Illustrate how there is "wisdom in the inward parts."

7. In your own words, summarize the steps involved with the explanatory filter method of detecting design.

8. Consider the mousetrap illustration of interdependence. Try to find 2 or 3 other objects or analogous structures in the room that contain similar interdependence.

9. Name 3 or 4 additional interdependent structures in the human body similar to those in table 16.1.

10. Finally, find a magazine article describing a recent outbreak of an infectious disease. If they are mentioned, analyze the methods used by the epidemiologists to find and treat the causative agent of the disease. See if you can find the "sleuth work" involved. Using these same methods and skills, analyze a published article on human origins, anatomy, or physiology. Do you arrive at the same conclusions as the author? Why or why not?

References

Behe, M. J. 1996. *Darwin's Black Box: The Biochemical Challenge to Evolution.* The Free Press. New York.

Bergman, Jerry, Ph.D. and Howe, G. 1990. *Vestigial Organs Are Fully Functional.* Creation Research Society Books. Kansas City, MO.

Brand, P. and Yancey, P. 1980. *Fearfully and Wonderfully Made.* Zondervan. Grand Rapids, MI.

Brand, P. 1991. *You Are Wonderful; Part #4, Hormones Video.* Norlynn A/V Services. N. Vancouver, B. C., Canada.

Cosgrove, M. 1987. *The Amazing Body Human: God's Design for Personhood.* Baker Books. Grand Rapids, MI.

Cuozzo, J. 1998. *Buried Alive.* Master Books. Green Forest, Arkansas.

Darwin, C. 1859. *The Origin of Species* (Reprint of first edition). Avenue Books. New York.

Dawkins, R. 1996a. *The Blind Watchmaker.* W. W. Norton and Company. New York.

Dawkins, R. 1996b. *Climbing Mount Improbable.* W. W. Norton and Company. New York.

Dembski, W. 1998. *The Design Inference.* Cambridge University Press. Cambridge, England.

Eidsmoe, J. 1987. *Christianity and the Constitution.* Baker Book House. Grand Rapids, MI.

Eakin, R. M. 1982. *Great Scientists Speak Again.* University of California Press. Berkeley, CA.

Glasser, R. J. 1976. *The Body is the Hero.* Random House. New York.

Gould, S. J. 1980. *The Panda's Thumb.* W. W. Norton and Company. New York.

Gould, S. J. 1999. "*Dorothy, It's Really Oz*: A Pro-creationist Decision is More Than a Blow Against Darwin." *Time Magazine, 154 (8)*: 1-2.

Gray, N. 1901. *Gray's Anatomy, fifteenth edition.* (Editors T. P. Pick and R. Howden). Barnes and Noble, Inc. New York.

Guyton, A. C. 1991. *Textbook of Medical Physiology, eighth edition.* W. B. Saunders. Philadelphia, PA.

Harvey, W. 1995 (reprint of 1628 edition). *De Motu Cordis: Anatomical Exercises Concerning the Motion of the Heart and Blood in Living Creatures.* Dover Books. Mineola, NY.

Jackson, W. 1993. *The Human Body: Accident or Design?* Courier Publications. Stockton, CA.

Katz, D. 1972. "Tonsillectomy: Boom or Boondoggle?" *Detroit Free Press*, April 13, p. 1-C.

Life Magazine Eds. 1997. "A Fantastic Voyage Through the Human Body." New York. *Life Magazine, 2*: pp. 59-81.

Menton, D. 1991. Eye Analogy on Creation Science Home Page. Web Site Address. http://emporium.turnpike.net/C/cs/.

Morris, H. M. 1988. *Men of Science, Men of God.* Master Books, Inc. Green Forest, AR.

Morris, H. M. 1995. *Defender's Study Bible, (KJV).* Word Publishing. Grand Rapids, MI.

National Academy of Science Editors. 1998. *Teaching About Evolution and the Nature of Science.* National Academy Press. Washington, DC.

Nester, E. N., Roberts, C. E., Pearsall, N. N., Anderson, D. G., Nester, M. T. 1998. *Microbiology: A Human Perspective, second edition.* WCB McGraw-Hill. Boston, MA.

Nuland, S. B. 1997. *The Wisdom of the Body.* Alfred Knopf. New York.

Paley, W. 1802. *Natural Theology.* Lincoln-Rembrandt Publishers (Reprinted in 1997). Charlottesville, VA.

Parker, G. 1996. *Creation: Facts of Life.* Master Books. Green Forest, AR.

Ryrie, C. 1994. *Ryrie Study Bible, Expanded ed., (KJV).* Moody Press, Chicago, IL.

Shakespeare, W. 1992. *Hamlet.* Dover Thrift Edition. Dover Publishing. New York.

Sproul, R. C. 1996. *The Invisible Hand.* Word. Dallas, TX.

Stevens, J. 1985. Quoted by David Menton (1991). *The Eye on Creation Science Home page.* Technical and In depth Papers. http://emporium.turnpike.net/C/cs/.

Strong, 1948. *Strong's Exhaustive Concordance of the Bible.* Royal Publishers, Inc. Nashville, TN.

Tortora, G. J. and Grabowski, S. R. 2000. *Principles of Human Anatomy and Physiology,* ninth edition. John Wiley & Sons, Inc. New York.

Tortora, G., Funke, B. and Case, C. 2000. *An Introduction to Microbiology, seventh edition.* Addison-Wesley: San Francisco, CA. Longman.

Van de Graff, K. M. 1998. *Human Anatomy, fifth edition.* Wm. C. Brown Publishers. Dubque, IA.

Wells, J. 2000. *Icons of Evolution: Science or Myth?* Regnery Press, Washington, DC.

Yancey, P. 1990. *Where Is God When It Hurts?* Zondervan House. Grand Rapids, MI.

For Further Reading

1. Alcamo, I. E. 1996. *DNA Technology: The Awesome Skill.* WCB McGraw-Hill. Boston, MA.

2. Brand, P. and Yancey, P. 1993. *Pain: The Gift Nobody Wants.* Harper Collins. New York.

3. Brand, P. and Yancey, P. 1980. *Fearfully and Wonderfully Made.* Zondervan. Grand Rapids, MI.

4. Brand, P. and Yancey, P. 1984. *In His Image.* Zondervan. Grand Rapids, MI.

5. Behe, M. J. 1996. *Darwin's Black Box: The biochemical Challenge to Evolution.* The Free Press. New York.

6. Cosgrove, M. 1987. *The Amazing Body Human: God's Design for Personhood.* Baker Book House. Grand Rapids, MI.

7. Cuozzo, J. 1998. *Buried Alive.* Master Books. Green Forest, Arkansas.

8. Darwin, C. 1979. *The Origin of Species* (Reprint of first edition). Avenue Books. New York.

9. Davis, P. and Kenyon, D. 1993. *Of Pandas and People: The Central Question in Biological Origins.* Haughton. Dallas, TX.

10. Gillen, A. L, Sherwin, F., and Knowles, A. 1999. *The Human Body: An Intelligent Design.* Creation Research Society. Hull, GA.

11. Gray, N. 1995. *Gray's Anatomy,* fifteen edition. (Editors T. P. Pick and R. Howden). Barnes and Noble, Inc. (Original Edition, 1901). New York.

12. Guyton, A. C. 1991. *Textbook of Medical Physiology,* eighth edition. W. B. Saunders Philadelphia, PA.

13. Harvey, W. 1995 (reprint of 1628 edition). *De Motu Cordis: Anatomical Exercises Concerning the Motion of the Heart and Blood in Living Creatures.* Dover Books. Mineola, NY.

14. Hole, J. , Shier, D., Butler, J. and R. Lewis 1996. *Hole's Human Anatomy and Physiology,* 7th ed. Wm. C. Brown Publishers. Dubque, IA.

15. Lubenow, M. L. 1997. *Bones of Contention.* Baker Book House. Grand Rapids, MI.

16. McMillen, S. I. 1963. *None of These Diseases,* 1st ed. Old Tappan, NJ: Fleming H. Revell Company.

17. Morris, H. M. 1995. *The Defender's Study Bible.* World. Grand Rapids, Michigan.

18. Nester, E. N., Roberts, C. E., Pearsall, N. N., Anderson, D. G., Nester, M. T. 1998. *Microbiology: A Human Perspective, second edition.* WCB McGraw-Hill. Boston, MA.

19. Nilsson, L. 1985. *The Body Victorious.* Delacorte Press. New York.

20. Nuland, S. B. (editor) 1998. *Exploring the Human Body: Incredible Voyage.* National Geographic Society. Washington, D.C.

21. Nuland, S. B. 1997. *The Wisdom of the Body.* Alfred Knopf. New York.

22. Parker, G., Graham, K., Shimmin, D., and Thompson, G. 1997. *God's Living Creation.* A Beka Books. Pensacola, FL.

23. Paley, W. 1802. *Natural Theology.* Lincoln-Rembrandt Publishers (Reprinted in 1997). Charlottesville, VA.
   (Also available as *Paley's Watchmaker* edited by Bill Cooper (1997). New Wine Press. West Susex, England.)

24. Parker, G. 1996. *Creation: The Facts of Life.* Master Books. Green Forest, Arkansas.

25. Tiner, John H. 1999. *The History of Medicine.* Master Books. Green Forest, Arkansas.

26. Saunders, J. B. and O'Malley C. 1950. *The Illustrations From the Works of Andreas Vesalius of Brussels.* Dover Books. Mineola, NY.

27. Silvius, J. E. 1997. *Biology: Principles and Perspectives.* Kendall Hunt. Dubque, IA.

28. Thomas, L. 1986. In Pode, R. M. (Editor), *The Incredible Machine* (pp. 6-8). National Geographic Society. Washington, D.C.

29. Tortora, G. J. 1994. *Introduction to the Human Body: The Essentials of Anatomy and Physiology,* third edition. Harper Collins College Publishers. New York.

30. Tortora, G. J. and Grabowski, S. R. 2000 *Principles of Human Anatomy and Physiology,* 8th ed. John Wiley & Sons. New York.

31. Tortora, G. J. , Funke, B. and Case, C. 2001. *An Introduction to Microbiology,* 7th ed. Redwood City, CA.: The Benjamin/Cummings Publishing.

32. Van de Graff, K. M. and Fox, S. I. 1998. *Concepts of Human Anatomy and Physiology.* 5th ed. Wm. C. Brown Publishers. Dubque, IA.

33. Van de Graff, K. M. 1998. *Human Anatomy,* fifth edition. Wm. C. Brown Publishers. Dubque, IA.

34. Watson, J. 1968. *The Double Helix.* Atheneum Publishers. New York.

Glossary Used in *Body by Design*

acidosis — A serious physiological condition in which hydrogen ions overwhelm the buffers of the blood, resulting in a life-threatening low pH.

adaptation — Creationists use this term to refer to a short-term change in the response of a body system as a consequence of repeated or protracted stimulation; whereas, evolutionists use this term to mean adjustment to environmental demand through the long-term process of natural selection acting on the genotype.

adaptation package — Biological organisms are more than the sum of individual structures; their ability to function successfully is due to an entire "package of parts."

alkalosis — A condition in which there is an increase in alkaline substances in the blood, especially sodium bicarbonate.

all-or-none principle — In skeletal muscles, individual fibers contract to their fullest extent or not at all. In neurons, if a stimulus is strong enough to initiate an action potential, a nerve impulse is propagated along the entire neuron at a constant strength.

alveolus — An individual air capsule within the lung; the basic functional unit of respiration. Alveolus may also refer to the socket that secures a tooth.

analogy (analogous structure) — A body part similar in function to that of another organism, but only superficially similar in structure, at most. Such similarities are regarded not as evidence of inheritance from a common ancestor, as in homology, but as evidence only of similar function.

anatomy — The branch of science concerned with the structure of living organisms and the relationship of their organs.

articulation — The junction of two or more bones. It can also mean "fit together."

asepsis — Freedom from infection; condition in the body that is free of pathogens, as in wounds or surgical incisions that are free from pathogenic bacteria, fungi, viruses, protozoans, and parasites.

ATP (Adenosine triphosphate) — The universal energy-carrying molecule manufactured in all living cells as a means of capturing and storing energy. It consists of adenine with a sugar, ribose, to which are added, in linear array, three phosphate molecules.

autonomic nervous system — The branch of the peripheral nervous system (PNS) that has control over the internal organs. It is divided into the parasympathetic and sympathetic nervous systems.

axon — The process of a nerve cell that transmits impulses away from the cell body of a neuron.

biochemistry — The scientific discipline concerned with the study of chemical reactions that occur in organisms (they explain the metabolic processes of life in the language of chemistry).

B-lymphocyte — Specialized leukocytes processed in the bone marrow (or bursa equivalent); these cells give rise to plasma cells that produce antibodies.

bone marrow — The soft sponge-like material in the cavities of bones. Its principle function is to manufacture erythrocytes, leukocytes, and platelets (formed elements of blood).

blind watchmaker — Richard Dawkins' metaphor for non-intelligent, purposeless, natural selection; expressing the idea that design characteristics seen in living things are not like the intelligent purpose and craftsmanship associated with watch-making.

blood — A modified connective tissue consisting of formed elements that are suspended and carried in plasma (a straw-colored liquid consisting of water and dissolved solutes). These formed elements and their major functions include erythrocytes (oxygen transport), leukocytes (immune defense), and platelets (blood clotting).

capillary — A microscopic blood vessel that connects an arteriole and a venule; the basic unit of the circulatory system.

cascade — A series of chemical reactions, or events, that involve interdependent reactions.

cell — The basic unit of structure and function in living organisms.

chorion — The extraembryonic membrane to which the placenta attaches.

chromatin — The extended form of chromosomes during interphase. They are threadlike structures in the cell nucleus consisting primarily of protein and DNA.

chyme — The mass of partially digested food that passes through the pyloric sphincter in the stomach, into the duodenum of the small intestine.

coagulation — Refers to blood clotting. The process by which platelets and soluble plasma proteins interact in a series of complex enzymatic reactions to finally convert fibrinogen into fibrin. It works on a positive feedback cycle.

commissures — Bridges of neurons that connect the brain hemispheres.

compound traits — Interdependent parts working together in an organ or system.

correlation (complementarity) of structure and function — The close relationship that exists between a structure and its function. Structure determines function.

convergent evolution — Evolution of similar appearances in unrelated species.

corpus callosum — The most massive of the brain commissures and typically the only one severed during surgery for epilepsy.

Darwinism — The theory that all living things descended from an original common ancestor through natural selection and random variation, without the aid of intelligence or nonmaterial forces.

dendrite — Nerve cell process that conducts impulses toward the neuron cell body.

design — The purposeful arrangement of parts; a plan, a scheme, a project, or a purpose with intention or aim.

dialysis — Refers to the process of separating molecules of different sizes using a semi-permeable membrane.

digestion — Hydrolysis. The process by which large food molecules are broken down into simpler ones, thus being able to be absorbed through the epithelium of the GI tract.

DNA (deoxyribonucleic acid) — Nucleic acid found in all cells (except mature red blood cells); the genetic material that specifies protein synthesis in cells.

Drosophila — Genus of fruit fly that has been used in genetic gene expression testing for over a century. The species most often used is *Drosophila melanogaster.*

E. coli, Escherichia coli, — An enteric bacterial species used in many biological research projects which inhabits the intestines of humans and other animals. Proliferation can cause newborn meningitis, diarrhea, and urinary infections.

electrolyte — A substance, such as a base, salt, or acid whose molecules, when in solution, separate into ions. Such a solution is capable of conducting an electric current.

embryology — The biological science which deals with the development of an organism.

emergent properties — Properties found in living things that show that the sum together is greater than the separate, independent parts.

enteric bacteria — Bacteria that reside in the intestinal tract. Most of these bacteria are not harmful to the human body and many are mutualistic with humans, providing valuable vitamins and breaking down nutrients. Many of these beneficial bacteria are now called "pro-bacteria."

erythrocytes — Red blood cells.

evolution, (evolve) — Mere "change in living things over time"; but also meaning descent with modification, and particular mechanisms to account for change such as natural selection and gene mutation.

gene pool — The total genetic material in the population of a species at a given point in time.

extracellular — Outside of a cell or cells.

genome — The total DNA for a given organism.

gradualism — The view that evolution occurred slowly over time, with transitional forms grading finely in a line of descent.

Great Physician — This is Jesus, the God-Man who heals men/women of physical disability, infectious disease, emotional and spiritual disorder. Restores men and women who are sick to health. Gives dignity to those who are ashamed of their condition.

Haversian canal — The longitudinal channel in the center of an osteon.

hemoglobin — The pigment that gives red blood cells their characteristic red color. It functions in the transport of oxygen and carbon dioxide.

hemophilia — Refers to several different hereditary deficiencies of coagulation.

homeostasis — A state of body equilibrium, or the maintenance of an optimal, or stable, internal environment of the body.

hormone — A chemical substance produced in an endocrine gland and secreted into the bloodstream to cause an effect in a specific target organ.

homology (homologous structure) — A body part with the same basic structure and embryonic origin as that of another organism. In evolutionary theory, it implies the common ancestry of the two. In creationism, it implies a common design.

hyperventilation — State in which there is an increased amount of air entering the pulmonary alveoli, resulting in reduction of carbon dioxide in blood.

hypothesis — In scientific method, 1) an educated guess, 2) a tentative explanation, or 3) a proposition that is to be confirmed by test.

immunodeficiency — An impairment of immunological function which leads to greater susceptibility to opportunistic infections (e.g., SCIDS and AIDS).

immunity — A specified defense against a disease.

integration — The coordination of excitatory and inhibitory signals and processes received by the cell body and processed at the axon hillock.

intelligent design (cause) — Any theory that attributes the action, function, or structure of an object to the creative mental capacities of a personal agent. In biology, the theory that biological organisms owe their origin to a preexistent intelligence.

interdependent parts — Body structures that are interdependent on each other. The body is one unit, though it is made up of many different types of cells and tissues. The body parts work together, cooperate, and cannot exist without each other. This resulting condition of these parts working together is that the sum of the actions is greater than the separate, individual actions.

irreducible complexity — Interdependent parts of living (and non-living) things that cannot be reduced further without losing their intended function (e.g., mousetrap parts working together).

Jehovah Rapha — The God who heals. The God who makes whole and the One who restores a life of calamity to a life of dignity and usefulness.

lactose — A disaccharide of glucose and galactose, or simply, milk sugar.

lamella — A concentric ring of matrix surrounding the canal in an osteon of mature bone tissue.

large intestine — A major part of the gastrointestinal tract consisting of the colon, cecum, rectum, and the anal canal.

leukocytes — White blood cells.

lipid — Compounds that do not mix with water, including fats, phospholipids, and steroids.

lymph — A clear, plasma-like fluid that flows through lymphatic vessels.

macroevolution — The hypothesis of large-scale changes, leading to new levels of complexity. A large change from one kind of plant or animal to a different kind (e.g., microbe to man). Also called vertical evolution. It is the idea that all living forms are related as branches of one ancestral "tree."

medulla oblongata — Section of the brain stem controlling blood pressure, heartbeat, breathing, and other important functions.

membrane — A thin layer of soft, pliable, and often permeable tissue.

metabolism — The chemical changes that occur within the body.

microevolution — Small-scale genetic changes, observable in organisms. A small change within a specific group (e.g., Darwin's finches; antibiotic-resistant bacteria). Also called horizontal evolution.

M. leprae — *Mycobacterium leprae* causes peripheral nerve damage and it is the species of bacteria that is responsible for leprosy (Hansen's disease).

monocytes — Largest of white blood cells. They are phagocytic and differentiate into tissue macrophages.

morphology — The form or structure of an organism.

mosaic — Patterns and designs showing contrasts among colors, pigments, structures, and/or organisms in their environment.

mutation — A relatively permanent change in the DNA involving either a physical change in chromosome(s) or a biochemical change in the order or number of nucleotide bases in gene(s).

mucociliary escalator — The mechanism where cilia of mucous membrane cells move particles along respiratory membranes and down the throat, where they are swallowed.

natural selection — Process in nature where one genotype leaves more offspring for the next generation than other genotypes in that population. The explanation is that the elimination of less-suited organisms and the preservation of more suited ones result from pressures within the environment, or competition, or both.

negative feedback — A primary mechanism for homeostasis, whereby a change in a physiological variable that is being monitored triggers a response that counteracts the initial fluctuation.

nephron — The functional unit of the kidney, consisting of a glomerulus, convoluted tubules, and a loop.

Neo-Darwinism — The concept of Darwinism with the addition of mutation, population, and Mendelian genetics.

nerve impulse — Electrochemical change (action potential) traveling along a neuron.

neuron — A nerve cell.

nucleotide — The fundamental structural unit of a nucleic acid, or DNA, made up of a nitrogen-carrying base, a sugar molecule, and a phosphate group.

ontogeny — The development of an individual.

order — A fixed or definite plan and system.

organ — A structure of the body formed of two or more tissues and adapted to carry out a specific function.

organ system — A group of organs that work together to perform a vital body function.

organism — The living body that represents the sum total of all its organ systems working together to maintain life.

organization — A unified coherent group or systemized whole.

osteon — A group of osteocytes and concentric lamellae surrounding a central canal, constitutitng the basic and interwoven unit of bone tissue; also called the Haversion system.

pathogen — Technical term for germ, or germ-causing microbe, such as virus, bacterium, or protozoan that may be disease-causing.

phagocytosis — The process of engulfing other organisms; the particle containing vacuole fuses with a lysosome whose enzymes digest the food. An example of this is macrophages eating bacteria and other invaders of the body.

phylogeny — The racial history of an animal, person, or plant.

placenta — The organ of nutrient and waste exchange between a mother and the fetus.

plasma cell (plasmacyte) — A mature antibody-secreting B-cell found mainly in lymph nodes.

plasticity — The ability of the brain to do long-term adjustments to long-term changes.

positive feedback — A physiological control mechanism in which a change in some variable triggers mechanisms that amplify the change.

physiology — The science of the functioning of living organisms.

physiochemical forces — Naturalistic view of how blind, mechanistic forces, through chance and natural selection, over millions of years, may explain the irreducible complexity of anatomical structures and physiological functions of the human body.

pseudostratified columnar epithelium — Tissue that has cells (like bricks on end) with relatively large cytoplasmic volumes.

pyemia — Pus-forming infection.

recapitulation — The idea that development in the embryo or fetus replays evolution. Ernst Haeckel first stated this idea in his so called "biogenetic law": ontogeny recapitulates phylogeny.

reticular formation — A complex brain network that arouses the cerebrum. It is also a site for the integration of various brain signals.

retinal pigment epithelium (RPE) — A structure in the posterior portion of the eye that maintains the photoreceptor structure and function and is necessary for optimal vision. It provides nutrients for the retinal cells and enhances new cell growth in the photoreceptor region of the eye.

selective advantage — A genetic advantage of one organism over its competitors that causes it to be favored in survival and reproduction rates over time.

septicemia — Blood infection by bacteria, such as *Streptococcus pyogenes*.

simple columnar epithelium — This tissue has cells with relatively large cytoplasmic volumes, and is often located where secretion or active absorption of substances are important functions. Their cells are shaped like bricks on end.

simple cuboidal epithelium — This tissue is specialized for secretion and makes up the epithelia of the thyroid gland. These cells are like sugar cubes in shape and secrete hormones into the bloodstream.

simple squamous epithelium — This tissue has relatively leaky tissue. These cells (shaped like floor tiles) are specialized for exchange of materials by diffusion.

small intestine — Long, tube-like chamber of the digestive tract between the large intestine and stomach; divided into three areas.

speciation — The development of a new species by reproducing their ancestral population, resulting in the loss of interfertility with isolation of organisms from it.

sphenomandibularis — A muscle that was recently discovered by cutting a cadaver from an unconventional angle and exposing an unfamiliar muscle connecting the mandible to the sphenoid bone behind the base of the eye socket. It is thought to stabilize the jaw during chewing rather than actually moving the jaw.

STDs — Sexually transmitted diseases.

synapse — Region between two nerve cells where the nerve impulse is transmitted from one to the other, usually from axon to dendrite.

systemic pressure — Arterial blood pressure during the systolic phase of the cardiac cycle.

stasis — The constant morphology of a species over a long period of geologic time.

synergism — Usually refers to properties found in non-living things (especially chemicals) that show the sum together is greater than the separate, independent parts. (Occasionally refers to properties of organisms.)

tight junction — Junction between epithelial cells where the membranes are in close contact, with no intervening spaces. Helps to maintain boundaries in cells.

tissue — A group of structurally similar cells performing a distinct function.

tissue trauma — This trauma is caused by the puncture of the skin; a severe wound that is internal. It is so named because the formation of prothrombinase is initiated by tissue factor (TF), leading to the extrinsic pathway. Response is very rapid.

T-lymphocyte — Specialized leukocytes processed in the thymus gland; these lymphocytes provide the body with specific cell-mediated immunity.

urinary system — The organs concerned with the formation, concentration, and elimination of urine (also known as the excretory system).

villus — A minute projection that extends outward into the lumen from the mucosal layer of the small intestine.

vestigial structure (organ) — A body part that has no function, but which is presumed to have been useful in ancestral species.

vitamin K — Fat-soluble vitamin K1 is found in foods, and K2 is produced by *E. coli*. They are needed for the clotting protein, prothrombin to form.

In this glossary, we define basic biological terms from a creation/design perspective. Included are words and terms which are used more than once throughout the book. This glossary clarifies word meanings that may have a specialized meaning in the context of creationism, anatomy, and physiology. For an extensive treatment of technical terms, we refer the readers to a standard medical, biology, and/or English dictionary (e.g., Webster). Some of the better medical dictionaries would include *Dorland's Illustrated Medical Dictionary*, *Mosby's Medical Dictionary*, and *Merriam Webster's Medical Dictionary*. In addition, I would suggest the reader consult a biology, an anatomy and physiology, and/or a microbiology textbook.

Index

About the Author

Dr. Alan Gillen is a biologist and zoologist with a doctorate in science education. He is an experienced biology instructor at both the high school and college levels. He has authored more than 25 papers and two books in biology, microbiology, zoology, anatomy and physiology, and medical issues. In addition to writing *Body by Design*, he has authored a companion book, *The Human Body: An Intelligent Design*. This book provides physiological evidence for creation. He has been active in bringing a biblical perspective in biology and medicine in the classroom and local churches for the last eight years. He is also a regular contributor to *Creation Matters*, a CRS newsletter. He is active in bringing a biblical perspective to biology and medicine in the classroom. Dr. Gillen is currently working on a college-level biology textbook with Dr. Chris Carmichael and Frank Sherwin. His professional interests include effects of exercise on the heart, blood clotting, antibiotic resistance in bacteria, and treatments for the common cold. Outside of the lab and classroom, he enjoys tennis and exercising. Dr. Gillen presently is a professor of biology at Liberty University.

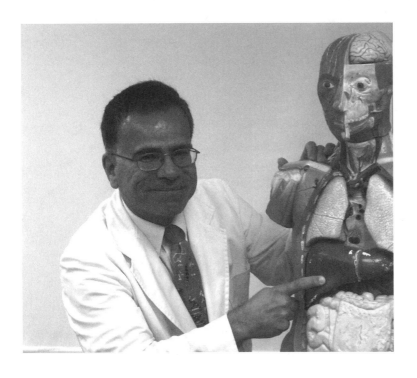

Afterword

In **Body by Design**, I have attempted to weave together a pattern that better explains the anatomy and physiology of the human body. In this book, I have described each and every body system, describing its basic structure and function. In each system, we have examined an interwoven part, pointing to intelligent causation. Creation concepts of adaptation, homeostasis, and interdependence throughout the body have been explored. I have attempted to keep it practical by providing clinical, both wellness and disease issues. Many of these explorations come from my own personal experience, either in my own life or a friend's life. I trust that you will see the pattern the Creator is weaving in your life and that you will also conclude that the human body was wondrously made as the Psalmist did. Hopefully, you can better see the tapestry being formed and fashioned in your life. The underpinnings may not only make sense in themselves, but the pattern above can be very beautiful as illustrated in the human body. Finally, it is my prayer that you will ask God what is His design and will for your life.